Christopher Hope was born in Johannesburg in 1944, grew up in Pretoria, and was educated at the Universities of Witwatersrand and Natal. His first book of poems was *Cape Drives* (1974), which received the Cholmondeley Award, and his first novel, *A Separate Development* (1981), won the David Higham Prize for Fiction. A collection of stories, *Private Parts & Other Tales*, was given the International PEN Silver Pen Award in 1982. His most recent novels are *Kruger's Alp*, which won the Whitbread Prize for fiction in 1985, and *The Hottentot Room*. A novella, *Black Swan*, was published in 1987.

Christopher Hope has lived in London since 1975. This is his first work of non-fiction.

Also by Christopher Hope in Abacus:

KRUGER'S ALP
THE HOTTENTOT ROOM

WHITE BOY RUNNING

CHRISTOPHER HOPE

ABACUS

AN ABACUS BOOK

First published in Great Britain 1988 by Martin Secker & Warburg Limited
Published in Abacus by Sphere Books Ltd, 1988
Reprinted 1989 (twice)
Copyright © Christopher Hope 1988

The three lines from 'Two Climbs' are reprinted by permission of
Faber & Faber Ltd from *Collected Poems* by W. H. Auden.

Printed and bound in Great Britain by
Richard Clay Ltd, Bungay, Suffolk

ISBN 0 349 10092 6

Sphere Books Ltd
A Division of
Macdonald & Co (Publishers) Ltd
27 Wrights Lane, London W8 5TZ
A member of Maxwell Pergamon Publishing Corporation plc

FOR KATHLEEN MARY McKENNA HOPE

Fleeing from short-haired mad executives,
The sad and useless faces around my home,
Upon the mountains of my fear I climb.

W.H. Auden
'Two Climbs'

Someday a grubbing historian may read the back files of South
African newspapers and marvel that such warnings should have
passed unheeded. But the fact is that the Transvaal Government
and its sympathisers had become indifferent to warnings followed
by no results and accustomed to prophecies unfulfilled.

J.P. FitzPatrick
The Transvaal·From Within 1899

CONTENTS

I

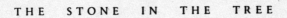

THE STONE IN THE TREE

THE BAR OF the one hotel in Balfour on Saturday night is a roaring place: a beery, echoing, concrete vault where dim, butter-yellow electric bulbs sway from the ceiling in the draught whenever the swing doors open to admit another customer and the whole room seems to tilt alarmingly. This is a small, nondescript Transvaal town, a *dorp*, population a few thousand, surrounded by rich fields of maize, just another stop on the national road running from Johannesburg, eighty kilometres behind you, down to the south coast, to Durban and the beaches of the Indian Ocean, six hours' drive away. Today the main road bypasses the town and robs it of its main distinction: no one needs to pass through Balfour any more. Gone are the days when lethal cavalcades of motor cars raced down the broad main street, pausing at the filling stations, days when it was, in a serious way, a place on the map.

If you believed your eyes, you might suppose that the Balfour Hotel possessed a restaurant, because that is what the sign above the front veranda tells you, and a ladies' bar, although no lady would be seen dead in the bar and should one be incautious enough to walk anywhere near this place a couple of heads will push through the tiny triangular window beside the back door and make a variety of outrageous suggestions. The heads belong to the four drunks, in sports shirts, khaki shorts and bare feet, who are playing snooker on the half-sized table which stands between the bar and the dart-board. The snooker players take these liberties because real ladies, which is to say – White women – are not to be found near the Balfour Hotel on a Saturday evening, and certainly would not be deceived by the faded sign which promises them a bar of their own.

Not only does the Balfour Hotel lack restaurant and ladies' bar but there is really no hotel either. But there is, just off the *stoep*, a noisy tavern which sells a good deal of booze and has some rooms attached to it, though these are not easy to book and are hardly ever used since the main coast road bypassed the town. The bar is crowded with White men drinking ice-cold lager, triple brandies and Cokes, or double cane spirits weakly diluted with a variety of mixers ranging from lemonade to ginger ale. There are three species of drinkers: on the stools around the big curved wooden bar are the taciturn imbibers who chase their brandies with lager, farmers who bring their teenage sons with them, fair-haired barefoot boys straight off the tractors, silently sipping orange juice. These serious drinkers do not linger, they swallow, nod and depart. Behind them stand the local football team, cheerful young men still in their red jerseys and white shorts, their ears rubbed raw from the scrum, knees scraped by the tackles of the afternoon game, knocking back a few rounds of beer to rinse the dust of the rugby pitch out of their mouths. Over at the snooker table the drunks pot and miss, show no signs of leaving and you can tell just by looking at them that they have been here since mid-afternoon and plan to make an evening of it.

I have come to Balfour because this is where I began. My Irish grandfather was mayor of this town many times in the 'twenties and 'thirties, and my family was once at home here for reasons which are as characteristic as they are curious. I have driven the hour from Johannesburg, arriving on a Saturday afternoon in mid-April to find the Balfour Hotel unprepared to receive a guest. The fact that a reservation has been made serves only to increase the scepticism of the clerk behind the desk, a frowning woman who assures me that I have found her here quite by chance and no record of my booking exists. In case I should wish to take the matter any further she is quick to tell me that she is only 'helping out', and if this fails to deter, that she has just 'stepped in' to assist the owner who is 'unavailable', as well as being 'out of reach' and is not expected to return in 'the foreseeable future'. The way she delivers these warnings suggests that he might never return at all – at least not while I am here. She stands looking at me: thin, tense, dark-haired and defiant. Something in her manner and the jut of her chin intimate that this is my chance to re-think my idea of spending a night here; it is something that can very easily be done, as she demonstrates with a gesture towards her book; the blank space makes clear that I am not expected. I have only to walk away and no one will ever be any the wiser. In reply, I take out my pen; I even ask about breakfast. From the light in her eye I realise I have given her another weapon. Breakfast is a problem, she says, on Sunday.

'What's the problem?'

'It's the current.'

'Do you mean the electrical current?'

'Yes. At eight o'clock on Sunday mornings they cut off the current. It's very hard to cook breakfast.'

I say I will risk it. With a shake of the head she pushes the book across to me and asks for a signature. I sign. She hands me the key to my room, a great metal tooth wired to a piece of wood brown as a beetle's wing and shaped like the triangular wafers they stick in ice-cream. A waiter is summoned to help me with my bag. He steps out of the shadows with a look approaching despair on his face, a wizened little Black man dressed in a red jacket and black trousers so old and rumpled they blend with the shadows which hang about everywhere in the hotel because the little yellow lights never reach below the waist. The waiter is astonished by the order to assist me. His role in life is to carry drinks between the bar and the gloomy little lounge. Carrying luggage is a job so far outside his scheme of things that he must feel the earth tremble at the suggestion. He shakes his head incredulously when I attempt to hand him my case and gives a deeply apologetic laugh mixed with a note of sadness, and strokes my sleeve as one might soothe an idiot child. Eventually I pick up the case myself. He stands and watches me carrying it upstairs and begins fanning me vigorously with his metal tray, either in the hope that this might bring me to my senses, or because he believes the cool breeze at my back will somehow help me to get the load upstairs.

On the first-floor landing there are paintings of seascapes screwed to the walls. White-capped waves tower above an icy green swell. Perhaps in the days when people still stopped at the Balfour Hotel these acres of ocean reminded holidaymakers on their way to the Durban beaches of the pleasures, or perils, that lay in store for them. But in the dark of the stairway they give off the hard, baleful gleam of pictures that know they are never looked at.

I had asked for a room with bath and a bath there is, but it does not work. The radio offers four channels but only one of them functions and cannot be switched off, I discover, but only turned down; so it goes on playing Afrikaans dance music through a scratchy accompaniment of static which makes it sound as if the notes are being forced through a thick beard. The only other diversion is the Gideon Bible, which has been used to kill flies. Their dried, flaky corpses embroider the red plastic cover. The business of the dry bath and the single channel radio that never stops rather affects me, principally because they are familiar symptoms of Africa – and this is what makes them so unfamiliar in South Africa which, after all, prides itself on *not* being part of Africa, but as being a place where the radio might be stultifyingly boring yet reception is always sparkling, where the plumbing works, where there might be racialists thick on the ground but they bathe often, believing cleanliness to be not only next to godliness but very close to apartheid as well. The sages teach that everywhere else in Africa tractors may rust in the fields and railway lines stop dead in the veld, but this is not supposed to happen in South Africa. Perhaps in the Balfour Hotel they are trying to erode these old prejudices; certainly the place could fit into any African country you care to mention. Possibly the old notion that even the worst of ours is better than the best of theirs really is breaking down. Anyway, this hotel is nothing more than a name, it could be painted on the veld, a figment of someone's imagination, built and run by absent owners who had once seen a picture of a hotel and taken it from there.

The bedclothes smell of dust and outside my window doves are loud in the oaks. As night comes on they call more loudly, long, blushing, trilling notes, like telephones ringing in the trees, until one by one they stop abruptly, as if the calls are being answered. Somewhere below I can hear a booming roar which, at first, I think might be a boiler somewhere deep in the belly of the building, but which, I am to discover, is the sound of the snooker players in the downstairs bar.

Arriving in the peace of a Saturday afternoon the town, in the way of many small South African towns preparing for the long silence of the Sunday to come, lies as if stunned in the brilliant sunshine and the sky has that polished gun-metal sheen so characteristic of the Transvaal highveld as autumn draws on. Though blazingly warm for mid-April the heat carries an almost imperceptible sharpness, a most delicate razor's edge to the faint breeze; a touch of steel on the warm neck which reminds those who feel it that the sunshine is really just for show and summer has gone. The main road, running north to south, is broad and empty, lined with one-storey shops, filling stations, a municipality building in yellow brick, and two banks, Barclays and Standard. Rumours reaching observers abroad have suggested that such financial institutions are pulling out of South Africa. If so, the news clearly has not yet reached Balfour. The only things moving in the main street are the election posters roped to the lampposts, showing once vividly coloured photographs of the candidates, now fading in the sun. A sense of weariness stamps the posters, the candidates' smiles seem stiff. We are already three weeks into this campaign, another three to go before White voters set off for the polls on May 6th. The posters are strapped to the lampposts at a height which makes it difficult to interfere with them. Mutilating your opponent's posters is a traditional sport at election time; but of course nothing is too high when you possess a ladder and a bit of determination and, doubtless, these posters are patrolled regularly since there is so much time still to run and the parties contesting this seat will be taking no chances. The colours of the posters are all noticeably alike; this is because they all use a great deal of orange, a colour which dominates the South African flag since it combines uneasily with the other two colours, white and blue. The effect of this combination is to induce, at least in me, an unsettled feeling, not unlike motion sickness – odd sensation in a country where so little moves.

The flag is revered as a sacred symbol combining, at its very centre, the flags of the former Boer Republics of the Transvaal and Free State, as well as a tiny Union Jack, reminders of vanished and glorious independencies on the one hand, and hated imperial domination on the other – twin themes which retain their potency in this country where history is re-lived with a vengeance and the defeat of republican ideals by the British, not once, but twice in the Boer Wars of 1880 and 1899, stirs bitter memories. The furies still ride and their shapes will be glimpsed soon enough through the shot and shell of this all-white, autumnal election of 1987. Altogether there are 470 candidates nominated to fight 166 seats. Another twelve seats are nominated. Whites comprise around fifteen per cent of the population. What is known is that the ruling National Party will win. It always does. Most of the country's three million Afrikaners and increasing numbers of English-speakers, who together total around one and a half million, support it – though this time that support is widely expected to be shaken as never before.

High on the telephone poles the election posters rattle drily: smiling pale faces, barred and stamped with slogans, flags and party logos, which resemble tribal markings, the facial scarification of the White African tribe. Identifying the contesting parties in these bruising encounters takes unusual skill. You want first to identify the species. It is a bit like reading spoor in the bush, following the signs that show which kinds of game have passed this way. It has been over a dozen years since I last observed a White South African election at close quarters and the signs are now even more confusing, but I have, as a single advantage, the fact that I can recall almost all of the others except the first and most fateful in 1948 when I was four years old and the Government of Afrikaner Nationalists came to power. I carry the effects of that election within me, rather as one might wear the marks of some fateful atomic explosion imprinted on the genes, locked in the marrow. Those of us born in the aftermath of that explosion grew up amid the fall-out. Subsequent elections revive memories of the original blast which we have, perhaps, suppressed – memories not from the mind, but those that lie just beneath the skin.

Today, all the political parties have reduced their names to initials and their messages are more encoded. Chief among the parties still is the National Party, or NP, its members familiarly known as 'Nats', political home of the Afrikaner, the force which has reigned supreme these forty years, now the natural party of government, the party which invented constitutional apartheid, confident possessor of over two-thirds of the elected seats in the House of Assembly in Cape Town where Parliament sits.

To the right of the National Party stand two proudly reactionary groupings: the Conservative Party, alias the CP, and the tiny *Herstigte* (the Reconstituted or Reformed) National Party, known as the HNP. The CP and the HNP attempted to form a loose coalition for the election but failed to do so despite assistance rendered to this end by what might be called the military wing of the far-right Afrikaner groupings, an organisation known as the *Afrikaner Weerstand Beweging*, the AWB or, in English, the Afrikaner Resistance Movement, which is to the Conservative Party what the IRA is to Sinn Fein. The AWB has all the trappings of the militias that once brought terror to the streets of Germany in the 1930s. This organisation, with its swastika of the three sevens toe to toe in a circle, its red, white and black flags and its enthusiasm for guns and muscle, is known in English as ARM, one of those unhappily appropriate coincidences so familiar in South Africa, the best known example of which dates from the time when the secret police were designated the Bureau of State Security, and came to be known as BOSS.

The aim of the White Right is to return to the dogmas of racial purity which have guided Afrikaner Nationalists during their decades in power, to revive the belief in total racial and cultural partition of the four main population

10

groups: Blacks, Whites, Coloureds and Indians, and to restore segregated amenities ranging from separate beds to segregated lavatories. Now of course it may seem to the naïve visitor, to the child, or to the fool, that the Government of South Africa has made only the slightest concession towards the Black majority and the tiniest genuflection in the direction of racial mixing, but even this little is too much for the far right, who declare that the merest tincture of poison introduced into the sacred well of racial purity will kill the tribe. Their election posters trumpet their anger and frustration:

FIGHT INFLATION
STOP INTEGRATION
SAVE THE NATION!
WE'VE HAD ENOUGH!

It requires a particularly warped imagination, shot through with the most macabre humour, to portray the governing National Party as the agent of racial betrayal. Is this not the party of the men who invented apartheid? Of Dr Daniel François Malan, its first leader, who took his people from the oppression and penury of the 'thirties and 'forties into the promised land of power in 1948? Is it not the party of the unabashed White supremacist, Johannes Gerhardus Strydom, who entrenched that power in the 'fifties? Of Dr Hendrik Frensch Verwoerd, the dreamy, unyielding visionary who formulated the philosophical concept of grand apartheid known as separate development? Of Balthazar John Johannes) Vorster, who declared in the sixties that the National Party was not merely a political movement but Afrikanerdom on the march?

This may be a small-time Transvaal town, but it is the country seats which provide the Government with their power-base and not the great cities. And the Transvaal is the province which dominates the country; the place where power resides, the lair of the political wild-men. 'Be kind to animals' say the bumper stickers, 'Hug a Transvaler!' There is more truth in bumper stickers than was ever dreamt of by official propagandists.

Among the new opposition forces, originating in the governing National Party, but distinct from it, is a group of three who call themselves Independents. No one seems quite sure on what platform this trio is to stand, and it appears to be the intention of the aspiring independents to keep their politics as vague as possible, even to the extent of denying that they are against the National Party, and to oppose only its leadership. The best known of the three is the former South African Ambassador to London who has proved himself a powerful champion of the good faith of the South African Government and the benefits of apartheid, defending the indefensible with an unblushing tenacity which suggests, if nothing else, that he has a fine future in politics before him. He combines an articulate manner with a truculent edge, truculence is something a Nationalist politician carries before him like a pike; government in this country has always been a matter of walking loudly and carrying several large sticks. He is bound to be a popular candidate. His appearances on British television were widely appreciated in South Africa where they were shown repeatedly to local audiences, who had for so long endured the dismal spectacle of their representatives abroad being either apoplectic or incoherent when facing the press, that the sight of their man giving as good as he got made a very welcome change. Starved as people have been of international sporting contests, these gladiatorial encounters between, in one corner, the Ambassador to the Court of St James and, in the other, the effete, pinko wimps of the foreign media, have brightened many a long South African evening. Yet it seems the confusions of political terminology in South Africa are contagious, for one British newspaper I saw recently, clearly affected by its glimpses of the asylum, dubbed this odd triumvirate of independent candidates the

South African 'Refuseniks'. It was meant, I suspect, as a compliment, but is so wildly inaccurate that any real Russian 'Refusenik' would be entitled to sue.

Consider, then, the parties of the White, predominantly Afrikaans, political establishment. Reading from the governing party outwards, their respective strengths in terms of seats are:

National Party: 126
Conservative Party: 18
Herstigte National Party: 1
Independents: 2

These are the figures and one clings to the figures. For what else is there? Everything else in this election will be rhetoric, threats, whistling in the dark, ominous silences . . . so I cling to the figures. I have them now, *before* the election, and I shall have them afterwards. Only they count. The differences between the establishment and the right-wing parties may be expressed by a kind of historical analogy: the National Party represents something akin to the Middle Ages; to its right the Conservative and Herstigte National Parties together yearn for a return to the Dark Ages. Within, but somewhere to the left of the National Party, a series of as yet unconfirmed sightings suggest the possible presence of a group of 'New Nats' who, together with the Independents, represent a desire to move the country not so much towards a Renaissance, but at least into the late Middle Ages.

On the left of the political divide stands the official opposition, known as the Progressive Federal Party, dubbed the PFP. The use of initials, in its case, is particularly unfortunate because there is something oddly pneumatic about them – to say them is to sound like an air-pump – or, worse, like a leaking tyre. With its twenty-six seats it is a small but vocal grouping, the party of the monied middle classes, predominantly English-speaking, urban, faintly liberal. Its most distinguished member is Mrs Helen Suzman, now the longest-serving member in the South African Parliament, a tribute to her courage and persistence, but also a sign of the long years during which the PFP has been wandering in the political wilderness without ever hoping to supplant the present regime. It is a feature of the Government's longevity that few can now remember a time when there was the slightest chance of beating the Government in a General Election and it is precisely its enormous parliamentary majority which has changed the National Party, once so enthusiastic about extra-parliamentary action, into a devoted supporter of the ballot box. And it is also precisely these long years in power that have made it so determined not to advance the facilities to anyone else except, perhaps, the fragmented and depressed White minority opposition. Indeed it is possible that the Afrikaner National-ists derive a peculiar pleasure from allowing the Progressives the dubious privilege of being sentenced to perpetual opposition in the bitter knowledge that they can never win. The PFP has been so long the bridesmaid and never the bride that its chief difficulty is knowing how to keep its posy fresh. Long years in the wilderness have taken their toll and young White radicals who were once natural PFP supporters are increasingly disillusioned with White politics, while the professional classes, from which it has always drawn its support, are voting with their feet and leaving the country for Canada and Australia in what has become one of the most alarming flights of technocrats, businessmen, doctors, dentists and engineers since the Sharpeville shootings in 1960. For this reason the PFP is sometimes known amongst its opponents as 'Packing for Perth'!

The Progressive Federal Party has formed an alliance in this election with the New Republic Party which holds five seats. The NRP is the remainder, the rump and relic of the old United Party of General Jan Christian Smuts who lost the fateful election in 1948 and so delivered the country into the hands of the White tribes of Afrikaner Nationalists, and the great darkness which fell on the land. The fate of the supporters of the old UP, or the SAPS, as its adherents were sometimes rather usefully known, in another of those cruelly appropriate ironies of South African politics (after the old South African Party to which they had once belonged), was to wander through the political desert singing and whistling at election times to keep their spirits up, while praying for a miracle to restore them to their rightful place upon the pinnacle of government. Yet, with each successive election, after that catastrophic defeat in 1948, they sank steadily, haemorrhaging votes to the National Party, and though they pledged themselves anew with admirable conviction to the destruction of the Nationalist Afrikaner Government and all its works, anyone with half an eye could see that they were dying on their feet. I think it came as something of a relief when the poor thing suddenly lay down one day and expired, donating what live members it still possessed to the National Party, the Progressives, and the New Republican Party.

This election has a peculiar fascination. Almost certainly it will be the last all-White election ever held, and I have an overwhelming desire to be in at the death. Undoubtedly something is going to die in this election, though what it is, or who it is, remains to be seen. In any event it cannot but be interesting, for election times in South Africa are something like springtime in England, when you can actually see life stirring in the undergrowth. In the White springtime of a South African election, politicians are wont to skip and gambol and to say the most interesting and even irresponsible things. So as I stand today on a street in Balfour murmuring to myself the names of the leaders of the National Party I find the sonorous boom of the syllables strangely comforting: Malan, Strydom, Verwoerd, Vorster and Botha. These are the men who have led the country since 1948. I recite it constantly; it is my White Magic, the charm I use to keep away the evil spirits: it is my mantra for election time. I can remember them all, as if it were only yesterday. But then that is not difficult. It is always yesterday in South Africa. When the present Government came to power I was four years old. Next year the Government will be forty. Will they give a party? Will I be invited?

Why come for an election? Why come at all? Because the place is a fever, an infection, a lingering childhood disease I simply cannot get over. Perhaps part of it is due to the fact that I am of that generation which knew no other way of life but that of the crusading segregation which came to be called apartheid. My generation are the children of apartheid. We were brought up with no other options, it was years before we discovered that this had not always been the case. We did not think about it; we lived it. Nothing could be more natural. My first glimpse of Black people told me not that they were Black but that they were strangers, and there were so many of them; for reasons I simply could not fathom, the world was full of strangers, working in the kitchens, walking in the streets. There were, it is true, hints that things had not been like this always; even as a child I knew that there had been a time when things were different. What told me so was not any explanation handed down by an adult; the message did not come in the form of words at all. I learnt it in the faint air of regret that I detected in the faces of the Black strangers who lived around us; I felt it in myself. I stared at the aliens who seemed so at home and wondered how they managed to be so close to us and yet somehow so removed? Why was there this distance detectable in people apparently so near at hand? These questions, which one felt more than formulated, must have come seething up in my mind around about the age of three and four, just at the time when the present Government came to power, the people who today rule, the tribe which decided that time should be stopped and put into reverse and the incendiary contact between people of different races

16

should be curbed, and then extinguished. Of course I knew nothing of these policies at the time, and I knew nothing but them in the years that followed. I learnt very early that the world one looked outward to, and forward to, was shot with shadow where Black strangers glanced at me with a baffled look in their eyes, or, worse still, with great cheerfulness and affection. 'Natives', they were called. How strange to be a native in Africa! That such people, whom one knew to be poor and strange, should seem sad was regrettable; but that others should seem unconcerned was positively alarming. So, as a child, I looked behind me, for behind me was a world of light and warmth – symbolised by my grandfather.

It was some time during the Boer War of 1899–1902, when the British Army took on an enemy composed of irregular forces, mostly farmers, in the world's first real guerrilla war, that my grandfather, Daniel McKenna, a poor lad from Waterford, Ireland, son of a lowly sub-constable, disappeared into the blue, somehow got aboard a ship sailing for South Africa and never went home again. A reputation for daring and quixotic courage marked the boy from the start. On his way home from Sunday Mass in Waterford one day he saw a man struggling in the river and plunged in fully clothed to pull him out. For ruining his only suit he earned a thrashing from his father (who rejected the story as preposterous), and a medal from the Royal Humane Society in London, 'For endeavouring to save life from drowning', the citation reads in graceful script. When the Mayor called a special meeting in the town hall to present the boy with the medal, his father sat there 'so turkey proud you'd have sworn he'd won it himself...' goes the old family story. Somehow I feel that young Daniel McKenna did not much regret leaving the sub-constable behind him.

———

17

Amongst his fellow-passengers aboard ship was Robert Baden-Powell, an accomplished and energetic imperialist who would go on to become the hero of the Siege of Mafeking (1900) and founder of the Boy Scout Movement. By contrast my grandfather, an incandescent Irish Nationalist, went on to spend the war breaking horses for the British army, an occupation which he shared with a variety of odd characters, including the American film actor Tom Mix. When the war ended in 1902 with the defeat of the Boers, my grandfather turned to his only other resource, a native talent for 'pub-keeping', headed for Balfour and bought the only hotel in town on an unsecured loan miraculously advanced by the Standard Bank. This suggests that, along with a feel for horses and a way behind the bar, the man possessed another valuable gift – a persuasive tongue, and indeed it was this that the citizens of Balfour were to appreciate most of all. Dan McKenna was a lovely talker.

I have often wondered what drew him to a place like Balfour. Perhaps, after a difficult and dangerous war, a quiet place in the country seemed attractive. In the early years of this century Balfour was certainly that; a tiny hamlet on the railway line from Johannesburg to Durban, a siding where farmers gathered to ship their maize: one street, a few houses and a station; a village no more than a few years old and not called Balfour at all, but known as McHattiesburg, the sort of name you associate with a Gold Rush town, and indeed gold was discovered on a farm not far distant, but it did not last. It is a pity about the change of name. After all, McHattiesburg *sounds* like something; it has a ring to it. It was only around about 1905 that this railway siding was dignified with the name of the Earl of Balfour – until that year British Prime Minister – and no doubt a flush of patriotism among the victors of the war against the Boers led to the change of name. My grandfather, of course, would have known Balfour, not as British Prime Minister, or even as philosopher and author of two works with engagingly contradictory titles (*The Foundations of Belief* and *The Defence of Philosophic Doubt*) but as Chief Secretary for Ireland from 1887 onwards – a desperate time for the Irish people.

I sometimes think that statesmen ought to be made to live for some years in the distant towns of conquered lands to which they allow their names to be affixed. I am sure that there was also considerable disquiet among the Boer population of Balfour when the change was made; because even then they were in the great majority and it must have seemed to them a bitter thing, this habit among victors of renaming towns in their own glory. Later developments were to show that it was a lesson Afrikaans South Africans had not forgotten.

If, as seems possible, the Boers were put out by the change of name, I can imagine that it seemed a far greater travesty to my grandfather. After all, the Afrikaners were a young nation in a new country and Britain had only fought them twice, even if the detestable English had plagued the country from the first occupation of the Cape right through to the invasion of the Boer Republics of the Orange Free State and the Transvaal. But for my grandfather, to whom the ghost of Cromwell was everywhere to be seen and warned against, this display of British chauvinism in what had been a remote place may well have led him to feel that, not content with hunting down the Irishman over the centuries, the intrepid English even pursued him to his pub in the African veld. This fellow-feeling, or shall I say this mutual loathing for a common enemy, goes some way towards explaining the cordiality and amity in which my grandfather, the Irish/ English-speaking Catholic, lived amongst his Afrikaans Calvinist neighbours. Bitter men have long, if unreliable, memories. In my grandfather the citizens of Balfour would have discovered someone whose detestation of England was both more intense and more deeply entwined in history than

19

theirs. And out of this discovery there developed, between the Boers of the nearby farms and the Irish pub-keeper of the local hotel, an alliance which was to benefit both for many years.

In the bar of the Balfour Hotel on this Saturday night patrons pack in as darkness falls. The serious drinkers on the stools around the wooden bar talk little, swallow their doubles, down their chasers, nod and leave, their silent sons padding behind them. The members of the rugby team, well into their third and fourth beers, are regaling each other with stories about women. Particularly enchanting to them is the joke about a Japanese named Sadie who, for various reasons, is having a baby. Only this phrase in the conversation is in English, everything else is in Afrikaans. But Sadie's baby is a catchword, a phrase so charged it bends them double with laughter. The serious drinkers look coldly upon this frivolity. Across the echoing cavern of a room the snooker players continue to weave around the table in their short-sleeved shirts, pushing beer bellies importantly before them; by now they are incapable of hitting a straight ball and spend a lot of time cursing, falling over or lying on the table, still pulling at their brandies and Cokes – and making a little Coke go a long way. The few dedicated drinkers remaining cup their glasses with protective hands and guard their conversation, which divides more or less equally into farm talk and politics; the subjects are not always distinguishable. A man with a great half moon of a belly, wearing a little blue pork-pie hat, drinking a triple cane spirit and lemonade, is telling the man on the stool beside him about the trouble he has been having with a tractor driver His friend, who has skin the colour of aged teak, nods sadly and swallows his beer very slowly:

'Yes, they're a lot of trouble.'

'That's what I say,' says the man in the pork-pie, 'they're a
lot of trouble. Especially when you consider the trouble you
have with them.'

'And the work you have, showing them how to do things.'

'Exactly,' says Pork-Pie. 'So in the end I had enough. I got
up on the wheel and I knocked that uppity kaffir right out of
the cab. Just like that!'

He mimics his assault and shows how the driver tumbled
into the road by swaying dangerously on his bar stool.

'Nothing but bloody trouble,' his friend agrees.

'What could I do?' Pork-Pie demands plaintively. 'I told
him nicely, but he didn't want to listen. He just didn't want to
listen!'

This conversation is deeply instructive. There is a
dimension to the relations between Black and White people in
South Africa little known among foreign observers who
imagine that the relationship is based on simple domination.
Domination is, of course, its foundation, but to think that
there is nothing more to it is to miss the metaphysics of South
African race relations and the missionary zeal with which the
religion is preached in bars, prisons, courtrooms and election
battles. The underlying metaphysics of the relationships
suggest that if God be pleased to see it so, Black and White
will enjoy equality in the world to come. Or perhaps it is more
sensible to talk of *worlds* to come, of separate but equal
paradises with linking corridors or inter-leading doors by
means of which the souls of the masters will mix freely with
those of their former servants. But before the Chosen enter
the world to come there is the struggle in the fallen world of
here and now in which the White Afrikaner is divinely
charged with the protection and moral uplift of his Black
brother. Thus it is that, to most observers, the admission: 'I
knocked that uppity kaffir right out of the cab,' will sound
like an aggressive action, a brutal assault by the boss upon his
employee. But this is a misconception and, in part, explains

the resentment with which the South African Nationalist complains of interference by the 'outside world' in matters it does not understand. For although the Afrikaner's religion enjoins him to succour his Black brother, the moment he embarks upon this he finds it easier said than done; instead of co-operating in his salvation the Black man proves stubborn, subtle, perverse, recalcitrant and proud, and try as you may to help him, he finds ways of resisting. So it is finally, more in sorrow than in anger, that one is forced to, well ... *chastise* the simple soul in order to correct his thinking and improve his demeanour. It's always done reluctantly, as a last resort, after much pleading with the man to see the error of his ways, but it is in the end usually what things come down to – a fist, a boot, a bullet. It must be understood that what underlies the conversation of the man in the pork-pie hat and his nut-brown friend is genuine sorrow, wounded feelings and sad frustration at the unwillingness of the driver in the cab to be shown the light. If you watch the doleful expressions, sorrowful head-shakings and tongue-clickings as the story unfolds, if you hear the incidental music beneath the exchange, you know that these farmers truly expect the Black man to be the death of them one day ...

And of course, in ways perhaps unsuspected, they could be right.

The barman turns to me: 'You new to town?'

I tell him 'yes' and 'no'. 'My grandfather owned the hotel once. The *other* hotel.'

The man on my right, perhaps reassured that the stranger in the bar can speak Afrikaans, despite an English accent, and is after all related to the village, now turns to me.

'That's the old hotel, you mean. There on the other side of town, under the railway bridge. The Indians got it now, you know. There's nothing to be seen there now.'

The loss of my grandfather's hotel to the Indians apparently moves him obscurely because he buys me a drink and introduces himself. His name is Philip and he wears grey shorts and a short-sleeved Aertex shirt through which the black hairs of his chest protrude like a strange crop. His most remarkable features are his ears, because they look quite extraordinarily like the handles of a Greek amphora; they are large, loopy and, in a curious way, very beautiful ornaments to adorn a weather-beaten head, rough as a fence post. I ask Philip what he thinks is going to happen in the General Election in a few weeks' time. He rubs his chin, sighs and stares into his brandy. Over at the snooker table a vat-shaped man in very short white shorts is attempting a difficult shot and has folded himself across the centre of the table and squints along his cue at the white ball. Behind him one of his friends bends down and, unseen by the sportsman, aims his cue into the opening in the fat man's shorts and makes as if to pot a testicle. The other players double up with laughter: 'Pocket billiards! Pocket billiards!'

Philip tugs at a shapely ear. 'If you ask me about this election, I think old P.W. is going to see his arse.'

By this jaunty abbreviation he refers to the State President, P.W. Botha, who was once Prime Minister but now under the new Constitution combines within his stern and polished person the roles of Government leader and Head of State. He is also sometimes referred to as 'Pee-Wee Boots' and also as 'Pete the Weapon', an echo, or repercussion, from the days when he served as our gun-hungry and bellicose Minister of Defence. So much for P.W. The earthy reference to the position the President is expected to assume when the election is over is not some bluff compliment to the political dexterity of the man, nor some hint of the degree of subtlety needed in order to attain the position suggested – not at all. Philip means that the State President, and by implication the governing White National Party, is heading for deep trouble.

'You see,' says Philip, 'I am a CP man.' He strokes the black hairs protruding through the Aertex holes as if strumming an instrument. 'We're the future.'

I protest: 'The National Party hold over one hundred and twenty seats in Parliament. There are only one hundred and seventy-eight altogether. Everybody knows they're going to get in again, just as they've done for forty years. And the rest of us will just have to do what we're told.'

He pulls at his cane and Coke. 'Yes, they'll win, and then they're going to take us down the road to Black government and I tell you, my friend, when that happens you're not going to see me or my friends.'

'Where will you be?'

'We're going to get in our trucks, or we'll climb on our horses and we're going back to the veld. Like our fathers did. And you know what we're going to do there?'

'I have no idea.'

'We're going to take our guns and we're going to fight, just like we did before. Against the Blacks. And the British. It will be the old days all over again. When the kaffirs came looking for trouble they got it. Right? So when the Government comes looking for us, we'll be waiting.' He dropped his voice. 'We'll be the terrorists then.'

Philip, otherwise such a Neanderthal political thinker, genuinely considers himself to be the Future. He also considers himself a horseman. I don't know which prospect is the more alarming. He wishes to move forward into the future by returning to the past. He wishes to return to the old certainties of Verwoerdian apartheid where everyone and everything was segregated and the State was run upon the principle of the forcible separation of the different racial groups into camps, ghettos, towns, suburbs, beaches, lavatories, beds, churches and graveyards. Now the fact that the changes made to this ideal separation have been no more than tinkerings, that the present Government, far from doing away with it, is attempting to modernise apartheid without abandoning it – this carries no weight with Philip. It is not the nature of the changes that Philip and his friends object to, it is that there have been any changes at all. It is not for nothing that the leader of the Conservative Party, Dr Treurnicht (the name translates, with that unhappy aptness so common here, as 'Sorrownot'), is also called Dr No. The Conservative Party, the HNP and the Afrikaner Resistance Movement (the AWB) stand in the great tradition of naysayers in Afrikaner history from the first settlers who said 'No' to the emancipation of the slaves and trekked into the unknown fastness of Africa; 'No' to the heretics who claimed the earth was round and 'No' to the poltroons who insisted on the equality of all people; 'No' to the British and their grasping, gold-stealing ways; 'No' to foreigners, outsiders, and imperialists; 'No' to integration, immigrants, missionaries, Catholics, Indians and Jews; 'No' to votes for non-White people; 'No' to mixed bathing, to Sunday sport, to television, to Coloured cricket players; 'No' to *Black Beauty*, television, raffles and Namibia; 'No' to the outside world and the mongrelisation of the sacred White tribe of the Afrikaner. An ability to see the future as if it were the present put into reverse joins Philip and his party to the old Boer leaders of the nineteenth century, and to Paul Kruger in particular who, after his defeat by the British, sat in lonely exile at Clarens by the shores of Lake Geneva and wrote a last testament to his countrymen, warning them that if they cared for their future they should look to the past.

TRUST THE NATS AGAIN? Demand the posters of the White Right – NEVER!!!

Philip sits peering solemnly into his drink and fondling his lovely ears. In his aerated shirt and bare feet, it is difficult to imagine this man getting up in the morning, never mind saddling his horse and heading for the hills, bandolier of ammunition around his shoulders and his rifle oiled and ready.

And it would not do much good to talk to Philip about Kruger's bitter exile in 1900 and the historical roots of the struggle for South Africa, although he speaks directly from the Krugerite tradition. Philip, like most South Africans, does not read history: history is something you fight, not read. Yet there is about him a reflection, pale but authentic, of the ferocious stubbornness and resolve of the Boer which the rest of the world, as well as the political opposition within the country, have ignored or derided – to their cost. But there is also a genuinely new note in Philip's politics which has been absent from legal parliamentary opposition in this country since the late 'forties when the present Government came to power. It is the threat of force, of armed violence, and there is no doubt that he means what he says.

It is getting late. The rugby team have drained their glasses and slipped into the warm, velvet autumn night. Philip has clearly said his piece and will say no more. The snooker players are now so stupefied that they have given up any attempt to hit the ball and instead wander about the table like sleepwalkers or blind sentries patrolling a small courtyard, their snooker cues carried like emaciated rifles, at the port. It is time to leave. No one remarks on my departure – why should they? – they know who I am now; I am the man whose grandfather once owned the hotel on the other side of town which the Indians took over. And so to bed. I climb the stairs that smell of fly spray. The seascapes have set like green jelly on the walls at the top of the stairs. The radio in my bedroom has shut down for the night, though it cannot be turned off, and buzzes quietly to itself. Outside the window the wafer-thin, grey-white moon hangs unhurriedly about the sky with a cheap, metallic sheen to it. And there is something about the way it dawdles across the heavens that is most eye-catching. It moves so slowly that if this were an English moon you might say it was loitering with intent; but of course this is not England. That this little town is called Balfour should not deceive anyone; nor should the fact that the next stop down the railway line is called Nigel: it is just another pretence. Names, mere names. Official signs and designations are not to be followed if you expect to find your way about South Africa. For that matter, the town on the road before you arrive in Balfour happens to be called Heidelberg, but the songs they sing there don't come from *The Student Prince*. Such names represent moments when the wing-tip of European history brushed against the face of South Africa, leaving the faintest of impressions. I get to sleep at last but I am awoken at about three by a seething, rushing wave of sound flooding the great flat plain outside my window. At first I think it must be the sea, until I remember where I am and recognize the sound of an approaching train. And I recall then the old family story about how my grandfather had been responsible for seeing to it that the train came this way at all since it had been the intention of the old colonial authorities, when planning a new line from the goldfields of Johannesburg and the Reef, down to the great port at Durban on the Natal south coast, to bypass little Balfour altogether. The Afrikaner burgers lost no time in dispatching my grandfather to argue their case with the Government, in those days entirely British, knowing that he spoke the King's English with precision, which they did not, while sharing their deep abhorrence towards all kings and their accoutrements.

In the gloomy dining-room downstairs the next morning all the blinds are drawn and the water in the vases holding the little bouquets of plastic flowers has long since dried. Across the way the bitter desk clerk of the night before glares at me from the foxhole of the serving hatch, and the radio is tuned unremittingly to the Afrikaans station, and the Dutch Reformed Minister, the Dominie, in that peculiar, high-pitched sing-song voice, is calling on the faithful to prostrate themselves before the Lord. At five minutes past eight precisely the weak little lights overhead go dead. My enemy smiles from the service hatch.

'There – what did I tell you?'

The demented bar-waiter, still in his blood-red coat and black trousers, still with his metal tray, watches from the door, nodding in enthusiastic agreement at the prophecy fulfilled. I get up, collect my bags, pay my bill and leave. As I drive away down the main street I imagine them folding up the hotel and packing it back in its box, fuming as they do so at the foolishness of the stranger who believes this place to be a hotel merely because the sign outside says so.

So it is that down the road I go in order to discover the old Balfour and my grandfather's hotel, down the road and through the dip and under the railway bridge, to the lower end of town, a place quite literally across the tracks, for the railway line forms the boundary and when I have crossed it I find myself in Indian country. Once I have passed under the railway bridge I turn left into Station Street and I am in another world, or rather I am in the world that was before this present one existed. My left turn into Station Street carries me back in time to an epoch before the introduction of classical apartheid. Station Street runs west to east and the main street in Balfour runs north to south, so you might imagine a kind of earthquake had occurred to swing the town on its axis like this. Station Street, now without its station, once the only street in town, follows the railway line faithfully down to the giant grey and yellow tubular elevators where the farmers bring their maize; a thriving trade, for this is prosperous farming country. The doves call in the oaks and I observe that the oaks are planted in regular patterns around Balfour, hinting at another, more gracious and rather ambitious time when such symmetries were appreciated and certain people had high hopes of McHattiesburg, dreamt no doubt of expansion, progress and enlightenment. Early in the century there were people here who felt as the settlers in other parts of the New World had done, that the country, having come through a bitter war, was over the worst and poised for expansion. They had good reason for thinking so, for up the road, just a few hours' drive, lay Johannesburg with its prodigious goldfields. The struggle between Boer and British had been long and unforgiving, but it was over, and despite my grandfather's sympathies for the Boers he must have felt that a modern South Africa was in the making and he was present at the birth of something great and new. Only such confidence can explain why a penniless young man drifted into McHattiesburg one day, set up a table and chair opposite the single hotel in Station Street, then called the Grange Hotel, studied the flow of clientele into the bar and on the basis of this unusual market research convinced the bank manager to advance him the money needed, with which he bought the establishment. And there are still hints of solid prosperity to be read in the sturdy whitewashed ruins of Station Street which must have made this confidence seem well placed.

In 1910 the four provinces of Southern Africa, the Transvaal, Cape, Natal and the Free State, were joined by an Act of Union and became a young country of enormous wealth and potential. These developments clearly affected my grandfather's view of the country – and also probably softened his fierce republicanism. His elder brother, a Sinn Fein activist, had been shot by the British back in Ireland and my grandfather sent for his younger brother, Michael, to join him. With Union the British had departed, handing back to the Boers the land they had conquered at such cost in men, *matériel* and military reputations, possibly quite unaware that they left behind a reservoir of bitterness, a lake of anti-British feeling to which the Afrikaner Nationalists would come and drink for another fifty years. I think sometimes that although his Irish nationalism helped my grandfather to understand, support and encourage the Boers in their struggle for freedom, his need to believe in the advent of a new South Africa prevented him from understanding the depth of mutual hostility felt by Boer and Briton for each other. This was a time when it seemed to many that out of the bitter conflict of the Anglo-Boer struggle, a real transformation was taking place.

One can trace the reasons behind Daniel McKenna's confidence to the leaders he supported. Pre-eminent was General Louis Botha, a Boer leader of genius whose guerrilla tactics sustained the Boers in the Transvaal with dazzling ingenuity in the last months of the war. And what a wretched, messy end it was. The Boers unable to accept they had lost and the British seemingly unable to force a conclusion. Botha was among the signatories of the Treaty, eventually signed in Pretoria, when peace finally came in 1902, and he survived the near despair of his followers to become the first Prime Minister of the Union of South Africa in 1910. Here, it seemed, was a leader worthy of support, a man of international standing, a statesman determined to forget and forgive, to bury the past. Botha was to support the British in the Great War of 1914. My grandfather must have agreed because, when South African troops sailed for France, his younger brother, Michael, was among the volunteers, his fare paid by my grandfather. Although it is unlikely that his suspicions of the British had in any way lessened, it seems he genuinely believed that there was now a new dispensation in South Africa and that under the leadership of Botha he was no longer Irish but truly South African.

He was quite wrong. The very qualities which Dan McKenna, and the outside world, admired in General Botha inspired in the breasts of devout, bitter Afrikaner Nationalists only anger and detestation. I will not say that the writing was on the wall, for the writing has always been on the wall. But

30

there are so many walls and the trick is not to try and read the writing but to take very careful note of the walls. The politics of South Africa are not, and never have been, literate: they are mural.

However, in the beginning it must have been different. After 1910 and Union under General Botha my grandfather was happy and prospered in the Grange Hotel in Station Street. He revelled in his small success, he enjoyed gambling, and raced horses, flourished in the camaraderie of the hotel bar; he was civic-minded, gregarious, generous with credit to his customers to a degree which explains both his popularity and the fact that while he was comfortably off, he was never to be rich. He went courting my grandmother, Mabel Brokenshaw, who lived in a nearby hamlet, dressed in a white suit, astride a huge black horse. He loved singing and dancing, raised five children, plied a variety of trades, considered standing for Parliament and bought parcels of land in and around Balfour in the sure expectation, never justified, that their value would rise. His commercial sense, like his political nose, was rather soft, although his boundless energy and his considerable personal charm were usually enough to help extricate him from his mistakes and to blunt the edge of his disappointments.

I have only the briefest of memories of him; in fact I do not remember him so much as a person but as an area of warmth, as a shining kindness. I have two photographs which show him young and old. In the first he is about twenty: handsome, dark-haired, with large, round, dark eyes and a thick droopy moustache, and an eager, intense and yet slightly anxious look about him, his expression a mixture of bravado and shyness which together make for an attractive air of vulnerability. The second picture, which was taken thirty or forty years later, shows him wearing a morning suit with a rose in his lapel. Perhaps it was taken at the wedding of one of his children. His hair is still thick, but grainily white and the moustache less full, but the face, though that of a substantial, successful man, still reveals about the gentle eyes, darker now, and deeper, a haunted, strangely baffled look.

The remains of the Grange Hotel are still to be seen about halfway down Station Street. The entire front with its gables has gone and so has the long veranda and the bar. Only a few rooms behind the façade remain, and beyond them is a jumble of out-buildings, including a large corrugated iron shed in which one of my uncles ran a Saturday bioscope at a penny a seat, in which local patrons willingly endured not only the stifling heat of the tin hall, but the frequent collapse of the projector. There is today a feeling of neglect in Station Street combined with signs of energetic commercial spirit. Garni's shop remains though the old man is long gone, Mystry is still here, as well as Mohammed, so is Hajee's Fashion Paradise, and Timol's Material Corner, all families my grandfather knew, friends and business acquaintances, some of whom still remember Dan McKenna. Across the road from the hotel the full length of the street was once lined with gangers' cottages for those employed on the railway line, and of course there was the station itself. A solitary ganger's cottage remains; a small, curiously pretty little corrugated iron box with a water tank up on the roof, like an oddly flat chimney. It looks like a doll's house.

I came to live with my grandfather in Balfour when I was a baby, in the last months of the war. My father had been killed flying missions in North Africa and my grandfather took in the young widow and her son and gave us a small flat at the back of the hotel. It seems that I took to hotel life with enthusiasm and soon became a feature of the pub, propped on the end of the bar and assured of constant attention by eager conversationalists who bought me lemonade, for which I was given my own small glass, and who fed me peppermints. Remembering my experiences in the 'new' Balfour hotel I am not tempted to romanticize the quality of conversation I must have heard in the bar of the 'old' Balfour hotel, but by all accounts it brought me along at a fine pace and it seems I was a very early talker. As the pub mascot I was treated with considerable kindness by the farmers and miners from thereabouts who petted me, helped me to crawl, extended my babyish vocabulary and generally exemplified, I suspect, the magnanimity of thirsty men who had found a congenial watering hole (and there was no other for many miles) where the beer was cold and the landlord tolerant and who wished to express their appreciation. I also benefitted from that well-watered goodwill on which charities rely when they put collection boxes for lifeboat funds and guide dogs for the blind on bar counters. When I fell dangerously ill, I was nursed back to life by the Black cook. I was put to school amongst the beer drinkers, and went shopping at the Indian stores. In South African terms this amounts to an unusually rounded upbringing. Presiding over it all was an indulgent Irish landlord who extended credit.

And at first he certainly prospered. If I cast my eye down the Balfour mayoral roll, I see his great period was the early 'twenties when he was voted back year after year. He makes another appearance in the late 'twenties and again in the early 'thirties. He is Mayor one final time in 1943–4. I have the feeling that even well into the 'thirties things must have gone his way. One Boer general succeeded the next as Prime Minister: Botha gave way to Hertzog and Hertzog to General Smuts. Hertzog was, it is true, a somewhat difficult Nationalist, but with the fusion between his National Party and the South African Party of General Smuts in 1932, it must have seemed as if a broad-based coalition pointed the political way ahead. And it is reasonable to suppose that the Boers who drank in the bar of the Grange Hotel, patted my blond curls, bought me lemonade and introduced me to the limited but pungent vocabulary of the bar, would have returned the affection of the Irishman who supported their cause.

And this points to a genuine tolerance in the early days of the town since my grandfather was, to all appearances, the triple manifestation of the enemy: he was an immigrant, he spoke English and, perhaps worst of all, he was a Catholic. Despite these considerable drawbacks, it was Dan McKenna whom the burgers sent to the new South African Government, now restored to its former capital in Pretoria, to plead their cause, just as they had once sent him to persuade the old colonial authorities that the railway line should continue to pass through Balfour.

Yet I cannot forget that my grandfather, by his optimism alone, showed just how foreign he was in his habit of taking people as he found them. The very worst one can say of this, in retrospect, is that it was probably a mistake to make presumptions of fellow-feeling and camaraderie, or of the beneficial effects of material progress. A 'real' South African would have known that the brief, gusty enthusiasms which distend the thin-skinned surface of South African life are based on nothing more than wind, on hot air; bitter memories are the real heart of politics. It must have distressed this Irish optimist that he lived to see the day when taking people as you found them became an arrestable offence and the physical expression of feeling, under certain circumstances, became, quite literally, a crime. I admire his faith, even so. In the early decades of this century there was perhaps a chance of beginning to forget the old quarrels and moving forward and outward into the world. Station Street in the 'twenties and 'thirties was a mixed area (what they call today a 'grey' area) and embodied a degree of racial toleration. The pattern was as follows: Whites ran the show, though there was also numbers of 'Poor Whites' reduced, during the Depression of the 'thirties and by the discrimination of other, usually English-speaking Whites; there was a settlement of Indians, a community obliged to become small traders since all other occupations were closed to them and they suffered the animosity of both Whites and Blacks; then there were of course the Blacks, the large majority, who provided the cheap labour. This was the pattern not only of Balfour but of the country generally. This is not to suggest that English-speakers, as they proved in their governments in both the Cape and Natal, were any less racially prejudiced than their Afrikaner counterparts; indeed, they were often more vulgarly and shrewishly disposed towards the 'natives' than the Afrikaner who lived and worked with them. But the whole basis was not yet imbued with the mysticism or the rigid dogmatism of later arrangements. It must have seemed to my grandfather that the natural divisions of Station Street would persist and that while it was expected of the Government, in the event of riot or disaffection, to keep the natives in their places, custom and tradition were themselves sufficiently powerful to hold the line. Furthermore, it would have been surprising if people had foreseen in the 'twenties and 'thirties that the Boer guerrillas, having gained their own liberation, were to gather themselves into a movement which would begin with considerable dedication, enthusiasm and religious intensity to deny to others that freedom for which they had fought so hard.

By 1939 the view from the bar at the Grange Hotel must have been pretty rosy. General Smuts had taken South Africa into war against Germany. His old rival General Hertzog, unable to support this alliance with the old enemy, Britain, withdrew from the Government coalition and his National Party faded to a memory.

There were, however, other readings of history. To the angry young radicals among the Afrikaners, Hertzog had been little more than a traitor ever since he joined forces with Smuts in the early 'thirties. With the unlamented passing of Hertzog's old National Party, a new 'purified' National Party, a rough, unlovely thing, was awaiting the day and the hour to be born. If Hertzog was seen as having deserted the *volk* then Jan Smuts was beneath contempt to the young men who joined the newly-constituted National Party of Dr Daniel François Malan and who pledged themselves to the defence of the purity of the White Afrikaner tribe, the cleansing of the Boer breeding stock, the victory of Hitler, the reclamation of Boer independence, the excoriation and, where possible, extirpation of the English and their influence, and the return of the country to the religious, racial and national ideas of Boer leaders of the past. They looked in particular to Paul Kruger and the spirit of the trekkers who had turned their backs on the hated British in the Cape, opened up the country and stood alone against the massed Zulu armies at Blood River and other places. A shrewd, if somewhat prejudiced, observer of the Boers, Rudyard Kipling, pronounced upon the hidden programme of the Boer Nationalists with a prescience which extends right down to the Soweto of the present day. He wrote in a letter to his friend Dr Conland of Boer ambitions: 'They want to sweep the English into the sea, to lick their own nigger and to govern South Africa with a gun instead of a ballot box'. It could not have occurred to Kipling that the ballot box was also within their grasp.

But to those who looked outwards, the Second World War must have seemed considerably more important than a little local difficulty on the home front and, in 1939, Jan Smuts reigned supreme. When the war ended his position seemed unshakable. The outside world came to recognize the former Boer general as a world statesman of great gifts, close ally and adviser of Churchill and he was on hand to help draft the Covenant of the United Nations. The farm boy who only went to school at twelve, a brilliant and ferocious Boer leader in the struggle for freedom, had become one of Britain's most loyal and active allies, a forward-looking, liberated leader in the mould of General Botha. Little wonder my grandfather was so devoted to him. No wonder, either, that among the members of the newly 'purified' National Party of Dr Malan he was hated and reviled with a loathing not seen in South Africa before or since; not at any rate, until the formation of the new right-wing Afrikaner movements a few years ago; those fanatical groupings – such as the Conservative Party and the *Afrikaner Weerstand Beweging* – of which my drinking companion Philip of the amphora ears is a supporter. They feel for President P.W. Botha precisely the same, undiluted hatred the Nationalists once felt for Smuts – 'the handyman of Empire' – as they derisively called him, back in the 'forties.

In 1939 a considerable body of Afrikaner opinion opposed the war which was called 'Smuts' war'. Numbers of people joined organisations such as the *Ossewa Brandwag* (the Oxwagon Brigade) and set about acts of sabotage; there were declarations of support for the Axis Forces and parades held in expectation of a German victory. My grandfather's position may be gauged without difficulty. His sons enlisted, his daughters married airmen and before long he was having to make arrangements to accommodate his recently widowed eldest daughter and her baby son in one of the rooms at the back of the Grange Hotel. Yet many years earlier there were straws in the wind which might have hinted at a looming catastrophe. In the 'thirties the Dominie came to Balfour. These ministers of the Dutch Reformed Church were preachers of racial exclusivity, Calvinist rectitude and the dangers of modernism, Anglicization and miscegenation. Dan McKenna's time in Balfour may thus be divided into two phases: BC – before the Dominie came, and AD – after the Dominie. In the beginning my grandfather had been a popular, much respected figure. Dan McKenna (BC) had his heart in the right place: civic leader, Boer supporter, former mayor, redoubtable spokesman on behalf of the local farmers in Government councils. But Dan McKenna (AD) stood revealed as a closet Englishman; for after all, that was the language he spoke. His Irishness was neither here nor there.

The Dominie was not a geographer. The Dominie's job was not to address himself to the world, but to condemn it as a snare and a folly.

Worse still was the fact that my grandfather was a Catholic and Roman Catholicism was listed among the great dangers stalking the Afrikaner people: it was a swelling theme. These 'dangers' represented forces intent on polluting – by racial, cultural or religious means – the stainless blood of the tribe. Dangers were always and everywhere present: there was the ever-present 'Black Danger', there was the 'Yellow Danger' – the Asian menace from the East – and there was the 'Roman Danger', the Popish plot whereby Catholics, particularly in Boer communities, supposedly worked to captivate and carry off unsuspecting Afrikaners to the Church of Rome.

Another warning sign might have been the geographical shift in the town itself to which my grandfather cannot have been blind as numbers of white people began moving across the railway tracks. The station moved too, and my grandfather, with customary zeal, bought land in the empty veld where the new station was to be built. There were even plans for a new hotel across town, as Station Street and old Balfour itself was increasingly abandoned to the Indians and poorer Whites. Perhaps some inkling of what was happening penetrated my grandfather's resolute optimism, for at about this time he bought a house in the faraway northern suburbs of Johannesburg.

Station Street today is, then, much as we left it. That is part of its charm and its sadness. It is a ghetto, certainly, but it is not a slum. The street has about it a curious serenity which is possibly due to the fact that it does not have to pretend any longer; it is now the Indian quarter and sections of it rejoice in evident prosperity. The only really ugly buildings are the motor showroom at the entrance of the street, on the site that was once my grandfather's office, and the municipal-looking mosque of orange brick at the far end of the street. The

Indians are pleasant and self-assured; beautifully dressed children scoot up and down on their bikes. No doubt White housewives still come up here to shop for material, clothes, cars, and to visit the perpetual sales which glitter in the dress shops and bazaars. Sustained neglect has preserved some relics of former times. Along one side of the street a number of façades retain characteristic gables, thick whitewashed walls, broad verandas; and over them all broods a kind of dreamy peace which is strangely attractive. The old bank which lent money to the indigent Irishman with no prospects and no security is still to be seen. It is used now as a storeroom and through the dirty window I see Victorian desks and old ball and claw furniture piled up to the cobwebby ceiling.

If you wish to find White people in Station Street you must look behind the Grange Hotel. There you will find a cemetery: it is very small, surrounded by a concrete fence, beautifully neat and utterly abandoned. Glancing at the gravestones it looks to me as if the last burial took place here in the mid 1970s. Clearly certain white families who had long ago left the area continued to return, to claim their burial plots. Death and the ever-present bargains in the shops are the only things which draw Whites back to Station Street. The headstones show dates from well before the turn of the century and I am struck by the fact that even then the majority of the names are Afrikaans. At no time have English-speakers in Balfour numbered more than a handful. The graves, solid affairs of marble, have sunk over the years into the iron-hard red soil. Headstones lean this way and that and a family of mongooses have taken up residence beneath the stone 'sacred to the memory of the family Vermeulen'. Little glass pots surmounted by artificial flowers are broken and the glass jars in which other floral offerings were sealed have a cloudy, milky film clinging to the inside of the glass which looks, when you first see it, like condensation, as if these blooms had miraculously preserved their moisture over decades. Closer inspection reveals instead a chalky precipitate, possibly the effect of strong sunlight on the glass, rather than the ghosts of the flowers that once adorned these graves. There are no tended graves; wind and rain scour the mounds, no one from the other Balfour across the tracks remembers those who lie here. Yet there are flowers to be seen in the graveyard, purple and pink blooms, growing wiry, wild, unchecked, flourishing with a ferocity that suggests recent rains, pushing up through the marble, shouldering aside the headstones: as always, in Africa, a brief, rampant, irrepressible blossoming. The centre of the graveyard is a memorial stone, a granite column which displays half-way up its tapering shaft of rough, grey stone a roundel with the head of a springbok. On the marble base of this little cenotaph are carved the names of the 'men of Balfour' who fell in the Great War of 1914–18, 'their duty bravely done'. There are eight names in all, led by that of Michael McKenna, my grandfather's younger brother, who died of his wounds at Arras.

To the right of the little graveyard, in a great circle of oak trees, is the cricket field, a bumpy, sandy, tussocky oval on which two teams of Indians in snowy whites are playing a needle match. It turns out to be one of the last fixtures of the season. The outfield is in a woeful condition, full of bumps, boulders and patches of knee-high grass. The contest is between 'the boys' and the 'oldsters'. The wicket itself is a mat laid between the stumps. The oldsters are batting and they're having much their own way, cracking the ball across the bumpy outfield to the intense enjoyment of the spectators who have parked their cars around the ground. On the table two trophies gleam proudly, awaiting the winning team and the 'Man of the Match'. This league is of long standing. In the old days, when the races still mixed in Station Street, my uncles played for these teams. Now the club and its field struggle to survive. It's one of the lesser symptoms of the neglect of Station Street and its community which, despite its bright storefronts and its beautifully groomed children, suffers dreadfully from over-crowding; it is without official funds or planning permission or allocations of new land to house the growing population which struggles to find living space among the backyard rooms, sheds and lean-tos where the Indians must live on, somehow, in the houses the White men left behind, an insecure and unpopular minority whose culture the Whites do not understand, whose large families they distrust and whose prosperity they envy. The state of the cricket field is a very sore point amongst the players. Despite repeated requests the town council will not contribute to its upkeep although they own the land. When you think about it the local council, composed of White Afrikaners, has any number of reasons for sitting on its hands. First and foremost is the fact that Indians are, well, *Indian* . . . and if that were not enough the field is used for that most English of sports, cricket; and, in any event, the council undoubtedly regards the community as quite prosperous enough already; if they insist on desecrating the Sabbath with this lunatic English pastime then they must pay for it themselves.

'But we won't pay for it,' one of the older members tells me, 'it's a matter of principle. It's the council's job to keep this place up. We roll the pitch, we maintain it in a playable condition but the field is theirs and they should look after it. They won't even lend us their big mower. They have this beautiful, huge mower for their own playing-fields but they won't lend it. We have to use little lawn-mowers to keep the grass down. And they won't give us more land for houses. You see how it is here. All we have is Station Street with sometimes three families to a room. But they won't listen to us. It's useless talking to them. We do talk to them, of course, but they don't want to know.'

The batman strikes the ball sweetly into the covers where it hits a patch of grass, rebounds, and bounces hip-high across the field. With the next ball the batsman, who has been doing considerable damage, is bowled around his legs and the fielding team erupt in excitement. The oldster with me applauds a fine innings.

'Damn good knock,' he says. 'Up the oldsters – we'll show them!'

I come away reluctantly from this peaceful, rural, oddly English scene preserved by the Indians of Station Street as a kind of living museum which reflects the way things were, and still are, in Balfour. A game of cricket played out under a high blue African sky is one of the examples of the way in which the extraordinary disguises itself beneath the everyday surfaces of life. The game is an import from the days of Empire; but then so are the Indians themselves, imports, brought in to work the sugar plantations of Natal in the middle of the nineteenth century. So what appears to be a simple game of cricket is neither simple nor a game. It has a political and a religious dimension. Indians may stay in Balfour provided they live in Station Street; they may pay taxes so long as they do not demand value for those taxes; and they may play cricket, though they should not expect that the choice of the game will be popular among the guardians of the town; and they may even play on Sunday, which, for the White Afrikaner community down the road, is a day of rest. But they should not be surprised if this challenge to the Sabbath serves to emphasise their alien cultural habits. And for their part, these competing teams drawn from the three hundred and fifty Indians of Station Street continue, in white flannels and caps, to assert their right to exist: they are making a claim for normality.

There is a third layer of unreality to be encountered that recalls the strange case that we are. Today, being Sunday, it is not in evidence and so I must retrace my way down Station Street, turn right, descend beneath the railway bridge and drive to the other end of town, passing the filling stations, the shops, the banks and the election posters waving from the telephone poles.

As I am about to leave town, I pause to admire the giant Dutch Reformed churches, which guard the exit from Balfour. Set well back from the road on lush green lawns and where, judging by the lines of cars parked outside, well-attended services are in progress, these churches constitute, I suppose, the Dominie's triumph. What began as a spot of trouble for my grandfather ends in these triumphant statements in orange face brick and soaring spires. They are without doubt the grandest buildings in town, not quite as tall as the grey and yellow grain elevators, but more important. Their tall delicate spires stab the gleaming sky. It is very curious that a religion so concerned to give theological justification to the earth-bound policies of segregation, so intimately involved in the workings of the temporal State and its White government, should build churches in the form of rather plump rocket ships, that a church so immovable and unyielding in its theological opinions, so heavily grave, should erect as its places of worship buildings which strain for the heavens, which seem to yearn to fly.

Originating with the Dutch missionaries who accompanied the earliest White settlers to the Cape of Good Hope in the seventeenth century, strengthened by an infusion of Scots Presbyterians in the early nineteenth, the 'Kerk, came to its full flowering in the mid-twentieth century when the National Party made Government policy of the Church's faith in the divine nature of racial separation, a policy it has supported, promoted and sustained with sober enthusiasm for three centuries. There are rumours that the Church is beginning to detach itself from the policies, but, like so much else, I doubt if the news is being preached in Balfour. The Church is divided into three sisterly varieties, the *Nederduitsche Gereformeerde Kerk*, the largest of the trio, and two smaller entities, the *Gereformeerde Kerk* and the *Nederduitsche Hervormde Kerk van Afrika*. Though doctrinally distinct, these Churches may be regarded as one body, known locally as the D.R.C., representing devotion to the ethnic immaculacy of the Afrikaner tribe. The mere initials have been enough to strike gloom into liberal hearts. Until recently the Dutch Reformed Churches have taught that not only is it plausible to serve both God and apartheid, it is positively required. Taken together they represent the National Party at prayer and despite the theological differences between them the outsider would have difficulty telling them apart – as indeed would insiders who have felt the political effects of their faith in a God who created an elected few and decreed that they be served by the unelected many who would be hewers of wood and drawers of water. The Church is not solely against racial mixing, it is also against raffles, Sunday fishing, Catholicism, liberalism, modernism. Its influence is profound and may be felt from the cradle to the grave – although not always in that order. You may test its mettle if you travel, say, to one of the founding churches of the Reformed Communion, such as the one in the village of Tulbagh down in the Cape Province, where the Mother Church is found, a modest, whitewashed Cape Dutch chapel, a place where the death in life, which is segregation, persists in the graveyard where the White faithful and their Coloured servants occupy separate resting-places in the apartheid of the deceased. Doubtless those who laid them here believed that they would continue to occupy separate sleeping quarters in Paradise. The spirit of division reaches its apotheosis in the townships, locations and squatter camps in what we choose to call modern South Africa. The great Dutch Reformed churches of Balfour tower prosperously in the brilliant morning sunshine, as confident and as important as the banking temples of Barclays and Standard down the road.

I take the road away from town for some ten minutes, over

the ridge, and into the location where the Black people of Balfour live or, perhaps more accurately, are hidden. In this sprawling collection of brick houses, huts and hovels exist eighty thousand people, nearly three times the population of the White town. Now the triangular configuration of a place like Balfour begins to emerge, and not only Balfour but every town and city across the country, in the Transvaal and Natal and the Cape Province (with the possible exception of the province next door, the Orange Free State, which is proud of the fact that no Indians are permitted to live there). For the rest, the pattern established here applies generally: Whites at the top of the town, Indians down under and Blacks over the hills and far away, out of sight, out of range. And yet this Black location is the source of energy, the powerhouse, the machine, the reservoir of labour without which Balfour would not exist. The world has heard of Soweto but perhaps what is not known is that every town and village in South Africa has its own Soweto. It is these residential divisions of the races which are likely to be the most enduring legacy of forty years of energetic, classical apartheid. They are the result of something known as the Group Areas Act which shortens to the unlovely acronym GAA, which, in turn, is the sort of noise that fierce men make when they jump out from behind trees to frighten children. GAA is the absolute cornerstone of the territorial separation, the concept of each to his own, which is the bitter fruit of the Nationalist Victory of 1948. And its effects upon this vast slum are clear: what is remarkable is not its size, its poverty – but that you would not realise that the place was here, unless you knew where to look. For the White inhabitants of Balfour the Black location does not even contrive to spoil the view. The only place from which it might be glimpsed would be the top of the very proud steeple of the Dutch Reformed Church, and it is unlikely that sightseeing tours to that vantage point are being planned.

Though I can recall nothing of the political upheavals of 1948, yet swirling, fragmentary images and impressions rise in my mind like surfacing trout when I think back to that time. The election itself was too generalised and vague a catastrophe to register particularly, though I am sure that the impact of the Nationalist victory on those around me, notably my mother and grandfather, and the widespread feeling of gloom and apprehension, must have communicated itself to me. But there were other unsettling factors which would have given to the period an alarming aspect. It was around this time that I exchanged my seat on the bar stool in the old Grange Hotel for a room in a pleasant house my grandfather bought for my mother in the northern suburbs of Johannesburg: perhaps, too, I was becoming aware of the fact that my father was dead. I had been too young ever to have remembered him but I think we sometimes become aware of a great loss only when attempts are made to replace it; it is the shock of the substitute which alerts us to the irreplaceable value of the original. My father had been a pilot in the South African Air Force and he died when his bomber crashed in the desert war against Rommel ('Up North' as the Western Desert was bewilderingly called) where the South African forces were heavily engaged. Yet though I was too young to know him, this had the effect, a few years later when I became aware of it, of making the sense of loss greater and more difficult to comprehend or accept. I took possession of a single memento, a photograph of a mild-eyed, pleasant young stranger, wearing an Air Force cap at a rakish angle, and a faint, boyish smile. His name was Dennis Tully and he was an Irishman, another quixotic victim of a war fought on behalf of a former enemy, just as my great-uncle Michael had been in the earlier conflict in the First World War in France.

News of his death had taken some years to reach me, I suppose, but it was at last brought home with the remarriage of my mother. I do not think, either, that I registered anything definite about the marriage, but the flux of sensations and emotions bombarding me became more fevered and inexplicable; the big new house was filled with strangers and I experienced what I now recognise as a feeling of profound dislocation, so radical that I sometimes think that the effects are still with me. I remember becoming fascinated with heights and walls, in that order. I discovered that however high the wall was between myself and the boy next door, it could be surmounted if sufficient stones, bricks or tree branches were piled on top of each other. I looked up the scaly trunks of the immense palm trees growing astonishingly out of the front lawn and longed to climb them because something told me they were taller than anything else for miles around; so tall that they disappeared into the heavens where a boy might likewise vanish if only he could climb that high. I suspect that the story of 'Jack and the Beanstalk' had something to do with it because my grandfather had an inexhaustible supply of such stories. Perhaps, altogether, these feelings amounted to a deep feeling of unease, possibly unhappiness and desperation, although, of course, I would not have recognised any of these emotions, still less been able to do anything about them. I think also that our removal from Balfour and my friends in the bar, the remarriage of my mother and the belated discovery of the death of my father, all combined to give me the most frantic need to escape. Now the means of escape open to a four-year-old are limited at the best of times but I was lucky, for close at hand lay a means of flight more effective and long lasting, and, ultimately, more potent than anything dreamed of in the fairy tales upon which I doted.

It was about this time that I learnt very quickly, and hungrily, to read. How and why it came about with such rapidity I do not know. Perhaps the impulse nurtured by my grandfather's way with words and his love of a good story, or the unconventional efforts of my former drinking companions in the Balfour bar to increase my vocabulary in unexpected ways, and unusual colours and unlikely pungencies, or the efforts of kindly aunts who pushed books into my hands and helped with the sounds, or all of these things, or none of them, I do not know. All I know (and knew then) was that I had in my hands a means of escape which no one could ever control. I knew I could not be stopped. Of that reading I can remember only the verses of A.A. Milne and, one day, putting together a long name – Stevenson – each syllable pealed like a bell, and when I put them together a carillon rang in my head.

It was as if a bird had blundered into a small room and flapped helplessly against the walls and ceiling until somebody, seeing its plight, opened a window. I did not know why I felt these waves of exhilaration each time I sat down with a book, but I knew at least that I was off and elsewhere. It was sometime later when I also realised that what had been placed in my hands was not only a means of escape and a source of infinite pleasure, but a weapon of incalculable power. The giddy rush of excitement I felt at realising that I could piece together the signs on the page into sounds, and the sounds into words and the words into some kind of meaning, brought on an emotion of joy so fierce that at times I felt almost sick with the pleasure and possibility of it all.

It was Marcel Proust, that great diagnostician of the sugared palliatives of time, who remarked that it is when we are at our most vulnerable that we take our most irrevocable decisions. I took my reading raw and strong, I took it like a mind-expanding drug and I began very early a career as a reader. It was to be many years before I could kick the habit sufficiently to realise that what I really wanted to be was not a reader but a writer.

The killer year was 1948. It did for a lot of people, my

grandfather among them. The house he had bought in Johannesburg, in a suburb called Parkview, was on the green and leafy northern side of town, a big comfortable place with a corrugated iron roof, a wide veranda of red flagstones, rolling lawns and high walls. It is from this period that I date my only memories of him. A fragmentary image has him offering me money to buy an ice-cream. The ice-cream cart is passing the front of the house and I can hear it going by because the Black man pedalling his tricycle with its big white ice-box is ringing his bell which has a fat, rusty, irresistibly urgent jingle to it and my impatience mounts as I watch my grandfather digging in his pockets, I am in an agony of anticipation as to whether he will get the money out in time and whether my short legs will still catch the ice-cream cart whose bell grows fainter with every second. This image of my grandfather accords with the general impression I retain of him as source of warmth; he sits somehow at the back of my life not so much as a person but as a radiant force of nature and I recall him rather as one might a good fire in a cold room; it is as if I have absorbed the warmth of his personality into my bones and stored it there, rather in the way one remembers days of uninterrupted sunshine. I think I must have basked in his kindness.

In my second memory he is ill. I know this is so because I have been told that he is very sick and that I am not to disturb him. We are in a room, probably a hospital, and my grandfather lies in a bed with very high legs. Everything about him is ice white: his face, the bed, the blankets, his hands on the coverlet. I sit on the floor and the sunlight pours in through the French windows with that African profligacy that makes one feel quite light-headed. I can smell the wax polish used to buff the wooden parquet flooring into a golden dark gleam in which my reflection appears, showing me to be another colour altogether, a glowing brown me. The bedside is crowded with relatives and I remember thinking how

onerous it must be for my grandfather if he is not feeling well
to have all these people gathered round his bed peering at him.
Surely, I reason, my grandfather wants them to go away? I
wait for him to ask them to do so. But he does not say
anything, he just lies there on the high bed and speaks to no
one, not even to me; he does not even turn his head. I never
know whether he even sees me sitting on the floor in the
sunshine. This seems sad but understandable, seeing how he is
hemmed in on every side.

In 1948 Jan Smuts had called a General Election which he
was widely expected to win, just as he had helped to win the
war. The soldiers were back from Italy and from the desert
war in North Africa; they were expected to support the
Government. The Afrikaner Nationalists under Dr Malan
fought the election on colour, on fears of miscegenation, on
what was called 'Swart Gevaar' (Black Danger); they revived
feelings of bitterness and accumulated grievances going back
to the Boer War of 1899, and beyond, back to the first
'freedom war' of 1880, back to the memories of over twenty
thousand women and children dead in the British concentration camps at the end of the second Boer War, back to the
Great Trek. Against all predictions the campaign carried the
day. Malan formed a tactical coalition with another, smaller
Afrikaans party and their majority was just five seats but it
was enough – a new government was in control and a new day
was at hand. The incoming administration of Dr Malan wore
its distinguishing marks proudly: it was 'pure' Nationalist,
Calvinist, racialist, isolationist and one hundred per cent
Afrikaans; it did not see itself as having a mandate but rather a
mission which was to remake the country in its own image. It
based its course for the future triumphantly on the past. The
ghost of Paul Kruger had come back to Pretoria. Of course
there were among the onlookers those who considered this to
be a temporary setback. Smuts himself was amongst them. In
fact it was very much more than an extraordinary election

result – it was the start of the Afrikaner revolution.

It should be understood that the White opponents of the Nationalist regime divide into two camps: there are the ameliorists and the stoics. The ameliorists are forever prey to what Arthur Kepple-Jones in his prophetic little satire *When Smuts Goes* (written in fact some time before Smuts went) referred to as 'irresponsible optimism about the future' and warned his readers to guard against it. The ameliorists are quite astonishingly undaunted by disaster and quick to take comfort where they can. They saw the beginning of the end for the present administration after the Sharpeville shootings of 1960, they talked of one more push after the Soweto riots of 1976, and they began organising for liberation during the State of Emergency of 1985. They are the party who still take the view that the 1948 result was an aberration; that the Afrikaner Nationalist Government is a hiccup of history which will be forgotten in the infinitely patient time scale of African development. And perhaps it will, given time, though, as John Maynard Keynes pointed out, in the long run we shall all be dead. The same ameliorists look for a new progressive grouping of opposition forces to oppose the Government, after the elections on May 6th.

The stoics, on the other hand, intend merely to endure. They look on the forthcoming elections in May with foreboding and recall that the Ayatollahs of apartheid have reigned now for four decades and the effects of their extraordinary forty-year programme of human engineering will be felt for many generations, whatever political changes may occur.

My grandfather lived at a time when the ameliorists were in the ascendant – he was, I suppose, one of the first of them – although he was not deceived by the results of the Nationalist victory of 1948: he did not draw comfort from their slim majority. I do not know what he said, if he said anything at all, but his behaviour was more eloquent than any opinion he may have offered. He took to his bed, inconsolable at the news that Smuts had gone, and lay there for three days. Whether he turned his face to the wall I do not know but it would have been appropriate: the wall-builders had come to town. The result undoubtedly hastened his end and soon afterwards he was dead. His reaction may seem flamboyantly emotional, excessively Irish, but this is what makes it seem not only fitting but very South African, for without appreciating the degree to which bitter emotion infects all political matters in South Africa, one understands nothing. Perhaps another way of putting it is to say that South African politics are, in fact – and this my grandfather may have recognised towards the end – very Irish. It is interesting to note that the author of the 1948 victory, Dr Malan, and the leader of the newly 'purified' Conservative Party, Dr. Treurnicht, were both former ministers in the Dutch Reformed Church.

Our new house was in Parkview, a pleasant, shaded, tranquil suburb of Johannesburg where, as its name suggests, there was doubtless a time when the gentle slope upon which the houses are built offered a view of the large park at the bottom of the road. This is no longer the case for the oak trees have grown up and the gardens have matured but even then Parkview must have been soft and green and it is not difficult to understand the attraction which it held for my grandfather. When he bought his house here he was merely following his Irish sentiments and the street names called him home: there is Wexford, and nearby is Wicklow, and Galway is not far away – broad, grassy, wooded avenues quite heart-rendingly tranquil and as emerald as Erin.

As I walk down these streets today, the realities of South Africa seem miles away, although there are tell-tale signs: election posters tied to the trees. This is a predominantly English-speaking suburb – prosperous middle-class, liberal – and the posters celebrate the White opposition party, the PFP. Worth noticing are the burglar bars on the windows of the large, gracious houses, the variety of security walls surrounding the properties, the dogs growling in the yard, the servants sitting out on the pavements. This lush, serene enclave is a long way from Ireland and we are in South Africa in late April. In a few weeks' time the White voters go to the polls. This will be the first election to be held under a State of Emergency which has become a permanent fixture; and it is vigorously applied; censorship is fierce and people are told very little. They wish to know even less. Rumours abound. The line of servants sitting out on the roadside falls silent as I pass. A White man walking about in the middle of the day could mean trouble. Some of the properties higher up the road are absolutely vast: fifteen or twenty rooms, acres of garden, mellowed stone, great mansions set back from the street. They are so enormous one wonders how people can keep them up. I remember they filled me with awe when I was small and walked these streets; I never saw anybody in their rolling gardens and I imagined they must be occupied by giants or millionaires. Today there is still no one to be seen in the beautiful empty acres, which remain as mysterious as ever.

We lived in Kerry Road in the years after the War. The house stands as we left it forty years ago; it is utterly neglected and even the paint is flaking off the corrugated iron roof. The giant palm trees still tower in the front garden. It is curious the way my grandfather's properties have been preserved by neglect. Of course he would not have approved, he was all for getting on, getting ahead, moving forward and he would not have liked to have seen either his hotel or his house, in which such zest for the future had been invested, go to rack and ruin in this way.

I had a Black nanny, of course, although mine was not at all the usual run of the species. For a start he was called George. Male nannies were rare, if not unknown. Certainly no one I knew possessed one and they were decidedly inferior in the scale of things. Proper nannies were female and could be graded by costume, serenity and dignity. At the top of the tree were nannies who did nothing else, and looked and dressed the part; gentle, ample, mature women who sat on the grass in the park overseeing their little charges who burrowed into their sides like a litter of suckling puppies. Then there were the part-time nannies who were actually cooks or housemaids in real life, wore no uniform and were seldom out of their teens. Boy nannies were so low down the scale they were virtually invisible.

George was a good, cheerful fellow. He went about in bare feet, wearing a tunic with a clumsy, square-cut neck and scarlet piping, and long, very ugly linen shorts. I wore a sailor suit. Together we walked down to the park in the afternoons. I think he was probably the gardener, or perhaps he worked in some junior capacity in the house. But in the afternoons he became my nanny. The park at the end of the road is one of the great attractions of this area with acres of rolling lawns, ponds, small woods and a big ornamental lake as well as swings and slides in the children's playing area. My nanny George used to push me on the swings or, more accurately I think, I used to push George on the swings and we must both have enjoyed this reversal of roles because I do not recall any complaints until one day in my enthusiasm I moved forward as the swing was coming back and collected it full in the mouth, scattering teeth across a wide area of the park. George carried me home and my mother's look of horror is with me still.

George, being a gentle, helpful soul, and no doubt moved by my mother's distress at my bloody, gaping grin, resolved to do what he could about it. The next morning before breakfast he appeared at the house, held out his hand and there, displayed on his palm in all their milky perfection, were my missing teeth. He had been up at dawn scouring the wiry kikuyu grass beneath the swings for hours until he had reclaimed my lost dentures. I felt then, and still do, very touched by his efforts. There was of course nothing to be done with the detached teeth, and I would one day grow another set, but it was an imaginative and kindly act. Later I thought that perhaps George knew a thing or two about the nature of South African life and he realised that a White boy who could not show his teeth was not going to go very far.

It was much later still that it occurred to me that my games with my nanny George had been quite illegal because the playground, indeed the park itself, was out of bounds to Black people. Until a few years ago, when the more grotesque notices were removed from public places in the middle of large cities, there were large signs around the play areas warning that these were reserved for children of the 'White Group'. They were not for nannies, male or female. But this rule, along with so many others, was frequently flouted and it was the irrepressible urge to get round such regulations that gave to life its only possible colour, warmth and excitement at a time when the dogmas of purified Afrikanerdom were spreading like a killing mist. A stroll through a park would reveal more of the nature of South Africa than any number of facts or figures, it would also show the nature of the resistance to the racial phobias of the dominant tribe. It revealed how many of us began from the premiss that anything pleasurable, unexpected, unscheduled or piebald was almost certainly illicit. Once you knew this you understood how to proceed on the basis of the risks involved and you discovered that the dangers of breaking the rules were more than offset by the pleasures derived from doing so. At the centre of the park was a lake. In the middle of the lake was a fountain illuminated at night which gushed in ice-cream colours, lime-green and strawberry. It was said that the nocturnal fountain was the only place where colours mingled after dark. Police patrolled the grounds by night searching for illicit lovers.

In the park I saw not only nannies but Black barbers. On Saturday afternoons and Sundays their makeshift salons opened beneath the thick patch of blue gums not far from the swings. The clients sat on little three-legged stools, the barbers swathed them in great red and white cloths and each customer was given a fragment of freckled mirror to hold. Then the barber sharpened his cut-throat razor with rhythmic enjoyment on the leather strop dangling from a branch and set about the important business at hand. These were not haircuts in the conventional sense but complete shavings of head, jaw and chin which were scraped until they shone. There was gossip, guitar music, a little gambling on the side and a stream of banter between competing stylists. No one minded the small boy whom George took by the hand and led through the chattering, snipping, scraping barber shop beneath the trees. And I remember looking up and seeing everywhere black ovoids gleaming under the blue gums. It was for me a taste of another world, a way of life, easy, gentle, relaxed and a hundred years away from the White suburb across the road where I lived.

From that White, middle-class, English-speaking suburb came vociferous complaint; expressions of fear and concern at the weekend invasion by these travelling barber shops. But nothing, as I recall, was ever done to put an end to it. The White householders fumed and fell silent or they got so used to the sight that it became one of those many features of South African life which people no longer saw – either because they closed their eyes to it or because they looked away and pretended that it wasn't happening. It is often thought that pretence and self-delusion are products of the racial system in South Africa; the contrary is true and the well-developed capacity for deceiving ourselves is the basis upon which we begin. The determined refusal to see what is in front of our eyes has been essential for our political development.

Another feature of the park when I came here as a child, and for many years after that, was the traditional gatherings on Sundays of Indian families: this; too, was illegal. Their methods of deception were subtle but their arrival was flamboyant, for they came in vast limousines in acid green, pink or purple which lined the road beside the lake: entire families would step from their cars on to the grass verge, open picnic baskets, spread rugs and take the sun, always staying close to the cars, just in case the police intervened and a quick getaway was in order. They gained their places by the lakeside by force of custom, and by pretending to be invisible. Naturally the use of the facilities was forbidden to them: they could not hire the boats on the lake where the White Sunday sailors jostled each other in their dinghies and lost their oars, they could not use the lavatories, they could not even get a glass of water from the tea house beside the lake. But despite murmurs of disapproval from White residents the Asian picnickers kept on coming and they represented, along with the barbers, something of the real nature of this place, a rich sense of other, more human, possibilities.

In this country grass grows over the most granite developments, flowers spring from walls and, given time, trees will sprout from the roof. The sub-life of South Africa has its own ripostes to the rules and regulations of our masters. It raises insistent, inexorable arguments against which nothing and no one can stand indefinitely. However rigid the arrangements against racial mixing, a way through can be found and in South Africa people are too closely involved with each other to be forced apart for long. One might even suggest that those on the receiving end secretly cooperate to subvert the forces designed to separate them. Or, if you prefer, that the logicians of apartheid have always been thwarted by the thorough-going and, to my mind, magnificent, unreliability of human beings who, no matter how energetically you prise them apart, somehow contrive to get together again. Thus, when I pushed George on the swings and lost my teeth I can claim, in a small way, to have contributed to that subversion. However, I know that the

truth is that the system was failing even before George sailed
into the heavens and I ran forward, beaming toothily. Because
although you may attempt to confine your swings and slides to
children of the White group, you cannot have White children
without also having Black nannies, and so it is that White
children have presented nannies with what I might call a
ticket to ride, quite literally a *carte blanche*. It is an arrangement
both sides have been happy to exploit.

With the election in 1948 of a government determined to
put the whole business on to a modern footing we were in a
new era. The basis of these new developments was the
doctrine of pure apartheid which identified, and deplored, the
tendency of people of different cultures to mix, whether at
work, at play or at home. Previous White regimes had
disliked this mixing and even condemned it in public while
conniving at it in private. Such double vision in governments
before 1948 was not merely convenient, it was pragmatic in a
society in which the Black majority outnumbered the
governing White minority by many millions, because it
allowed the façade of dominance to be preserved while
turning a blind eye to the flourishing undergrowth of racial
mixture and the slow erosion of the boundaries between
races. Such had been the policies of the doomed regimes of
Generals Botha and Smuts upon which my grandfather had
placed so much reliance.

As it happened, I was closer to one of the prime movers of
the new system than I suspected. One of my near neighbours
in Kerry Road was a man with whose name, perhaps more
than any other, the world has associated the concept of the
rigid divisions between races. He was Hendrik Frensch
Verwoerd, possibly the most influential of all South African
leaders, and his life and mine were to run in a curious kind of
tandem for many years. I am in many ways a child of the
Verwoerdian era. However, at the time he and I held
different occupations: I was the four-year-old toddler who

took walks past his house each day to the park and the lake, accompanied by my nanny George; he was the editor of the official organ of the Nationalist Party, the newspaper *Die Transvaler*. This party organ stood in the same relation to the Afrikaner Nationalists as does *Pravda* to the Politburo in Moscow. What Verwoerd was doing in this English enclave beside the lake I do not know. I wonder if we met. It is possible. At any rate, I have always held the theory that this early proximity to the apostle of apartheid must have had its effects. Perhaps Dr Verwoerd frightened me as a child; perhaps he was the sort of man my mother warned me never to accept sweets from; I imagine that my nanny George had one or two things to say about him.

What strikes me now, as I look at Hendrik Verwoerd's old house on the corner of Kerry Road, is the fact that it stands on a spot which would have given the doctor, should he have chosen to have raised his eyes, a remarkably good view of the patch of trees where the travelling barbers met and, for that matter, of the swings where I lost my teeth, and he would have been close enough to the lake to have seen the vivid limousines drawing up with their Indian picnickers. If he had needed any reminder of the ways in which the old system of what I might call confidential racialism kept breaking down, with subsequent inroads into the heartland of White superiority, then the park was the place to show it to him. When Verwoerd and his party came to power it was precisely this nettle that was grasped. There was a religious zeal about their programme; what was hidden they would make plain, what was crooked they would make straight. Laws would be passed. It would be necessary to put yards or miles between different groups and then confine them to those areas – by legislation. If people would not part from one another voluntarily then they should be driven asunder. I often wonder if Dr Verwoerd might not have used scenes from the park in planning future campaigns.

We were not neighbours for long. Within a very short time
of Malan's victory in 1948, Dr Verwoerd, although he had
failed to win a seat in the election, was elevated to a seat in the
Senate, the upper house of the South African Parliament, and
moved on to greater things. Soon afterwards my mother
remarried and we moved across town to live in a raw, new
suburb built to house servicemen returning from the War and
which was called – without a hint of irony, but with a royalist
flourish which was intended to indicate its (and our) patriotic
English connections – Sandringham.

What operates here today is a variation of classical apartheid.
A few years ago, in 1984, the Constitution was remodelled
and now, instead of a single Whites-only legislature, there are
three: for Whites, Indians and Coloureds, respectively. It
could be said, then, that apartheid is dead; and in its place we
have tri-partheid. Behind the shifts in terminology lie the
figures, the numbers, the population statistics. At the heart of
our politics is numerology gone mad. The population is
currently estimated at 28.4 million. This figure is made up of
4.9 million Whites, 2,954,000 Coloureds, 884,000 Asians and
19,662,000 Blacks. Black people, without votes or Parliament,
regard this election as a fraud or a farce, or both. White
liberals also reject it and talk of not voting at all, or of spoiling
their votes. Such studied indifference, I fear, is the affectation
of the powerless.

Amongst committed White opponents of the Nationalist
Party it is being put about that President P.W. Botha has no
good reason for calling this election and they dispute his
explanation – which is to increase the size of his mandate.
This is already formidable because he holds 126 of the 166
elected seats, and 11 of the 12 nominated seats, an
overwhelming total of 137. The opposition parties, right and

left, between them hold another 52 and there are hopes that this number might be increased to 70 or even 80. It is suggested that the Government – for the first time in living memory – might feel threatened. Tails are up, hopes are high – and all opposition politicians agree that this election will be different. There is much talk of fluidity, of 'time for a change'. And indeed it is true that the ruling party machine is not what it was; unable to renege on its modest reform programme, yet unable to increase the pace, or scale, of reform. No wonder the opposition is in good voice and winds of rhetoric gust across the country. In the South of France they have the Mistral; we have something called the *Electoral* which until now has blown no one any good. But *this* time we may see the start of something new.

Consider the defensive postures of our governing politicians. Camouflage is something which, until now, would have been disdained. Like tree frogs or stick insects or chameleons, Nationalists are learning to merge into the background, they are adopting the strategy of the familiar – even more striking is that they are laying claim to ordinariness. They are beginning to dodge and weave and duck. It would be a pity if those who have brought the country to its present agony, out of a fanatical desire for racial purity and tribal survival, coolly calculated and remorselessly applied, should now be allowed to pass themselves off as mere politicians. This is the last time we may observe them in all their cracked grandeur before the White supremacy party turns into the 'justice for all' party. The revisionists are already stepping forward. The Afrikaner Nationalist is not – has never been they suggest – a sect devoted to the supremacy of the tribe, but only pro-Afrikaans. Pleas go out for greater understanding of a country with first-world aspirations and third-world problems. Probably nothing will prevent the sleight of hand. But such deceptions are less easily practised in election times because now the contradiction in Nationalist policy becomes visible. On the one hand there is the 'new' argument which says that, far from being the party of rampaging social engineers, the party is really just a collection of honest-joe politicos, bumbling along and doing their best. On the other hand, the country knows it has passed from the certainties of Verwoerdian apartheid to uneasy euphemisms of 'reform'. And they know that what the regime really requires is not understanding – but obedience.

For its part, the Government seems intent on winning handsomely. Just because you already have a lot it does not mean that more is not better. National Party politicians woo and warn the electorate at every turn. Their attitude to the opposition parties is one of amused contempt; they treat them as an irrelevance, an increasingly anachronistic minority whose sole use is to give dissenting White voters the illusion that democracy works, that opposition is possible and change can be achieved through peaceful, parliamentary means. But the demeanour of the Government speaks more plainly and suggests that those truly interested in power, that is to say those who hold it (the White Afrikaners) and those who seek it (the Black majority) know that the only real contenders, now or later, will be White and Black nationalists. Rubbing the noses of the liberal opposition in their own redundancy increasingly brings cries of protest from discomforted moderates who complain that the real adversary in the contest is being portrayed as the exiled African National Congress.

In fact it seems to me that the Nationalists are using an old and well-tested election ploy, something that has been a major plank in every election fought by this Government. What they are actually saying is that the Hun is at the gate, the barbarians are coming. This is called, indelicately but accurately, *Kaffirpolitiek* or *Swartgevaat* (Black danger). It is a tactic traditionally favoured by the Nationalists, deplored by the opposition and believed by the electorate. Precisely on cue the Foreign Minister warns of a campaign by guerrillas of the

African National Congress that is planned to coincide with the election – and promises it will not succeed.

In fact, there is a curious linguistic resemblance between all three White political groupings contesting this election: Nationalists, Progressives and Conservatives. All are united in their rejection of majority rule; this is the form in which the unthinkable is described: no one talks of Black rule. This is not seen as a rejection of democracy but as a rejection of something called 'majoritarianism', an ugly word which simply serves to emphasise the refusal to confront reality. New words are found to get around difficult words. The Conservatives speak of separate 'nations'; a euphemism which reflects a desire to tribalise our society still further. The Progressive opposition speak of rights and freedoms for all groups. The Nationalists talk about mutual responsibilities among all groups. Together the parties talk a language so fuzzy that it is really not a language at all but a kind of gas sprayed at the electorate in the desire to pacify them.

A visit to the Rand Easter Show, alas, no longer the colourful affair of former years, memorable among other features for a dramatic attempt to assassinate Hendrik Verwoerd. It used to be perhaps the major international event in the Johannesburg annual calendar and foreign countries vied with each other to put up the most expensive and outrageous pavilions. National pride was at stake. Today no foreign country would care to visit the Rand Easter Show, unless it was in very deep disguise, and the flamboyant pavilions are no more. The only foreigners prepared to break cover are Taiwan, always referred to as the Republic of China, Chile and, I have little doubt, Paraguay. New enlarged show grounds have been established out to the south west of Johannesburg, hard by Soweto. The crowds, today estimated at around eighty thousand, jostle and push their way through the giant exhibition halls which resemble aircraft hangars. Under the new dispensation, the crowds are mixed, and the restaurants integrated. This is faintly ironic since many of the Whites here will be ardent Nationalist supporters up from the country, increasingly likely to vote for the Conservative Party which opposes the new racial dispensation. At the exit gates there is a young man wearing a golf hat on the peak of which rests in coprophiliac splendour an extremely realistic light-brown turd. The sign on his hat reads: 'Shit Head'. Nobody gives him a second glance. Across the veld I can see smoke rising thickly into the air above Soweto.

'Maybe it's a riot,' someone in the crowd suggests calmly.

'Maybe someone is being necklaced...' says someone else. This gets an appreciative laugh.

Inadvertent moments of frankness. Standing in one of the Johannesburg constituencies for the governing party is an ex-spy who began his career as a police informer on the campus of Witwatersrand University. This was once a method of paying one's way through college adopted by any number of informers at major English universities. Some people worked nights in pizza parlours, other people spied for the Government. The ex-spy on television, patting his pocket as if searching for his revolver in an old and yet not discarded habit, gives something closest to the truth of the matter when he speaks of future plans by addressing his comments simultaneously to the fears of the White electorate and, over their head, to the originators of those fears, the Black opposition groups in exile. The candidate contends that 'White fear' must be taken into account if there are to be concessions made towards what are called 'Black aspirations'.

Suddenly a fierce light falls on the dilemma facing the

ruling party; it is promising in one breath both a loosening of the old rigidities while emphasising how very limited such flexibility will be. Lest there be any doubts about this, the President himself now declares that there will never be majority rule in this country and, therefore, there will never be a Black President. Such fatal contradictions are not exposed; perhaps opposition politicians feel that to do so would be too boring, too predictable or perhaps even too impolite, worse still – it may be that this is not far from the opposition's belief, as well. It is precisely these contradictions, the ability to say radically incompatible things in the same breath, that reveal the real nature of the politics here. A Government minister declares, in a week when a Government order has forbidden any protests over the detention of thousands of people and has even forbidden prayers on their behalf, that he is opposed to detention without trial. This from a member of a government which, since it introduced detention without trial in the 'sixties, has wielded the weapon with pugnacious relish! I feel as I would were a practising cannibal to tell me that he disapproved of human flesh. My range of responses is limited when faced with brazen absurdity, or hypocrisy enthroned; to laugh, or cry, or run. Or maybe to do all three.

Opposition voters, particularly the English-speaking, keep up their spirits by means of a diversionary tactic which might be called the 'Bonnie and Clyde Method'. This is a mixture of bravado and deceit, a form of whistling in the dark, and pretending things are not too bad. The Bonnie and Clyde Method dates from the time when a film of that name caused a considerable stir and the censors, on learning that it was a lively piece of work, immediately banned it. This was perfectly customary; however, this did not prevent people from reading about it, seeing pictures of it and learning of the new styles and fashions that it promoted. Many people went on to give 'Bonnie and Clyde' parties and to show an extraordinary knowledge of a film which none of them had ever seen.

This ability to live vicariously and to take comfort where one can is a distinguishing characteristic of South African life. Reporting favourable items with cheerful aggressiveness is another familiar trait, and so we are told by the newspapers that this country, which has not played cricket in the international arena for over a decade, now possesses the best one-day team. Naturally this assertion cannot be tested, but then testing rhetoric against the facts has never been widely practised. It is the rhetoric that matters and not the facts. And Black politicians are just as much hooked on the opium of rhetoric as are their White counterparts. The English-language papers vacillate beween extremely limited reports of current unrest: sixteen thousand railway workers on strike; a strike in the Post Office; reports of shootings in the townships; trains set on fire and up-beat accounts of sports, stocks and sex. All political reporting is controlled by the Bureau of Information which exists not to promote but to suppress information and to ensure that the public knows as little as possible about agitation and violence in the Black townships. There is no longer news in the usual sense of the term, there is propaganda and silence.

My morning newspaper today provides a fine example of the way in which some editors must operate in the far reaches of surreality. The editor runs what purports to be a front page story but which is in fact a series of allusions to some undisclosed event which would be of interest to investors and shareholders, were he allowed to print it, and he hints at rumours affecting the movement of certain shares. He may not say why he may not print it. His frustration is palpable, and culminates in absurdity.

So is there then really naught for our comfort? Well, there are, occasionally, cheering moments. A government spokesman, asked about his party's relations with Black people, answers with shining sincerity: 'We get on like houses on fire...'

It is necessary to recognise that present conditions are not a bizarre departure from better times but the logical consequence of a racial revolution unleashed in the late 'forties. Before that time the mass of rule and regulation had not begun to harden into a crust upon the surface of life. In former times and other places a sense of possibilities still existed. And, for me, that place was Sandringham.

In 1949, despite its name, there was nothing regal about the suburb of Sandringham except the streets, all of which commemorated English kings and queens, sandy streets newly made by shaving the veld away to show the red ground beneath, its surface flinty with pebbles. I lived in Henry Avenue which dipped steeply into Edward, and Edward led to Elizabeth. The water truck came on memorable visits, proceeding majestically down Henry Avenue, spouting water from its sides in a wonderful, curving tracery, thick whiskers of water skidding into the bone-dry dust, whipping it into a creamy, luxurious mud. Barefoot we ran whooping behind the truck, splashing through puddles in the ditches, standing in water to the ankles, squeezing silken mud between the toes. Newly washed street stones were surprised into baring their blue veins. The sense of release and freedom this gave me was enormous. In the giant blue seemingly unalterable days of my boyhood this magical capacity of the water truck to transform the stony, dusty surroundings in seconds, to have it running, flooding, hugely wet – before the sun destroyed the magic, baking the street back to dusty boredom – answered to some desperate need I felt for variety, change, movement. I applauded this brief Venetian miracle. It turned on its head the seemingly immutable law of parents and the weather which insisted on the hateful unchangeability of everything, as if the White Man's Burden was really to be always responsible, deadeningly regular and to serve out a life sentence of mind-numbing inertia in this hot, raw, untidy suburb in the veld. It was what the water did to the dust that so intrigued and delighted me and made me realise that other events and incidents could also supply surprises if you looked beneath the surface of things; if you did so you began to see that the real life lay in the unexpected and the illicit, in unforeseen arrivals, novel departures, in unclassifiable careers and dubious callings. I remember the secret visits of the night-soil men, never seen at all, but deeply appreciated and hugely admired, who came while we slept and removed the buckets of sewage, people of great decorum who left behind them only the scent of their visit, which we pretended not to notice. Not even the dogs barked. The coalmen, carbon black, black-hole black, sweat shining in the coal-dust, stripped naked to the waist, wearing on their heads a kind of hood or veil made of rather greasy sacking which gave them a faintly Egyptian look and made the whites of their eyes alarmingly brilliant. Then the dustbin men came, taking their leaden colour from the ashes dumped in the garbage cans in the backyard, running down the long driveways carrying the still-smouldering trash cans on their shoulders, whistling and kicking at the dogs who always chased them. Though large claims were made for their ability to tell the races apart, accidents happened with the dogs. Relatives were continually being bitten, neighbours were savaged by Wolf or Prince, Nero or Tamburlaine...

For all its claims to be a suburb of Johannesburg, Sandringham, out on the eastern outskirts of the city which had been itself until fairly recently a mining camp, was just emerging from the bush; it was frontier country and all around stretched the limitless Transvaal veld. Guns were in plentiful supply. Specifically, service revolvers retained by the returning soldiers, oiled and loaded and kept in the bedroom cupboard, beneath the socks, or behind the shoes. From time to time curious children found them, with lethal results. That was another occupational hazard. Dog-bites and bullets punctured the dull surface of things; better still, they came with stories attached and what made those stories interesting was that they ran contrary to expectation – dogs were supposed to bite postmen and intruders, not aunts. And guns were supposed to shoot burglars, not children.

There was also an air of political disaffection on the estate and that too was full of mystery. The soldiers returning from the war were mostly English-speaking Smuts supporters. Having risked their lives for the new South Africa they found on their return that their hero was out of office and a new government was installed, comprised of men many of whom had spent the war lighting candles for Hitler. It was a blow. Angry young men joined something called the Torch Commando which was formed in 1951. There must have been a strong contingent in Sandringham though I never myself set eyes on a member and I knew very little about their political feelings. It was the peculiarity of their activities which caught my eye. They ran through the suburbs by night, as silently as the night-soil men, and plastered all the letter-boxes with their symbol of defiance, a triangular torch shaped rather like an ice-cream cone from whose mouth issued a rosy flame. Whether this sort of thing worried the Government I do not know, but certainly the strange nocturnal mushrooming of paper torches delighted me. It seemed gloriously odd, such a wonderfully strange thing to do.

Henry Avenue leads down the hill to meet Edward and beyond that lies wild country, a stretch of veld running beneath a steep ridge, rutted and rocky. At the foot of the hill water flowed and made a great marshy area choked with high grass, gum trees, poplars and all the sturdy riff-raff that springs up wherever water is plentiful. In this swampy thicket, it was said, there lived bad men, gangs of burglars who raided the houses of the estate and against whom the guns and dogs were kept. At night they crept out of their lairs and set off on burglary expeditions; they were said to be terrifically adept at opening the windows of your house, they would insert a fishing rod – O the skill I attributed to those strange, shadowy robbers! – and whip your trousers from the chair, your wallet from the bedside table, even the blankets from your bed. I would have given anything to have watched these magicians at work. Needless to say entry into the wild thicket was strictly forbidden. But no one could stop me from watching from across Edward Avenue, staring into the triangle of grass behind the tall trees, waiting and listening for signs of the outlaws who hid there.

Twice weekly the Indian greengrocer roared down the dirt road in his green, open-backed van, pyramids of pineapples and avocados trembling dangerously, wadges of brown paper bags skewered like smoked kippers on the steel hooks hanging from the steel struts, with all the urchins of Henry Avenue running behind him, shrieking like banshees: 'Sammie, Sammie, what you got? Missus, missus, apricot!' The boy across the road threw open his large lawn for marathon games of cricket, though he spent most of the time in the lavatory; but his sister compensated by proving a mean leg-spin bowler. For no apparent reason I decided to stuff several stones up my nose and had to be rushed across town to the doctor, who retrieved them with a pair of silver tweezers, dropping them meticulously into a faintly bloodstained metal dish while he counted them like cherry stones: 'Tinker, tailor, soldier, sailor...' I felt curiously empty afterwards. Perhaps the monotony of it all had driven me to this form of self-abuse, for above all else I grew to relish the unpredictable and the mysterious: the raids of the Torch Commando, the little naked girl disappearing round the corner of her house in a flash of buttocks, the visits of the water truck and the night-soil men, the dancing dustbin collectors, the angling burglars in the forbidden marsh – all of them actors in the theatre of purest subversion; and, in a country where the deadening sameness of everything seemed so absolute, these eruptions took on the power of acts of God.

Today, in April, the plane leaves are just beginning to turn in Sandringham. The leaves when silhouetted against the polished blue sky are frog-shaped. There are no election posters in Henry Avenue, which has been tarred but otherwise is not much changed since I lived here. My old house hides behind a thick mass of overgrown hedge and creeper as if it were hoping not to be noticed or to retire from the world. The homes in Henry Avenue are modest places yet even they are protected, as is so often the case now in Johannesburg, by heavy grilles on the windows, bars on the doors, high walls, lights and sirens and I have no doubt that there are more guns than ever in the sock drawers. This is not new but is rather a frenetic continuation of an old policy; it was always the case that people in Johannesburg measured out their lives with burglar alarms. The business of home protection during the endemic violence of the past few years has become a great industry. Wall-top security spikes are in demand. 'Angled Right... To Bite Right', promises the advertising leaflet, 'Surprisingly attractive'. And, in a way, I suppose they are, the razored steel tines standing out delicately along the curved walls, as if the stone were baring its neck, showing metal hairs rising along the nape. People are, it is said, very 'security conscious'. There are uglier, shorter words to describe the overwhelming mood. Fear is one of them, but fear is a four-letter word not used here. At the bottom of Henry Avenue where it joins Edward I can see that the wild wood where the brigands lay in wait has been fenced off now; a tall concrete fence with barbed wire runs along its length for a mile or more. Behind the wall a lone cactus holds up two spiny fingers in an impertinent gesture at the houses across the road. The place is still a thicket, choked with trees and grass, and undoubtedly the war between burglars and householders continues. Fears of attack are not groundless. Horrid facts are usually to be found tucked away between the pugnacious sporting columns in the papers or are offered in the relentlessly cheerful tones radio announcers affect for both good news and bad. In the Johannesburg Reef area over the past six months, sixty elderly Whites have been murdered in their homes. And it is not only the old who are under pressure. Certain educational departments are issuing battle plans to teachers at White schools. The cadets who now pretend to be soldiers once a week in the playground may be trained for real action. Teachers are to be issued with instructions on difficult questions such as 'When may I shoot?' Training will be given on how best to mitigate the effects of a hand-grenade attack, and on the best method to be followed when your Principal is kidnapped by terrorists. There is also advice on how to avoid reading the wrong sort of books. Selected parents and staff are to carry firearms. Fierce dogs are more loved than ever. An advertisement in my paper makes this plea: 'Rottweiler Wanted. Cat 'flu took our last one . . .' The bereaved owner signs himself 'Devastated "Rotty" lover'. Fatal attacks by 'Rottys' are not unknown. Rumour has it that they can be trained to kill on coded command.

At right angles to Henry Avenue a small lane leads up to the single line of neighbourhood shops. The lane is still here, untarred, unkempt, full of blackjacks and luxuriant weeds, plenty of the tough, hoodlum grass you get after good rains in the back streets of Johannesburg, the sort of grass that throws its weight around. The shops at the top of the lane are little changed: butcher, chemist, liquor store. It is a peaceful scene. The 'Rug Doctor' is offering his services in the dry cleaner's. White housewives stride purposefully along the pavement casting little anxious glances left and right as if negotiating a narrow bridge. On the sloping bank of a grassy verge across the way lie circles of servants, cooks and nannies, taking the sun, seemingly in no hurry. Their crimson overalls paint the grass. The quick footsteps of the White housewives patter drily past the shop fronts where the newspaper headlines flapping on the boards carry echoes of distant thunder: 'Bombs in Gaborone', 'Soweto Strikes'; 'Invasion Threat'...

Across the road is the Jewish Old Age Home. I can remember this stretch of land before it was built over: dark green, rather gloomy, a mass of thick scrub and trees. The building of the Home caused a sensation in the servicemen's neighbourhood. This bronzed and gleaming building was colossal and even now it is a striking and generous piece of architecture. It was received with a mixture of sullen resentment and grudging admiration by the locals who looked on it rather as natives might when a party of raiding imperialists with advanced technology lands amongst them. The building was so much bigger than anything we had seen before and was said to appear from the air in its true shape, a giant Star of David. Still further along that road is the dynamite factory at Modderfontein, reportedly the biggest in the southern hemisphere. If that ever exploded we would go with it, we were assured by our elders in tones of some pride. It would also carry away the Jewish Old Age Home, and presumably they felt there was some consolation in that.

Beside the row of shops is a patch of waste ground. It used to be much larger and wilder but now it has been reduced to about a quarter acre of grass and a few trees, some rather sad poplars, ugly blue gums and one magnificent oak. I always had a particular affection for that oak – even thirty-five years ago it was a good tree to climb. It was to the oak that I made my way in 1952 when I learned I would be leaving Sandringham.

The reasons for the move seemed to me obscure and terrible, my stepfather worked for the bank and this was a transfer. Until then, to me, a transfer was something you moistened and then laid out on the back of your hand, lifting the corner carefully to show a picture of Popeye, or Superman in glorious colour. This bank transfer took place against my intense opposition. It seemed to me a mad, bad, dangerous move. I think part of the reason for my resistance was my attachment to Sandringham, its dogs, burglars and dustmen. Also I had discovered that it was possible to learn to read a place, a neighbourhood, in much the same way as you read a book. When you knew the trick you could let your eye run over the place and it told you stories in much the same way as the words on the printed page. I was loath to leave the book of the suburb called Sandringham, for that was the way I saw it, as an unfinished story. But the transfer seemed to operate under the sort of iron constraints that govern military postings and would not be denied. Besides there is little that an eight-year-old can do to stave off the inevitable in these matters, his opinion is not seriously sought. Consequently the feeling that I was a captive, a prisoner, increased, and so did the urge to break my bonds. What I was not to know then was the unexpected advantages which the move to Pretoria was to confer on me. If Sandringham was a chapter of surprises, then Pretoria was to be a volume more weird and wonderful than anything I could have imagined. But at the time this posting to the enemy heartland, the Boer capital of Pretoria, seemed a sentence to the salt mines.

My horror at the move sent me to the oak tree on the patch of wasteland and I placed in a hollow between two branches a stone. It was one of those roadside stones that washed very white and blue-veined when the rains fell. I put the stone in the tree because it was a way of leaving something of myself behind. Whatever else might change, the stone would wait in the tree for the moment I chose to return – patient, loyal, faithful and secret. While the stone remained in the tree something at least would stay the same.

I am very tempted to climb the tree now. There is every chance that the stone is still there, but – familiar presence – a tall barbed-wire fence protects even this scrubby patch of ground. Reluctantly I decide against looking for the stone. It is probably just as well. What would the passers-by think – the hurrying housewives and the lounging servants – if a middle-aged man began to climb an oak tree on a patch of wasteland?

II

VISITING THE ELEPHANT BIRD

PRETORIA HAS BEEN described as a city with one foot in the nineteenth century and the other in Woolworth's. This is amusing but not very accurate. I do not mean to suggest that I carry any great torch for accuracy; requests for accuracy in South Africa usually imply that an indictment is being drawn up. Besides, whoever adds so much as a jot or tittle of wit or gaiety to the perception of the strait-laced capital of South Africa should be clutched to the bosom of the beloved country, and congratulated. In the capital of apartheid diversion is to be preferred to accuracy, any day of the week. However, the truth is rather more interesting and, in a way, more grimly amusing. Pretoria is the mother of civil servants, a city of Calvinists, jacarandas, museums, monuments, police, politicians and uniforms; above all, it is the city sacred to the memory of Paul Kruger, President of the South African Republic, and the man who went to war against the British, not once but twice, in the First Boer War of 1880 and the Second of 1899. In the old fighting song so popular in the Boer War, and after, it is always Pretoria to which the soldiers are marching and it is Pretoria that 'rules the way'. And indeed it still does. Though a good deal smaller than Johannesburg, it is much more important. It is layered with diplomats. I can

remember when the unfortunate ambassadors were given
their own kind of diplomatic reservation in a Pretoria suburb
because someone realised that the day was not far off when a
black diplomat would be appointed by some mischievous
foreign state, and feared embarrassment and political
infection. Pretoria also bristles with military bases and
airfields.

There are another two capitals: Parliament may pass
legislation in Cape Town, while the judicial capital is in
Bloemfontein, but the real damage is done in Pretoria, in an
imposing pile set on a ridge, designed by Sir Herbert Baker to
commemorate the Act of Union in 1910 and known as the
Union Buildings. This is another fairly typical misnomer
because it is from here that the country has been divided and
ruled these past forty years. It is our very own Kremlin: a
bulky, red and orange declaration of British imperial power,
now in the hands of the ruling native tribe and still well placed
to frighten passers-by. Cycling past it as a boy I would avert
my eyes with a shiver, because it gave me the impression that
its wide stony arms were waiting to embrace me. Huge lawns
and gardens fall from it in a series of descending terraces to
culminate in the statue of a mounted horseman who draws
lawns and terraces behind him like a cloak. It has about it the
look of a prison or an asylum. It is instead a flamboyant
example of imperial architecture. The real jail stands at the
entrance to the city. And as for the asylum, that is called
Weskoppies and I remember it well because I played highly
unorthodox, but inventive, games of hockey against its
inmates on several occasions; they proved to be masters of a
certain kind of subversive enlightenment, demonstrating in
the course of an hour how a game with certain set rules may
be transformed into something rich and strange by taking the
rules as being no more than pointers towards a set of stunning
variations: scoring goals from *behind* the goalie's box, for
example, or playing *at* the referees on the understanding that

this made them move hastily away, thus increasing, sometimes by fifty yards, the size of the playing area.

My family's move to Pretoria, when I look back now, seems nothing less than foolhardy. It was alarming for all concerned for a Catholic to enter the holy city of Calvinism. My grandfather had done something similar early in the century when he moved to the little village of Balfour, admitted to all his unashamedly popish beliefs and set up his hotel among Boer farmers. But things then were somewhat looser. By the early 'fifties, when we moved to Pretoria, however, these matters had firmed up considerably and there was no way that you would be unaware, as a Roman Catholic, that you were venturing into enemy territory. And I soon discovered that to be an English-speaking Catholic from Johannesburg was a form of double jeopardy. The relationship, if that's what it is, between the two cities has been somewhat fraught for the past century. In 1886 gold was discovered in Johannesburg and drew with it what the Boers considered to be the deplorable rabble of Europe, itinerant gold diggers they called *uitlanders*, desperate for the barbarous metal. Until the discovery of entire reefs of gold, Johannesburg had been a Boer town. Pretoria and Johannesburg are not far apart, less than an hour's drive, but there is no feeling of closeness between the cities. When I arrived in 1952 I found myself in another universe: I had strayed right off the map of the known world and it was unlikely that I would ever be found again. I soon discovered that to reveal my origins was a mistake. What Pretorians felt about Johannesburg was probably best summed up by Paul Kruger who had taken a couple of looks at it; he suspected, correctly, that it represented the future and he didn't like it and spared no effort to tell his people so. It was Babylon, Nineveh, Sodom and Gomorrah, a city of gold, a place of *uitlanders*, a satanic brew of foreigners, Blacks, Jews, Englishmen and rebels. He kept his visits to Johannesburg to a bare minimum: on one memorable occasion he addressed a crowd at the old Wanderers Sports Club; at the end of his address his audience, who felt extremely aggrieved at the failure of Kruger's South African Republican Government to give them the vote, attempted to lynch him. After that the President did not venture back for years and, when finally coaxed to do so, began his speech with words which show that his suspicions had not dimmed: 'Burgers, friends, thieves, murderers, newcomers, and others...'

When, as an eight-year-old, I moved into a suburb in the east of Pretoria called Brooklyn, I began almost immediately to suffer from the first signs of a failure of faith – not in my Catholicism, but in the existence of my country as a real place. Though the process took some years to work itself out, it was inexorable. It was also bewildering and painful. It came to seem that a faith in the existence of the place also means, even if unintentionally, a belief in some of the sad, savage injustices which have been practised here, a belief, in short, in a kind of deity to whose dubious existence many victims have been sacrificed. So yes, I will say that the gradual, memorable diminishment of belief in the concept of South Africa as a place or a living entity, as a unity, as anything real at all, was for me akin to losing a form of religious faith.

It happened slowly; I began to have doubts, I did not tell anyone because I was unsure how the news was going to be received. Even then people had a lot of emotional capital invested in the concept; I also felt that the admission of these doubts was rather like confessing to deplorable morals. But being in Pretoria made the process both harder to admit and yet impossible to resist.

I had moved to Pretoria at a particularly significant time. The new Government was in control, memories of the triumph were fresh. You might say that people were still dancing in the streets because Pretoria, Kruger's old capital, was once again in the hands of its original owners. Except, of course, that no one danced in the streets, not in Pretoria, either then or now. In Pretoria street dancing is not the first thing that comes to mind. Anyway, the steets of Pretoria were full of Afrikaners: civil servants, policemen, soldiers, students – particularly students. Around Brooklyn where I lived we were surrounded by students. Next door was the suburb of Hatfield. Not far away was Sunnyside and down the road was a place called Arcadia. Hillcrest was nearby. But who would be so logical as to suppose that Brooklyn had, let us say, Dutch or American connections? Or that Hatfield resonated with the significance of the fact that this was also the name of the place where Queen Elizabeth I grew up? Did it mean, because there was a rather pleasant suburb called Hillcrest, that the countryside round about opened into dells and dingles, dales and woods and meadows? Certainly not. And even Arcadia was a long, long way from Greece; the only Greeks in Arcadia ran the corner cafés...

The problem I had with my disappearing country did not begin at home – it began in the far more mysterious place which we called 'overseas'. The problem was aggravated, in the happiest fashion, as was so much in my life, by my reading. The Pretoria Central Library supplied an unlimited number of books on fortnightly loan for the cost of a penny. I read without discrimination, to feed my habit; I read fiction, and my method was to begin on the right of a shelf and work my way leftwards. The chief benefit of growing taller seemed to me to be that more shelves came within reach. By the mid-fifties this gargantuan approach was somewhat more refined by the discovery that books could be read for their authors. Accordingly I read Jeffrey Farnol, Gene Stratton Porter, Dumas and Damon Runyon in quantity and repeatedly. It is not surprising that I developed a fascination for a world which was located almost entirely 'over there', in England, Canada, France and America; I had various personal, private visions of these places which no one else would recognise, but they

83

made a kind of sense to me. England was a place of fogs and
stallions and passionate love affairs, followed usually by duels;
Canada was mostly forest through which lovers wandered, he
had a withered arm and her name, I think, was Angel; France
was unimaginable, a place of moustaches and exclamations;
and America – well, America was dreadfully expensive.
Someone at school told us that a Coke cost a dollar – or was it
two? We shuddered.

Difficult though it may be to believe that I could live at
such a remove from my own country, I must say that I found it
preferable. Even then, in those far-off days, we knew that
anything that looked even remotely interesting, or lively, or
original was likely to be either unobtainable, illegal, or would
shortly be banned. It did not matter what these things were,
whether ideas or books or pictures. If South Africa existed to
do anything, it existed, as far as I could see, to disapprove of
these things. 'Overseas' was infinitely preferable. When, in
the middle 'fifties, the revolution that was rock and roll burst
upon us, the craving to be off and elsewhere was like a fire in
me. Naturally, I despaired of ever doing so. Perhaps this had
to do with the fact that I had read my way into the outside
world, dreamed my way into it and danced my way into it,
courtesy of the only guy on the block who could afford the
latest records. In those days kids did not get allowances,
teenagers had not yet been born and everybody over twenty
owned a demob suit and went around singing the 'Tennessee
Waltz'. They all wore perms, very red lipstick – smiled
widely and looked sad. *They* were the people from the 'forties
– the very word was like a knell. Looking at them, one
supposed they had been young, once, these creatures with
their rather tight hair and their very baggy shorts. Personally,
I had a theory that my parents were aliens from a distant
planet who had landed on earth and captured me and were
holding me against my will. I saw my parents as interlopers
from outer space – and so were all their friends. So in fact was

anybody who was over about five feet, and who remembered the War.

Such thoughts, dreams, books, are not a good preparation for life, not at least where I grew up. But there was worse to come. As I grew older the outside world seemed more outside than ever, further away, out of reach, unattainable. I began to despair, I began to think that maybe it was all a con trick, a fraud, a joke perpetrated by life, or God, or the Government and that, in actual fact, there was no such place as overseas and the earth was really and truly *flat* – just like Paul Kruger had believed – and that if you walked far enough in any direction, you simply fell off the edge, and that was not all, because when it happened the Government and the police and the neighbours gathered at the side of the chasm down which you had plummeted and shouted loud and long: 'We told you so!' And their voices echoed in the void, along with their cruel laughter. Of course I had met people who had been overseas; or at least they claimed to have visited places like Holland or Dulwich, even on one celebrated occasion, Detroit. But then people talked, didn't they? Somebody claimed that his mother had met the Pope. But could we be sure?

Perhaps my dilemma is explicable in what would be the reverse of Copernican terms. It was said by those in authority that there was at the centre of the universe a bright and flaming star around which a lowly planet like mine revolved. Call that dazzling celestial object – 'overseas'. That is the position from which one began. What happened in my case was that I began to wonder if this wasn't wrong, that perhaps there was no sun and that my lowly planet did not revolve around anything and that perhaps this cold and rather small and unfriendly planet of mine, at that time called Pretoria, was the only object in the heavens. In other words, maybe I was being set up by all these words and pictures that I read in my books about faraway foreign places, I was being taken in by the visits people were rumoured to have made. Maybe they were bluffing when they claimed to have seen New York? The more I thought about this the more convinced I became. Yes, I was being set up. I was the patsy. Those pictures of the Eiffel Tower? Forgeries. The films of Elvis Presley? Fakes. Stories of English duels, French moustaches and Canadian lumberjacks? Purest make believe. But then what about that boy in my class who claimed to have come from America? An impostor. It is true that until then he had seemed a rare creature, so rare that I suggested that we put him in a glass case and preserve him. But now I lost interest. I mean anyone could speak with an American accent. Even I did, from time to time. You learnt to do it from all those fake movies that we watched on Saturday mornings in the Café bio ... There was probably a factory churning them out, in a place like Brakpan.

So what did I do? Did I despair? Well, perhaps – but not for long. I decided that if the world was this one, and only this one, then I had better come to terms with it, study it, find out what *it* was so that I should know who *I* was. If we really were alone in the universe, then what was this world where I lived and where was it precisely? I did not absolutely abandon the hope that one day I might be able to test the hypothesis that the outside world existed, but that meant travelling and at that time any thought of doing so was inconceivable. It would have meant a journey equivalent to that needed to reach the nearest star in our solar system, that is how far away things seemed. There was no way one would live long enough to survive the journey and there was no guarantee that there would be anything there when you arrived. Besides, the idea of travelling such distances was absurd, I mean people made a big deal of it when they travelled to Durban ... So, for the duration at least, I was stuck, and I would have to examine what was within reach.

I started with the central question. The country in which I found myself was called South Africa. Did that mean that I was a South African? Well, yes – *but* ... But what? Well, it was more accurate to call myself an English-speaking South African. Was that all? No – I was also a White, English-speaking South African. Anything else? Yes, I was also a Roman Catholic, English-speaking, White South African. So that was me taken care of and I was something of a mouthful.

So then, let us take these Afrikaner students who surrounded us. Were they South Africans? Well, yes – they were Afrikaans-speaking South Africans. Was that all? No, more fully described, they were Calvinist, Afrikaans-speaking, White South Africans. Very good then. So far I had identified two sorts of South Africans. But of course there were more. There were Indians in Pretoria in those days. They ran the shops at the bottom of Andries Pretorius Street and they organised wonderful clothes sales. 'Buy one pink sports coat and get two pairs of charcoal trousers, three shirts and four socks... FREE!' What about those Indians? Were they also South Africans? Well, in a way, I supposed they were, they were also Asians, but they were not really what we would regard as South Africans. Of course, if you insisted, you could describe them as such but somehow it seemed and sounded so much better to call them, well, just Indians or shopkeepers ... or a variety of more demeaning names – coolies, or crooks – depending on your point of view. So the difficulties began to multiply.

But there were still more people in Pretoria, quite apart from the Whites and the Asians, there were also lots of Black people. Well, what were they? This got really difficult because they had lots of names. They were called natives, or Africans, or Bantu, and a lot more unrepeatable things besides. Yes, but were they South Africans? Well, perhaps it was better to distinguish them by tribe, to call them Sothos, Tswanas or Zulus? Yes, well, but *were* they South Africans? Well, not really. Of course there was nothing to prevent me from describing them, say, as Black, Sotho-speaking South Africans, if I wished to be pedantic about it. But if you tried being pedantic half the people in Pretoria would not have known what you were talking about, and the rest would have tried to have you arrested, because it made for all sorts of difficulties. It sounded even odder if you simply referred to them as South Africans. 'We have South Africans working in our garden'; 'We have South Africans looking after the children; doing the cooking, the weeding... the work'. The moment you applied the term to them it sounded so curious. Were they really the same people sitting on the side of the road playing guitars? Those people whom we would not allow into our parks? Or on our buses? Into our beds, our churches? Were they really South Africans?

No, it would not work and so we did not try. At the very best people felt we ought to call such people Africans, or natives, or Bantu, or more often as not, nothing at all. They were just 'them'. And if they were them, then who were we? Well, of course, we were 'us'. There were no other South Africans then, there were just them and us. All other claims to nationality were no more than polite affectations, pretensions, or threats. More often than not – threats. The main thing to remember was that we were 'us' and determined to keep it that way; and we planned to do it by keeping them 'them'.

Our little garrison suburbs, where the English minority huddled together for protection, with their deceptive Anglican connotations of green meadows and woods, were really battle zones deep within the hot hairy heart of Afrikanerdom. We were quite literally surrounded by the enemy; the flower of Afrikaner youth was being educated at the vast University of Pretoria which encircled us and we were nakedly exposed for what we were, not merely English, but Roman Catholics of a most exotic variety: our popish temples were everywhere, the Parish Church, called the Monastery; my school, Christian Brothers College, as well as Loreto Convent for girls, an elaborate Sea-Scout Hall, built of bricks in the shape of a ship, bows straining at the sky, five hundred miles from the nearest ocean; there were also the girls' hockey field and our rugby pitches, as well as crucifixes, priests in black cassocks and heavily swathed nuns; the Brothers' house and the Sisters' nunnery. Also on display were public professions of faith: street processions, clouds of incense, altar boys, bells, hosts, and beads. The Afrikaners examined us warily, prayed mightily for deliverance from the Roman danger in their midst and, practical as ever, began making plans to move us out.

Our Catholic Alamo occupied roughly four large blocks of prime suburban real estate, out in the eastern suburbs, hard by the spreading campus of Pretoria University, rapidly becoming the largest in the country and flush with funds from the incoming Government, which pressed upon the playing fields, church and schools within our holy stockade, unable for the moment to swallow us but beginning to spread round the sides of our small estate in a pincer movement, throwing up enormous hostels, sky-scraping boarding houses, for its prodigiously expanding student population. I think it is true to say that in the nine years I attended Christian Brothers College we all knew, despite protestations to the contrary, that we were going one way. We watched the shaven-haired, barefoot young men in Volkswagens and the well-scrubbed farmgirls in cotton prints blushing at our nuns and running giggling from the Brothers and priests who taught us, those strange men in black frocks. We saw how they looked on in horrid fascination at such public feasts as Corpus Christi where we paraded through the streets with banners, bells, and the sacred host held aloft within the golden sunburst of the monstrance. The entire construction of the Catholic community, its cultural foundation and its religious expression, was so thoroughly out of keeping with the sober Calvinist pieties of Pretoria that, looking back thirty-five years, I am surprised we survived as long as we did. It might

89

have been possible for my grandfather to live among his Boer neighbours, despite his language and nationality, at least in the years before the coming of the Dominie; but after 1948, with Nationalist Afrikaners in the ascendant, and we infidels in the middle of their holy city, any rapprochement was simply out of the question. Who wanted it? Or needed it? So we sat tight, an intensely Irish Catholic community, exclusive, self-contained, intimate – in short, a ghetto, an Irish Roman settlement in Africa, a tiny outpost of the one true faith deep inside enemy country. The only possible virtue of this exposed position within the Afrikaner laager was the affinity we felt for the far larger and more obviously despised Black majority who stood far outside the defences. I do not mean to compare our position; Black people were obliged to suffer under the crusading racialism practised as an article of Government policy against all our coloured countrymen, while all we received was a small, but sharp, education in the penalties of being a detested minority, a peculiar race apart. But it gave one something of an imaginative grasp of what the others must have felt. Relationships with Blacks were, none the less, narrowly confined: we met them as master and servant, or we met them as children playing with the children of servants, a more natural encounter. But of course children grow up, and the children of servants grew up to be servants.

It is hardly surprising that we were never quite sure where we were supposed to be. Sometimes we lived in Ireland, sometimes in Rome and very occasionally we remembered we were in Africa after all where, it was said, we were supposed to feel at home. But home for us was not a place but a parish, a holy see, a richly intricate weaving of institutions: the Sodality of Mary, the Third Order of St Francis; the troop of Catholic Sea Scouts; the Children of Mary and the Altar Servers Guild, as well as the badminton club, the Friday confessional and the Saturday night social in the Church Hall. Above all, we rejoiced in the certain knowledge that no matter how many of the enemy were ranged against us, we were the children of God, possessors of the one true faith. Contrary to rumours put about by the opposition we did not worship statues or adore the Pope; nuns did not visit priests by night, at least not to our knowledge. We did not sell indulgences or plot to return the Calvinist churches to the fold by stealth. We were a rock in a rough sea and that sea was teeming with sharks; we were a shining light in a hostile world and our position inspired in us a mixture of fear and pride which, I imagine, perhaps resembled, very faintly, the temperament of the early Christians in pagan Rome. Only, we were not meek. For we saw ourselves also as the church militant and we were going to go down fighting. They might pursue us with their giant hostels, their Volkswagens, their braggadocio. But *they* were also the heretics, *they* were the ones who would someday roast in hell. We would fight for the faith. When the Calvinists sent their cavalry over the hill we would be waiting to shoot them out of the saddle.

Next door, blessedly close, was the convent separated from the boys' college by a tall, sturdy hedge with spiky boughs loaded with bright red berries. All of the convent's facilities, its holy and profane delights, had hedges round them of one sort or another (or at least it seemed so) as if to remind us of the sacred boundaries between boys and girls drawn in heaven. Behind the hedges tall, rather scrawny but somehow very beautiful pine trees skewered the sky. The borders of our Catholic enclosure had been planted with these pines which flourished their crop of cones each year and dropped them like offerings at our feet as we stood after school watching the girls perspiring excitingly on the hockey field, pale-faced in their dark-blue gymslips, pounding up and down the sandy pitch which rang to cries of 'Sticks!' and 'Your ball, Imelda,' and 'Good shot, Monica!' while two nuns refereed from the touch-lines with fluting trills on their little silver whistles, flinging furious glances at the knots of boys grinning behind the thorny hedge. Of course the girls played for us and we knew it; we had eyes only for them and they knew it. But then so did the wiry, athletic nuns with their white sand-shoes flashing mysteriously beneath their long black habits.

The sense of exile we felt within our own country is something which has never left me. We were a generation who went into exile before we left home. Leaving does not increase the sense of loss, returning does not cure it. To some extent, I suppose we were a little like the Indians of Station Street in Balfour, an alien minority on the periphery of things – except that we were not on the periphery, we were slap-bang in the middle of it all. Like the Indians of Station Street we pretended to be leading perfectly normal lives, even though we knew by the way passing students averted their eyes that a community which believes in black frocks for men, bells and incense cannot, and will not, ever be normal. The assertion of normality was vital; we were rejecting the view that we represented some monstrous sub-species of the human race. We did not expect this to convince our sceptical Calvinist neighbours; we laid claim to be ordinary because in an abnormal society this is a strategy of defiance. Besides, it kept us sane.

College and convent were not exclusively Catholic; we took in whoever could afford the fees, and we were open to all Catholics in the city, whether or not they could afford to pay. The results were very mixed indeed, in religions, classes and nationalities. My school numbered in its community Anglicans, Jews, Moslems; my classmates were Syrians, Italians, Poles and Yugoslavs. We even had one American from the Diplomatic Corps. And because we were, in the wider sense of the word, such a catholic community we drew on a variety of talents. One of the Jewish boys frequently led prayers and an Egyptian was noted for his devotion to the Virgin Mary. But of course this sort of internationalism did us no good, it merely confirmed the suspicions of the Puritans amongst whom we lived. As far as they were concerned the whelps of Rome had been joined by the riff-raff of North Africa, the Middle East and Southern Europe. We were indeed the cosmopolis of Pretoria, we were part of the world – or say, at least, we constituted as far as I was concerned a certain proof, tattered, slim but lovely, that a world existed beyond the stockade.

It was an education of a sort. Not only did it teach us something about the dimensions of religious detestation but it gave us a thorough grounding in trench politics and an un-rivalled appreciation of the fact that South African reality henceforth was to be a matter of drawing lines. The giant pincers of the University crept ever closer, and we saw close up the draughtsmen of the new politics at work, at study and even at play. I spoke Afrikaans with almost the same facility as I spoke English – a necessary requirement for self-protection. While protesting our belief in the right of the other to be different, we detested and deplored each other's differences; but so long as they kept to their side of the line and we kept to ours an uneasy truce prevailed.

Even as early as 1952, as I was settling uncomfortably into my new school among Brothers whose Irish brogues were so broad one's ears buzzed with them, rough, red-faced men smelling of cigarettes, brandy and violence (the leather straps they carried in their pockets were laced with halfpennies for added impact); even then it was becoming clear that the new Nationalist Government was going to be no nine-day wonder. Pretoria became increasingly, and enthusiastically, a city given over to the practical implementation of the party's politics of racial partition which began with the concerted attempt to pass the entire population through racial filters: one for each group: Whites, Blacks, Coloureds and Asians, as well as the preparation of separate institutions to receive the victims of this experiment. In 1954 the smooth tactician, Dr Malan, gave way to the aggressive Mr Strydom, known alarmingly as the Lion of Waterberg. Malan had wanted, and won, power in order to begin the process of unscrambling the racial mix which had slowly and surely begun under the earlier administrations of Smuts, Hertzog and Botha. His successor, sure of power, now proceeded with the programme of grand apartheid and in the Union Buildings, high on its ridge, an army of bureaucrats laboured to divide the country. The numbers of civil servants, which had always been pretty impressive anyway, grew more so over the years. The *Volk* had elected the Nationalists into government and now the Party appeared to be repaying the debt by putting the *Volk*, wherever possible, into Government service. Henceforth, the country was to be run on the lines of a human zoo with different species confined to their own cages. And of course in the way of defenders of zoos, the organisers of this policy argued that they were not really imprisoning the animals but rather protecting their freedom and independence by preventing the exploitation of weaker species by the stronger. This was an argument which we Catholics heard with some interest and we had a grandstand view as the engineers of the new order set to work. It is, I suppose, correct to say that with the Act of Union of 1910 the country had achieved, after decades of bloodshed, the beginnings of a settlement, at least amongst White groups (for the Act of Union excluded the Black majority from political discussion); however, the new regime of 1948 came in on a programme which declared that the way forwards was the way backwards and they began dismembering that unity with a vengeance, secure in the knowledge that it was not only Party policy, but also God's will.

Pretoria, in the run-up to the General Election, now just two weeks away, is plastered with bunting, flags and posters.

Rumour has it that there is considerable conservative support for the right-wing parties among the functionaries of the Civil Service, frightened by what they see as radical changes in the traditional policies of apartheid as well as in the lower ranks of the army and the police. Since these are the most important props of the State, and since Pretoria is home to all three, it is not surprising that there should be a groundswell of support here for the White right, for Dr Treurnicht's Conservative Party and Eugene Terre'Blanche, and his Afrikaner Resistance Movement. However, senior police and army officers are not likely to represent any particular threat to the Government. No junta threatens. This is not South America (though the model looms dangerously) and besides, with the increasingly complex involvement of the military in political matters, at the level of the President's Security Council and on the shadowy 'Management Committees', the top brass are already incorporated into the Government machinery and undoubtedly the process will continue. On the other hand, absolute loyalty is no longer certain among lower-ranking civil servants, policemen and soldiers who represent fertile recruiting grounds for the White Right. Of course this is exactly what happened in the years prior to 1948, when neo-fascist, quasi-military organisations lent their support, and their muscle where it was needed, to the rising National Party: groups with such names as the *Ossewa Brandwag* (Oxwagon Brigade), the New Order, and the *Broederbond* (the Band of Brothers). What they did for the present National Party no doubt similar shadowy organisations are doing for their right-wing opponents today. Pretoria is made for this kind of sedition.

You will find so much rebuilding, I was told, when I set off for Pretoria. True enough. Enter the city from the south and you will pass Pretoria Central, the hanging jail. There is always work for the hangman here and new additions have been built which bristle with arms, cameras and guards. No jail is more notorious or represents a more obvious target and so the precautions are hardly surprising. Besides, such security measures are increasingly the rule even in private houses in the suburbs – it is as if the policy of imprisoning the population within racial limits has now reached its absurd apotheosis as people begin to build their own cages.

I had forgotten how many uniforms you see in Pretoria; there are soldiers, police, traffic wardens, nurses, every third person appears to have on a uniform of some kind and the city has the look of a wartime capital, a city under arms. This is not in the least to suggest that it is in any way bleak or depressing, quite the contrary – it has an almost disconcertingly ebullient air, it thrives, the streets are full of conscripts in berets which range from the most alarming shades of blue to cherry and purple. These young men, who do two years' full-time military training and serve for many years more in the reserve, are being drawn into the depressing argument with which this entire place is increasingly buttressed: 'Why does Pretoria exist?' It exists, I suspect, in order to defend itself.

I put up at an hotel close to the city centre and to a number of important historical sites – favourite visiting places of mine thirty years earlier. In the lobby this morning, quite suddenly and unexpectedly, two women come to blows in the foyer. They have walked in off the street where they patrol the sandy pavements beneath the jacaranda trees for custom. Perhaps they have fallen out over some client or one has been encroaching on the other's territory, because, before anyone realises what is going on, these two White whores are squaring up to each other in front of the reception desk. Both girls are dressed in very tight, moulded blouses and jeans, and both are barefoot. The tall, rather pretty girl with chestnut hair piled up on her head is being punched by a short, dark, business-like lady. The tall girl grapples with her, hitting back hard, while puzzled guests look on. The staff seem paralysed. Then both women are seized from behind by two Black waiters and lifted, kicking and screaming, through the hotel doors and dumped in the garden where the fight looks set to continue, but friends and relatives suddenly emerge from the shrubs and carry off one of the combatants. The Black staff who have ejected them are outraged; the Indian porter is scandalised and the White manager deeply embarrassed. The tall girl won't leave; she stands shaking and sobbing outside the glass doors and despite entreaties and promises she refuses to budge. When the manager threatens to call the police she encourages him to do so. She is clearly very worried and I have the feeling that perhaps she fears for her life. Leaving the hotel, I pass her opponent who is standing just around the corner, surrounded by supporters, also barefoot, all carrying what look like large sticks, but these are not sticks, they are heavy branches, torn from the nearby jacaranda trees. They hold the branches behind their backs rather furtively, though they are far too big to hide.

A little further on an albino beggar woman and child sit on the pavement. She has a skin of that pale, pinky translucent colour, or rather non-colour, with a dusting of freckles to be seen just beneath the skin. She is so pale, so chalk-white, it is quite disturbing. The child is pitch black, sturdy and very beautiful and perhaps four or five years old. The woman has her hand out, begging; the child plays around her feet and when she isn't looking he reaches into her bag and pulls out a toilet roll. His mother tries to grab it from him and while passers-by avert their eyes and hurry past, mother and child tug for possession of the paper.

Just around the corner you walk into history; that is the other thing about this place, history waits around the corner, like a beggar, a mugger, a whore. I've come to Melrose House, built in 1886. It was here that the Peace Treaty bringing to an end the Boer War was signed on 31 May, 1902. It is a handsome Victorian house set in extensive gardens, with palm trees and a large ornamental pond. The pond is beautiful; three swans support a column on which two Cupids stand lifting a basin of water in which a sparrow and a pigeon happen to be sharing a drink. White and purple lilies of great delicacy float on the water and between them I get glimpses of plump, intensely vivid goldfish. Over the whole prospect breathes that peculiar peace of South African gardens in the middle of the morning, in the middle of the week, in the middle of the city.

The interior of the house preserves the Victorian love for density of detail in the innumerable frills, flounces and comforts of an affluent, upper middle class family, as well as its abiding passion for new kitchen gadgets. You can see the room with its big table where the Peace Treaty was signed. Outside the door hangs a drawing showing the signatories to the document who include the Boer generals Smuts, Botha and De La Rey as well as the British warlord Kitchener and that arch-enemy of the Boers, Milner. This document not only put an end to the war but it extinguished the independence of the old Boer republics, the South African Republic of Kruger and the Republic of the Orange Free State, and it was regarded by many Boers with the same degree of bitterness and shame with which the Germans looked upon the Treaty of Versailles at the end of the Great War. It was memories of their own bitter anger which prompted Botha and Smuts to plead in vain with the victorious allies at Versailles to moderate their demands for punitive reparations from Germany, fearing that they were only storing up trouble in years to come. There were those among the Boers who vowed they would not rest until their country was theirs again, and the short tenure of leaders such as Botha and Smuts, to whom my grandfather looked for the future, turned out to be nothing but a temporary aberration.

It is curious that the prescience shown by the South Africans at Versailles deserted them at home. The mistake had been to suppose that with the signing of the Treaty the Boer War was over. In fact it was only just beginning. Botha and Smuts believed they could put the past behind them and head a united country. They believed in progress and forgiveness. But, to the fiery young Nationalists who hated them, forgiveness was weakness, progress an abomination and the best place for the past was firmly ahead of them. There is a story told about Smuts, trying desperately to come to terms with his electoral defeat in 1948, saying to a friend that all his old comrades had abandoned him. 'But how can they have done?' came the cruel rejoinder: 'They're all dead.'

Pretoria, then, is the city of the restoration and without some appreciation of the spiritual significance the place holds for Afrikaners it is not possible to understand the dark symphony of White South African politics: the Whiter the politics, the darker the music. If you do not at least glance at the shrines of the ancestors and look into the holy places of the tribal faith, you will grasp very little. You must also take account of the naming of places. It is, for example, helpful to know that outside the city lies the headquarters of the South African army and, appropriately, this heroic institution stands hard by the suburb called Valhalla. The naming and renaming of South Africa provides a particular joy for those who know how to read the text. Ironic coincidences make up the thread by which the political fabric is bound and bizarrely embroidered. The area occupied by Defence Force Head-quarters was once called Roberts' Heights, a name which commemorates that hammer of the Boers, Field Marshal 'Bob' Roberts. A name was slapped on the place in the late 1930s to exorcise these deplorable British associations, and to show that when the Boers came to power they remembered what the British had taught them about victory and did to Roberts' Heights what the British had done to McHattiesburg.

They called it Voortrekkerhoogte (Voortrekker Heights).

And in the city of monuments, there is the greatest of all, the Voortrekker Monument, which I am also visiting today. This immense bulky granite bunker on a low hill dominates the surrounding countryside, crowded with air bases and army camps, the greatest concentration of military power south of the Sahara. The Monument was opened in 1949 by Dr Malan and erected in homage to the founders of the Boer nation, the Voortrekkers, a permanent reminder to the Afrikaners that they belong, as the handbook says, 'to a nation of heroes'. The building is intended to endure a thousand years, containing within it a Hall of Heroes, an historic frieze depicting the triumphs and disasters of the early trekkers, a cenotaph, and a dome through which, on 16 December each year, the sun's rays fall upon an altar commemorating the death of Piet Retief at the hands of the treacherous Zulu chief, Dingaan, as well as the divine retribution for that betrayal symbolised in the victory of the Boers over the Zulus at the Battle of Blood River in Natal, on 16 December 1838. This victory is marked by a public holiday (another Sunday, really) with religious services and bellicose speeches between prayers. It used to be called Dingaan's Day, I remember, but this was changed, I suppose because it seemed to give too much to Dingaan, and was renamed instead The Day of the Covenant.

The place is a gigantic exercise in vulgar triumphalism and it looks like an inflated model of those radio sets they used to build in the 'thirties; it has a curious Art Nouveau look about it. Do not be fooled – this is the most potent shrine in Afrikanerdom. When it was inaugurated in 1949 someone took a photograph which shows the new Prime Minister, Dr Malan, preparing to perform the opening ceremony. Beside him stands General Smuts and I could swear the old man still has a rather dazed look on his face, as if the shock of his defeat has not worn off. Over a hundred thousand people crowded into the great open arena for the occasion.

All the more odd then, that on my visit today, I should find it closed 'for repairs'. However, a few discreet enquiries prove that this is a polite subterfuge. What is concerning the authorities, it seems, is the growing practice of the Afrikaner Resistance Movement to hijack the sacred sites of Afrikaner history and there to lambaste, before delirious audiences, the reforming policies of the present Government and to call for a new, independent, self-sufficient, all-White Boer nation. In the run-up to the election there are worrying reports that Terre'Blanche's AWB plans to hold a gigantic rally in the open-air arena. Even so, I must say that the significance of the closure is quite extraordinary because the gesture it makes towards the importance of such right-wing groups is unmistakable. This is rather like finding St Peter's closed because the Vatican fears a visit by a band of fiercely conservative Catholics – for that is all they are – a dissident fragment, according to the Government which denies vehemently that it pays any attention to the rise of the right-wing parties, denies indeed that they are rising at all. However, a Government official of my acquaintance is more forthright:

'Do you know what the letters A-W-B stand for? Afrikaners without Brains.'

This is interesting because I think I hear in his voice the same sort of contempt it was once usual to encounter among the British when they spoke of the 'stupid Boer'. The point about our conversation is that we are speaking Afrikaans. And I had never known it was possible to sound the 'English' note of contempt in Afrikaans. Things are changing.

'These lunatics, and that's what they are, want to strangle progress in this country. They want to suffocate us with their racialism.'

'And what are your plans for progress?'

'We want to reconcile the different population groups. We

know we've got a diverse population here. How do we reconcile that with the inter-dependence of different groups, while at the same time protecting the integrity of each of those groups so that they feel secure? We do it by creating joint structures, over-arching bridges, by means of which the leaders of each of these groups come together to form the Government of the country. The leaders of each group get together in a State Council and share power in the areas such as national affairs, law and order, defence and the economy. This will be our approach to the central problem facing us, which is: how do we stop dominating others without being dominated ourselves?'

This is offered in good faith. It is the sort of conversation that makes me want to go and stick my head in a bucket of ice-cold water.

Driving back into town I visit the Transvaal Museum, outside which hangs a huge replica of a pterodactyl, probably made of fibreglass. The magnificent white skeleton flies through the air with jaws agape, an impressive if somewhat alarming sight. People are drinking tea beneath its enormous saw-toothed beak. I am here to pay a visit to the Elephant Bird of Madagascar which is to be seen in a glass case in the Hall of Birds. As a boy I made trips to stare at the prodigious creature. This enormous fowl laid eggs much larger than those of the ostrich and weighed about half a ton. Its legs are massive, thickening from the knee into huge muscular thighs; it spent its time wandering about the swamps of Madagascar and doing pretty well. But over thousands of years the island climate became dryer and the change in environment was fatal for the Elephant Bird of Madagascar. It was just too big to run around on dry land and about 600 years ago it died out. The legs, or trunk, and a few massive eggs are all that remain of the Ozymandias of birds. But there is also an artist's impression of the Elephant Bird in the flesh, a very curious, hefty, thoroughly muscular creature, something like a gigantic ostrich, ridiculous to look at, I suppose, even comical. Next to it stands an even funnier-looking bird, just as extinct, the Dodo. 'The Dodo is dead', a notice above the familiar skeleton announces with bleak finality. I used to go and stare at the Elephant Bird and ask how anything so silly could have been born. For me, the people who ran the country, whom I saw from day to day all around me in Pretoria, were actually in heavy disguise; they called themselves White Calvinists but I knew that they were really the Elephant Birds of South Africa. And their nervous, English-speaking accomplices were the Dodos. Surely it would be simply a matter of time before both faded into oblivion; perhaps to be preserved just like them in a glass case in some museum somewhere, some day. It was only a question of waiting, I told myself. I did not pretend that I was going to be around long enough to see it happen because I knew that their demise was further away than anticipated, but it seemed to me certain even so.

Therein lay the nub of my predicament when I came to consider my own identity. The two White role models which I was offered as potential South Africans had turned into candidates for extinction. This led on to yet graver problems. For if we did not really stand up to close scrutiny, then neither did the country from which we purported to take our names. Having no South Africans meant no South Africa, whether or not the place happened to appear in the atlas.

There were some small consolations in this bitter knowledge. Consider again the question of names. Whites in this country have used them so often that we have over-familiarised ourselves with them, and I think we forget just how very demented the names are which are given to people. What on earth were we supposed to do with the word

'Bantu'? That was the official term by which Black people were to be known, according to Government direction: not Blacks, or Africans, or natives, but 'Bantus'. I had only to roll the word around my mouth to be overcome by a fit of embarrassment. What were intelligent people doing, making use of such a term? But there was more to it than that, because at the bottom of town there lived the 'Indians' and what sort of designation was that? And down in the Cape there were these 'Coloureds'. Coloured what? And if we felt embarrassed to go around using these ridiculous appellations, how did the people feel to whom they applied? When I made my discovery in the Transvaal Museum, I felt a whole lot happier about things, in an unhappy way, because even though it left me feeling a little lonely to know that there were no South Africans, I had instead a whole new set of creatures; the population of this country now listed, at least in my mind, as Bantus, Indians, Coloureds, Elephant Birds and Dodos.

No South Africans? No South Africa . . . that entity seemed to recede ever further into the distance as the quality of life took on, for me, an increasingly fictional character. It was as if the place was so absurd, so incredible, so terrifyingly funny that it was only by putting it into story form that you could believe in it. Not only that but it was perhaps the one way of making the bizarre quality of life in some way remotely reputable. Gradually I became more and more convinced that the country so confidently named amounted to not much more than a geographical convenience, a rallying point for political opinion, somewhere you assumed for the purposes of argument but which was, to anyone with half an eye, very little more than a nest of shadows. It was necessary to pretend to believe in it; it was as if we had been raised with the kinds of expectations which we associate with the great Russian landowners of the last century. We were taught to take for granted our absolute right of ownership to great estates while all the time knowing in our hearts that really we had only taken possession of the maps. Only the paper belonged to us. The real world where events occurred, people acted, lay elsewhere, so we could not lay claim to a history, all we had were politics, and if you discounted the politics; all we had left were fictions.

But I see now that the temptation to dismiss the Afrikaner as the elephant bird of Africa is to be resisted. In assessing the present circumstances it will not do to give way to the misconception of the British in the nineteenth century, or to the delusions of the sanctioneers in the twentieth, or to underrate the degrees of resilience, resourcefulness and determination that have carried this people and their Party through four decades of unchallenged government. Anybody who remembers the years following the Nationalist victory of 1948 and felt the gusts of acclamation with which the faithful cheered their leaders on their way will know that they were magnificently determined that no one would stop them. They set out to restore the legend, the potent myth, of trekker heroism; they revived bitter memories of the twenty thousand women and children dead in the British concentration camps, the flight of Paul Kruger into exile, the insolence of the Black man and the contempt of the English, but above all the calumny that the Boers were not much better than savages, an inferior species. All these slurs were to be rejected at last. Even so, a residue of this feeling exists today amongst enemies of the Nationalists, some of whom rejoiced a short while ago when the townships seemed to be burning out of control in 1985 and '86 and declared that the end of Afrikaner rule was only a matter of time. Those who put about this view are victims of the elephant bird syndrome. They cannot understand how the White Afrikaner revolution can possibly survive, they cannot believe that anything so absolutely preposterous, so ill-designed, so foolish, so absurd, should have existed at all. Therefore it is possible to detect in predictions of its imminent demise a note of fierce joy. However understandable such rejoicing may be, it is premature. The body politic of Afrikanerdom is far from moribund; for a people on their last legs they look remarkably vivacious. Any invitations to the funeral games, or preparation of the baked meats, is not advised. A stroll through the streets and suburbs of Pretoria will reveal a quite striking sense of energy and determination, as well as ample evidence of the prodigious military power of the White South African State.

Local critics of course persist, rightly and very bravely, with their attacks upon the present regime and it is sometimes thought that the Government's willingness to tolerate dissent is a sign of its political maturity. In fact, until recently when the State of Emergency was imposed, people could object and demonstrate and complain as much as they liked, on the understanding that it changed nothing. This attitude is based not on cynicism but on a clear-eyed reading of the nature of power. The policy was best summed up, as was so much else, by Paul Kruger when he faced the wrath of the foreign *uitlanders* of Johannesburg who angrily complained about their lack of voting rights and of the visible injustices suffered under the Government of his Boer republic:

'Protest! Protest! What is the good of protesting? You have not got the guns. I have.'

Kruger issued his warning in the 1890s and it echoes down the years and still applies in the 1980s, coarse, succinct, unpalatable, but the truth even so. Of course Kruger was so easy to dislike, he presented such a target, an extremely vulgar man, a buffoon, an anachronism, a man who genuinely believed that the earth was flat, disapproved of steam trains and when told that there might be gold beneath the city of Pretoria advised his people to leave it there, citing the trouble which the discovery of gold had brought to Johannesburg –

the influx of foreigners, capitalists, and Blacks. He was called by his friends and admirers 'Oom Paul' (Uncle Paul), though I suspect there were no very great avuncular qualities about him, and yet the caricatures of the British propagandists were deeply misleading. It is as if dislike made them quite blind and they obsessively emphasised his foolishness, even his personal ugliness. Here was the King of the Elephant Birds! Yet a glance at the man's face shows someone astute, bold and especially sensitive.

There are many faces of Kruger to be seen in and around Pretoria, many of them congregated in the holy of holies, the Kruger house, now preserved as a museum and tabernacle, a few blocks from the Transvaal Museum with its flying pterodactyl and its plump-thighed elephant bird. His house is not difficult to find; a modest little place it stands beside the very much larger and extremely ugly modern headquarters of the Pretoria Murder and Robbery Squad. It has a gable, a veranda and several dark little rooms crammed with heavy furniture and relics, the old man's bed, his Bible and pictures of his house in exile at Clarens on Lake Geneva. Outside on the veranda is a pair of white stone lions presented to Kruger by his friend the diamond millionaire Barney Barnato. An unexpected friendship, this, between capitalist and Boer. One of the lions is fast asleep, the other tries to look fierce but fails. Inside the house the air of reverence is claustrophobic, people speak in whispers.

A more public Kruger, in official regalia, sash and top hat of the State President of the South African Republic is to be seen up on a pedestal in the centre of town in Church Square. At the feet of the squat, sturdy figure, at the four corners, as it were, of his square, flat world sit four burgers, cradling their rifles. Kruger stares northwards – perhaps anticipating that this was the direction from which the ultimate threat would one day come. Yet it is a curiously peaceful group. If you ignore the riflemen at his feet he has the air of a man waiting for a train.

It is lunchtime and the White office workers from the government buildings and banks surrounding Church Square come hurrying by, they do not stop or look or linger, while on the lawns that spread out beneath the statue of Kruger Black people settle themselves, stretching out on the grass, invisible extras of South African life. Office workers pass by, careful not to look down. Into this square they have crammed in their thousands on occasions of great political achievement, armies of the *Volk* come to celebrate election victories and primary feasts of the Nationalist calendar. Pretoria is the city where the Afrikaner parades on behalf of faith and Party and, until very recently, the two have been virtually indistinguishable. But now others are beginning to parade. Not very long ago there took place in this city what was known as a 'March of Gratitude'. It was organised by the Afrikaner Resistance Movement whose members marched in silent tribute to the local Police Headquarters to pledge their allegiance and to assure the force of their support in their struggle against political subversion, a struggle, it was intimated, less than fully supported by the present Government. What made the march noticeable, indeed what made it illegal, is the present State of Emergency which forbids any gatherings of this sort. There were some who wondered aloud how it was possible for a small army of large men to march through the streets of Pretoria and not be anticipated? To this the police responded that the marchers had come upon them so unexpectedly, so silently, that they had been unable to prevent the gathering. It was further rumoured that the marchers carried torches but it seems the police, usually so attuned to the least sign of civil disturbance, simply had not the eyes to see them. Such evasions, prevarications and coded warnings are among the true delights of South African political life.

Into this same Church Square I can remember others coming in the mid-'fifties, intent on turning the place into a battleground, armies of ducktails, young men besotted by the latest rock and roll heroes, Elvis Presley devotees to a man, taking their name from the curious way in which their hair was combed around the sides of their heads and met at the back in a series of interleaving wedges. They came from miles around, these young men, wearing black, skin-tight stovepipe trousers, white and blue and silver sports-coats, string ties and knuckle-dusters. Their temple was across the road at the Capitol Cinema which showed the first rock and roll movies and where the manager and his usherettes patrolled the dark with torches to separate the courting couples in the back seats and police with dogs were called to stop people dancing in the aisles. These armies were opposed by the fresh-faced, scrubbed and devout students of the University of Pretoria who left their Bibles and their Volkswagens, enlisted in the army of Calvin, and took on the Presleyites in fierce running battles which shocked and exhilarated the city and continued, as I remember it, for nights on end, under the stony gaze of Uncle Paul on his plinth in Church Square.

It is interesting to see that the statue of Kruger was a gift of the millionaire Sammy Marks, given in 1899, the year before the old man was forced to flee abroad. Pretoria was abandoned to the British and the South African Republic collapsed into bitterness and despair. Intriguing to find another instance of Kruger's friendship with very rich English-speaking businessmen; one might have imagined he stood for everything these entrepreneurs most despised. Of course it is true that Cecil Rhodes hated Kruger but then Rhodes was, in a sense, a competitor. Kruger stood between Rhodes and the goldfields of the Witwatersrand and he loomed between Rhodes and the ideal of a unified British empire stretching as far as the Zambezi. Doubly curious, and even more bitingly ironic, has been the comparative rise and fall in the reputations of the two men. Rhodes, the prodigious entrepreneur, the colossal imperialist, has declined in

Southern Africa to nothing more than a memory and a grave in the distant Matopos of Zimbabwe; while his enemy, the vulgar, stubborn backwoodsman who left on a train for exile just ahead of the British troops preparing to march into Pretoria, has proved to be something of a winner.

This connection of Kruger and the businessmen clarifies something which has puzzled me for years. I have never properly understood the obsequious behaviour of English businessmen towards the Nationalist Government. Now I begin to see that the custom of bearing tribute to the Boer conqueror is of long standing and this no doubt explains the strength of the tradition, even today. And yet I doubt very much that the Afrikaner has ever expected anything material from the businessman; I cannot believe that Kruger would have treated either Marks or Barnato any differently had they not given him statues or lions. I am sure he distrusted businessmen even when they bore gifts. All that was, and is, required is obedience. The obedience of the English businessman is a wonder to behold. It is noteworthy and widely understood in the English-speaking business community that should the minister, whichever minister of whichever relevant department, instruct businessmen to jump, every individual thus addressed will leave the ground upon command and remain suspended in a characteristic feat of levitation for as long as it is the pleasure of the minister to require him to do so. What others might, perhaps unkindly, call a fawning complicity English businessmen tend to describe as 'realism', or 'behind the scenes negotiations'.

It is wonderful to have these mysteries resolved but sometimes the revelations one encounters on a stroll through White South Africa are almost too painful to be borne.

Those who live on the edge of things, the little groups too

small to make any difference, the Indians of Balfour, the Irish Catholics of Pretoria, those who exist in the loopholes, the interstices of an increasingly rigid, contracting society learn to keep moving. Movement gives the illusion of progress and, besides, if you keep dodging about, you present less of a target. It makes you nimble, edgy, alert to the slightest threat; your dream is always to be elsewhere. Through the 'fifties, as the University grew taller, closer, it pressed in on the Catholic ghetto in much the same way as the new machinery of apartheid was squeezing the life out of the old, loose and untidy racial mixtures, and we grew more wary and more nervous. But the nature of the pressure was very complex and this made our opposition more difficult because we kept picking up unspoken messages of reassurance on the sensors we wore mounted just beneath our very thin White skins. These subcutaneous messages were meant to console us, to tell us that the quarrel in the end was not with us because we were, when all was said and done, on the same side as the political masters of the country; even if we were not quite, well, blood brothers, we were certainly cousins above the skin.

Such secret epidermal consolations, not so much racial overtones as undertones, did not reassure us particularly, though their truth was undeniable. You knew it every time you sat on a Whites-only bench in a park, or got on a bus reserved for Europeans, or saw the servants of parishioners filing obediently into the last three pews in the church, designated by means of a neat little brass plaque screwed into the dark wood, and marked 'Reserved'.

And the map of the country, similarly, has spaces on it reserved for such people, millions of them, out in the bush and the Government lost no opportunity to remind us that we were so few and so lonely. What would happen if they massed for an attack? The message was frequent and effective. Though we resisted the call from skin to skin, we heard the call of fear. We did not detest the scornful glances of the Calvinists around us any less, but we feared the others more. Carefully engineered alarm accompanied political changes further north. In 1957 Ghana became independent – and it also became, quite literally overnight, a term of political abuse. 'Go and live in Ghana!' Nationalist politicians delighted in yelling at their liberal critics. And the Prime Minister, Mr Strydom, the Lion of Waterberg, went about roaring and seeking whom he might devour. The situation seemed increasingly hopeless.

Mind you, it was rumoured that the Prime Minister's health was poor. I remember telling my mother, in a spirit of considerable anticipation, that it seemed the brightest news in years.

'Don't talk like that,' she warned.

'But why not?'

'Better the devil you know,' came the terse rejoinder.

She was right. In 1958 when Strydom went, his place was taken by Dr Verwoerd. I remember looking at myself in the mirror and my mother's words sang in my ears. 'Now look what you've done!' I said to myself. After all this time my old neighbour had caught up with me; we were, in a sense, living on the same block again. Maybe, I thought, this is how my grandfather must have felt when somebody came along to the perfectly well-named village of McHattiesburg and renamed it after the sort of politician he had left Ireland to escape. In short, perhaps there was no escape.

But we had to try. Each had his own method: there were, in our tight little Catholic world, some who took to drink or crime or homeopathy; there were Brothers who ran off with other boys' mothers; there were boys who devoted themselves to the service of rock and roll, or stole car tyres, or went to jail, or gatecrashed parties with their pregnant girl-friends on the backs of their motor bikes. We were all a little mad, all on the run. Quite what we were fleeing was never mentioned, but there was enough fear around to keep us edgy; there was mortal sin and the massing Black hordes and the Calvinist ascendancy. Fear was a home industry. It was about this time that I first heard the following story: 'He was walking home, this guy,' the story went, 'late one night, in the middle of town; it was dark and he took the short-cut down an alley between two very tall buildings, a long alley. This wasn't a wise thing to do but it was late and he was anxious to get home. After a while he heard footsteps in the alley behind him. Of course he didn't turn round, he didn't want to show that he was nervous, but he began to walk just a little faster, because up ahead he could see the lights of the main street and he knew that up there he'd be safe. The steps behind him speeded up. That's when he broke into a trot – I mean who wouldn't? But the steps behind him matched his own. Well – that was it, he put his head down and ran for it. Behind him he heard the other man running. What's more, he was gaining! Then, with his heart pounding and the blood singing in his ears, the guy breaks into the safety of the main street and the bright lights – when, very close to his ear, right beside him, a voice says, amused, scornful: "Why are you running, White boy?"'

I can hear that voice. It is anything but threatening. The question it put was a joke, a practical joke, and the voice knew it. There was nothing to be afraid of, but all the same it was a question no one stopped to answer. It was a question to which there was no answer. Who told me the story? Did I make it up myself? I do not know.

In 1958, when my old neighbour Hendrik Verwoerd took over the running of the country, our small Catholic community in Pretoria in what now looks like a brave riposte, or an act of blithe unconcern or even perhaps outrageous

folly, began to build across the road from my school a
boarding-house for boys from distant parts of the country.
This at a time when the University had completed its
encircling manoeuvre and was beginning to tighten the noose.
Or was it an act of ludicrous defiance, an expression of faith in
a future we certainly did not have? Or perhaps it was an
assertion of our right to a normal life; after all the school
possessed no boarding establishment and there was clearly a
need for one. Possibly, the school authorities were inspired by
the gigantic hostels for Afrikaans students rising all around us
and they fell to imitating the enemy on the basis that if they
could do it, then, why so could we! On the other hand it may
have been that the Catholic community, having survived in
this place for many years, felt that our chances of continuing
to do so had improved in the light of the incoming Prime
Minister's policies, swiftly promulgated and rigidly applied,
that from now on each group would be entitled (which is to
say confined) to its own territory, or independent homeland.
Thus we too deserved our own little Roman, Irish Bantustan.
The fatal flaw in this argument, if it was ever contemplated
by deranged clerics deep in their cups, was that *our* homeland
was right in the middle of theirs – and they were not planning
to move.

Whatever the reasons that gave it birth, the boarding-
house or hostel was built. It was a modest place with two
dormitories, a chapel, a kitchen, study hall and games room
and, when it opened, in 1959, I was among the inaugural
intake of boarders. As if to emphasise still further their
distance from reality, those in charge of the venture imported
as the new Rector a man straight from England. He arrived
and was studied with astonishment. Despite the language we
spoke I do not think any of us had ever seen a genuine
Englishman. After a few weeks of mutual amazement the
community of Irish Christian Brothers discovered something
which of course they had always known: that the Irish do not

understand the English, while the Englishman, for his part, found himself utterly unable to communicate with the fifty wild colonial boys in his care.

The Rector came from a school which he referred to with languid pride as the 'Awtree'. It was several weeks before we worked out that what he meant was the Oratory. However, the exact nature of that place remained a mystery to us since the Rector assumed that the bare mention of the name would be quite enough to indicate its status and good breeding forbade any fanfares for his previous school. He was wrong on both counts. We had never heard of the place, nor did we understand the code of reticence in which he hinted at the classiness of his origins, but we gathered from his tone that it was a pretty superior establishment and we understood further, from his bearing alone, that he was used to being associated with superior establishments.

He was a plump man, as pink as a tongue, and he parted his thin brown hair in the centre of his head and wore a very English cassock, bulky and black, which emphasised his generous belly. His weak little eyes behind very thick glasses were continually screwed up against the cigarette smoke curling from the fags he chain-smoked, holding them in one limp hand which he bore before his belly, as if the cigarette drooping ash between the plump pink fingers was some emblem that preceded the important procession of himself. His public progress through the streets of Pretoria, when he insisted on wearing a small biretta squarely on his centre parting, in a town where even the most hard-boiled Christian Brothers chose to wear black clerical suits so as not to scandalise the neighbours, drew astonished glances from passers-by and jeers from the Afrikaans urchins who registered on their exceptionally sensitive, inbuilt spiritual Geiger counters that here was not merely one of those Catholic priests, but an Englishman to boot.

Communications between the Rector and his boys did not

simply fail, they never began. He grew paler and more remote
as he confronted the horrible discovery that he had fallen
among savages for whom not merely the Oratory, but the rest
of the world did not exist, neither Paris nor Italy, not pictures,
music, conversation or culture. Our gods were rugby
football, perhaps, and Elvis Presley certainly, girls in plenty,
rock and roll, and politics. Naturally we had nothing to say to
one another. The Rector began to speak ever more frequently
of 'the Awtree' as if by mentioning the sacred name he might
lift the spell that his hellish predicament was casting over him,
but it did no good, and so he began to withdraw steadily from
the daily affairs of the boarding-house. But before drifting
entirely into a world of his own he made a final attempt to
come to grips with the disastrous situation by appointing a
kind of second-in-command from among the boys, an
attractive young hoodlum feared for his fists and his temper
and deeply admired for his contempt of all conventional
morality. The Rector appointed him not for these reasons at
all but because by some strange, arcane reasoning he believed
the fellow to be an outstanding Christian gentleman. I
remember he made a famous speech to this effect before
handing us over to his tender mercies. We knew, on the
contrary, that the boy in question was barely Christian, had
never been a gentleman and devoted his time to drinking,
whoring, rock and roll and fast, possibly stolen, cars. Yet in a
curious way we welcomed the appointment, tired of the
anarchy that prevailed in the first months of the Rector's
ineffective regime. I suppose you might say that the Rector,
from then on, played Hindenburg to the Head Boy's Hitler.
He really was not present any longer but became a distant,
smoky, reproachful presence glimpsed at the end of corridors,
a plump, pink, grieving ghost.

But God is merciful. Some months later the Rector took
himself off on a recuperative holiday to Italy from where
news reached us one day that he had died, suddenly, of a heart

attack. It seemed to the hostel boys a blessed release, and I think we felt genuinely glad his luck had changed at last. Certainly I remember that we all appreciated the half-holiday which his unexpected death brought us.

The Rector had always been a Royalist of the most sentimental kind and, in a way, he was indeed lucky that he did not live to see, as we were obliged to do, the unrestrained celebrations which accompanied what is perhaps regarded as Dr Verwoerd's most considerable accomplishment: the Referendum of 1960, in which the White electorate voted to become a republic and broke for ever the hated links with Britain and ensured that Verwoerd entered the pantheon of Afrikaner heroes. The vote had been very close, 52.3 per cent in favour and 47.7 per cent against. But, like the election results of 1948, it was enough. Huge Afrikaner crowds celebrating beneath the blind stare of Uncle Paul in Church Square cheered the achievement of a dream long deferred. The Boers at last had regained their Republic. A new President was appointed and once again the country had at its head a man wearing the Kruger regalia of top hat and sash of office. When, during the Boer War, Rudyard Kipling had suggested to a friend that the Boer preferred to rule by the bullet and not by the vote, he could not have foreseen that there might be an even more unpleasant possibility, and that the day would come when the Afrikaner would find a formula which would enable him to use both.

The feeling among English-speakers was one of alarm and despondency; I don't think we felt particularly bad about the loss of the British connection, we were, even then, too South African to care much for that, but the coming of the Republic and, a short while thereafter, the decision to withdraw from the British Commonwealth altogether, cruelly exposed what had been one of my favourite illusions: the belief that we were part of the world. It is often forgotten, when people talk of isolating South Africa from the international community, that those who wish to do so are pushing at an open door. South African isolation began with that decision to become a republic and then to leave the Commonwealth. It was freely chosen, it was the preferred course of the majority of the White population who cheered it mightily. I walked among the banks of flowers piled at the feet of Paul Kruger in Church Square the morning following the referendum and I remember reading one of the grateful inscriptions left by an admirer: 'Thank you, Uncle Paul, for the lessons you have taught us from the past...'

A few weeks later Dr Verwoerd, still with the laurels of the new Republic fresh upon him, attended the Union Exposition at the Show Grounds in Johannesburg where he was due to deliver a major speech. He was seated in the main arena, the inner sanctum, the closest thing we had to a royal enclosure where the cattle were paraded for prizes and the best bulls were judged, lining up obediently with rings through their noses, each with its Black guardian standing silently behind it, a place of rosettes, ribbons and exotic hats and much vying for places in the members' enclosure. It was here that a trout farmer named David Pratt walked up to the Prime Minister and fired two bullets into his head. A third shot missed. Pratt was a Cambridge-educated South African, deeply depressed and politically frustrated. Despite the closeness of the range and two hits, Verwoerd survived the attack and, in consequence, was seen in devout Afrikaner circles as the recipient of divine protection, a sign that God not only welcomed the new Republic but had been on hand to save the life of its architect. Pratt was arrested and found to be mentally deranged and about a year later hanged himself in his cell. His desperate act in the members' enclosure has always seemed to me to represent the very last attempt by an English liberal to affect the course of South African political history, and if this resort to violence was widely deplored among the English-speaking community there was, in some quarters, the feeling that since he had gone to such lengths it was a tragedy that he had proved himself to be such a bad marksman. I suppose it is entirely appropriate that the English-speaking community of South Africa should list among their number a failed assassin with the name of Pratt. Such is the lamentable record of White opposition one might argue that Pratt is really our patron saint. The deep ambivalence felt by many people was wonderfully well expressed in a limerick that did the rounds at the time:

There was a young man named Pratt,
Who took a pot shot at a Nat;
He said, 'Had I known
There'd be so much bone,
I'd have bought me a bigger gat.'

The only slightly cheering incident in the whole dismal business was the news that one of Verwoerd's bodyguards had fainted during the shooting, though I seem to recall that the gentleman in question denied this hotly, on regaining consciousness, and claimed to have dropped to the floor in order to investigate his chief's condition.

After all this time away, I have forgotten the pleasant sandy sprawl of the Pretoria pavements of my old stamping grounds in the deceptively named suburbs of Brooklyn, Hatfield, Arcadia and Sunnyside; in summer they are thickly shaded by the jacarandas planted closely together along the length of every street and the profusion of purple blossoms in spring gives Pretoria a brief and uncharacteristic blazing flamboyance, a welcome counterpoint to the Black and White politics of its civil servants.

The place is tranquil and curiously unchanged; everything

seems just about as I left it over a quarter of a century ago; the Catholic ghetto is still here, at least in outward appearance, but it has succumbed to the sting of the scorpion, it is a husk of its former self, perfectly preserved but quite dead. The jacarandas are bare, as if in mourning. All is now incorporated into the gigantic campus of the University of Pretoria. Our buildings are here, only the names have been changed to protect the innocent, or the guilty. On the playground of my old school stands a skyscraper which purports to be part of the Agricultural Faculty of the University. Next to it, but no longer separated by the protective hedge, stands the convent, now a crumbling annexe of the Agricultural School, the cement is dropping out of the red bricks as if the glue that kept this old place together simply has not the heart to hold any longer. Apart from the skyscraper on the playground everything looks much as it was; even the bicycle sheds and the outside toilets and washrooms remain.

The school is built in colonial style, with great, red-stoned verandas, creamy pillars, a roof of red tiles, cool and airy corridors. It has the look of some forgotten fever hospital and it is now used as a suite of offices for the high-rise tower alongside. The door to the Headmaster's study is closed, the old steel grille has been dropped across the mouth of the tuck shop. In front of it is the steel rail, rather like the sort of thing used for tethering horses, against which we pushed and struggled, during the short recreation breaks of the school day, to buy buns and Cokes. Since these are the University holidays the building is quite deserted and no one notices that I go and stand in front of the Headmaster's door. He was a tall, horsey, handsome man with baleful yellow teeth, an arrogant gleam in his eye and rather full, always slightly wet, lips. To be sent to the Headmaster's study was to experience moments of exquisite terror; you passed through his door quite literally never expecting to emerge again. We boys, in the opinion of the Irish Christian Brothers who raised us, were like gongs, made to be beaten often and loudly and so they hit us with their bare hands, with sticks, with straps, with canes, with blackboard rulers, with books and board-pointers. But none beat us so meticulously or with such energy and unflagging enthusiasm as the Headmaster. He beat us without concern for status, rank or nationality; he was a cross between Mussolini and an avenging angel. His chosen instrument was a long, heavy leather strap, weighted with lead, polished by frequent contact with the backsides of generations of boys. He kept a collection of these straps and would sweep open the cupboard in his study with the air of a connoisseur about to display his collection of rare books or horse brasses and select from its rack the instrument he felt most suited to the offender, who would touch his toes in the middle of the study and be advised on no account to look back, a warning which we frequently found ourselves, rather like Lot's wife, unable to obey.

'It'll only make it worse for you,' he warned. And it did.

And he would gather himself in his black skirts at the far end of the study, lift the strap well above his shoulder and come rushing upon you like a mighty wind; you would actually smell his mixture of tobacco and aftershave as he brought the strap down with every fibre of his strength. He did not look on it as an unpleasant duty but rather as a special calling to which he was devoted. I think it was the first time any of us actually came across a real enthusiast and the percussive impact of the blows echoed down the broad, red stone corridors and boys in classrooms far distant trembled at the sound, fell silent and began to count the strokes which ranged from three, for very minor offences, to as many as twelve or, even as I remember in one celebrated case, to eighteen. College was a rough, tough, roaring place, run like a Wild West camp. Certainly the Irish Brothers regarded us as being little above the beasts of Africa and having been the first to plant the papal standard in this pagan veld, they were now called upon to civilise and save us from perdition.

Waiting now outside the Headmaster's door, as I last did I suppose thirty years ago, I recall it was precisely the waiting that was the worst punishment, worse than the beating, the pain and the humiliation that followed, because you waited on his summons, perhaps for five minutes, perhaps for an hour or more, quite possibly all day. You were in effect detained at the Headmaster's pleasure, in the way Royalty once had with lunatics and lepers. He was like God and you knew not the day nor the hour when the call would come. The Headmaster had taken the eccentric decision to master Afrikaans, which he spoke with quite alarming fluency in a thick Irish accent. He enjoyed military uniforms and led the corps of school cadets, sometimes inviting permanent force officers from the military base at Voortrekker Hoogte to attend parades at which he gave lengthy addresses while the Afrikaans-speaking officers listened in horror as their language passed through the furnace of his fiery Irish brogue. Perhaps this was intended to ingratiate us with the Army, but I fear it probably had the opposite effect; the last thing they wanted was that Roman Catholics should start colonising their sacred language – their *taal*.

Although today I wait a good fifteen minutes outside the Headmaster's door, of course no call comes. The place is silent, given over now in term-time to the study of the eradication of pests, to studies of drainage and irrigation. Whatever ghosts haunt these corridors I do not think they are likely to frighten the young Afrikaans students with their unshakable belief in God, P.W. Botha and racial purity.

Opposite the school buildings is the hostel where I used to board. It now bears a sign above the door which reads, in Afrikaans, 'Uncle Gert's Place – Cafeteria and Barbecue Restaurant'. Pizzas in the chapel, and a strong smell of sausage in what used to be our dormitories. What would our pink English Rector from the Oratory have made of this? In the

yard next door stand two armoured cars. Are they kept in case
the revolution breaks out in these quiet streets? Or perhaps
this is part of a new policy of opening a military base on every
block. Or simply because you never know when the Roman
Catholics might try to return?

And now here is the old Catholic Scout Hall, which is
pretending to be, according to the name above the door, the
J.J. Theron Hall. What is J.J. Theron to this place or it to
him? And what do the people think when they look up and see
this ship of bricks called Theron? It even has portholes, though
I notice that the anchors which once hung from the ship's
bows are gone. Inside, the nautical illusion continues, with
cabins aft, and a quarterdeck which we were expected, upon
entering the hall, to salute. I doubt that visitors continue to do
so. Behind the Sea Scout Hall is the School Hall, now called
for some reason 'The Mask'. Perhaps that is rather
appropriate because all the buildings are wearing masks;
Uncle Gert's Place, the J.J. Theron Hall, the buildings of the
Agricultural Faculty; all of them are, quite simply, impostors.

Our School Hall was built for reasons which were both
religious and political, if one can distinguish between them.
The Nationalist Government, in the late 'fifties, decided to
come out into the open and expressed strong feelings of dismay and distrust regarding all forms of mission education for
which, traditionally, the churches have been responsible in
South Africa. Mission education meant education by liberal
Whites of aspiring Blacks and, in many cases, it was often the
only education open to Black people. An extraordinarily high
number of people who were later to become significant
political leaders in the Black population received their
education in mission schools and colleges. The Government,
being nothing if not efficient, decided that the most telling
way of preventing this form of political sedition was to cut off
all Government funds from such institutions, and to remove
their charitable status. This measure was reinforced by

making it apply not only to remote rural missionary schools in the veld but to all private religious educational establishments. Since the Roman Catholics resisted this characteristic blackmail it became necessary to raise the money to fund all its schools by private means. This hall was built on the proceeds of a thousand tombolas. A gigantic industry of charitable events and fêtes, cake and candy sales, jumble sales, whist drives and dances got underway to raise the necessary cash to preserve our missionary schools and to save us from the ravages of the new Government education policy. This was known as Christian National Education and, needless to say, since it took as its first premiss the obligation to divide people of different races, it was not particularly Christian, never national and a travesty of education.

The hall is a handsome building with a large stage and proscenium arch at one end, and a gallery at the other, space enough for the seven hundred boys who filed in there every Monday morning for weekly assembly, a ritual which resembled the Nuremberg rallies, with a succession of minor speakers exhorting the audience to greater religious fervour, better academic discipline and overall Christian conduct and then, when it was decided that we were in an advanced state of receptivity, the Headmaster would make his majestic entrance on to the stage and cover the business of the week, pausing suddenly, unexpectedly, to order Jones or Hope, who had thought they were invisible at the far end of the hall or at the back of the gallery, to meet him in his study after assembly; this X-ray vision struck terror into his hearers and further added to his Faustian reputation as a man in league with the forces of darkness.

Perhaps the most desolate sight of all is the old hockey field where we used to watch the girls play. It is still an open space but all that remains of the familiar landmarks are the pine trees marking its boundaries. It is a parking lot now. This is a land of perverted compliments. It should be understood that

124

among the most impressive things about White South African universities are their parking lots which display a mechanical wealth and a devotion to conspicuous consumption generally well in advance of academic reputation. At least the pine trees are still here, and the old hedge behind which we stood to watch Merle, Imelda and Monica thudding up and down the sandy hockey pitch. The needles of the old, scrawny pines are just beginning to turn brown and the ground beneath the trees is thick with cones; sticky to the touch, giving off the peppery fragrance of pine resin.

Across the way, beside the former rugby field (another parking lot), stands the parish church, the Monastery. It is perfectly preserved, though its adjoining garden of olives has gone. The priest's house is now a student union building and both church and house are strikingly at odds with the tower blocks striding triumphantly across the bare landscape. Those who came after us ripped out the trees and the wild and overgrown jungle of a garden which once grew here, a thicket of surprise, wonderful undergrowth designed to get lost in, as we were to discover, an Eden gone wrong. All gone, shaved of green to the bare bone. A napalm of the mind has hit this place.

The old Church Hall, famous for fêtes, badminton, Saturday night socials, illicit smoking parties and a good deal of heavy petting in its dark corners, built for amateur dramatics, survives unchanged in its slightly garish orange brick, a grey stone plaque inside the front doors listing the dead of the Parish in two wars. Utterly empty today, only the floorboards creaking gently. In 1952 I came to my first production here, a school performance of *The Desert Song*, and was dumbfounded, delighted and disbelieving when I was told that the tall blond man who played the famous Red Shadow and who looked at least forty was in fact a schoolboy and so, even more extraordinarily, was the pretty girl with whom he fell in love. The realisation that struck me that night has been with me ever since. As I watched the Red Shadow galloping across the desert sands which rumbled in a fascinating way, I knew instinctively, despite the tinkling piano in the pit and the shaky stage scenery, that his world was more real than mine. I had that early, primal recognition, certainly ineradicable, that South Africa was impossible to come to grips with, it did not respond to probings or questioning, it refused to define itself and it declined to allow me to locate myself in it. I do not think this is a particularly unique experience. I feel, and others like me feel, that if we exist at all it is as a kind of hypothesis, we have no real weight, we are a theory unsupported by the facts. Our presence here is a result of a series of improbable historical accidents and yet our existence is accorded superior status which we are obliged to defend whether we wish it or not, and is guaranteed by a determined but demented tribe of indigenous Dutch Africans who believe they have a direct mandate from the Lord.

The interior of the Monastery church is eerie; the original atmosphere of peace and seclusion has been retained, while the building has been cleansed of its more outrageously Catholic symbols: the greater-than-life-size Christ who swung in agony upon his cross, hanging high above the main altar, has gone, but all the stained-glass windows are still here, rather flashy and somewhat vulgar stained glass, showing a variety of saints, ranging from a saccharine St Theresa to a virile St John. The three altars remain, although the tabernacles have been removed; and the doors to the four little confessionals at the back of the church are open to reveal that they are used as storerooms. I saw once in Paris the 'miraculously' preserved body of St Vincent de Paul. This church reminds me of it, beautifully kept, though lifeless, a mummified and rather waxy corpse laid out in a glass casket. Yet so much of it is still just as it was, the dark pews, the Stations of the Cross, and even the brass plaque marked 'Reserved' screwed into the third last pew on the right at the back of the church, which was the form employed for designating the area set aside for Black worshippers. As I leave I put some money in the box set into the wall and marked 'Holy Souls'. Obviously this place still has some sort of religious connection because there is a lectern standing up at the central altar, but I suspect it is also probably used now as a venue for the Debating Society.

A little further up the road I note with interest that the Anglican church of St Wilfred's has somehow survived the storm; it still possesses a resident minister and services are advertised. But I guess its chances of survival cannot be good. Directly over the road an enormous, new, aggressively modern Dutch Reformed Church designed by someone who clearly had dreams of Corbusier dominates the street. The church adjoins the police station which I remember very well as a modest red-bricked building with two faint blue lamps outside it. Times have changed, and it is now what one must call, I suppose, a 'state of the art' police station. It has lookout posts, video cameras, bullet-proof glass, steel gates and no doubt a dozen unseen security devices to protect it against attack. When I look at it I understand what is to be the new South African architecture, not fortress architecture, or bunker style of which I have seen examples springing up across the country in banks, building societies, factories, but these new bastions I know now are best described as 'neo-police station style'; it is undoubtedly going to be the dominant architectural mode of the 1980s.

Here they stand then, side by side, fortress police station and church, brother and sister born from the same brick. Once again this curious contradiction between the need for security and the display of faith, because the church is without doubt a handsome and confident building with its curves and flourishes and its unicorn's horn of a spire; while beside it stands its Siamese twin, the police station, locked away behind sophisticated defences. Nearby stands yet another small army post; perhaps they do, after all, intend putting a military base on every block.

Next door to the army post is the large municipal swimming pool where I spent almost every weekday afternoon. The water temperature today is a low sixty-nine degrees and the place is virtually empty. Everybody learnt to swim at this pool and the chief instructor, as I recall him, was a great leathery walrus of a man burnt black by the sun who was never known to enter the water but taught generations to stay afloat. He was much later suspected of an excessive fondness for little girls and left town under a cloud. But then a number of people who used the pool had unfortunate careers. Perhaps it was something in the water? Besides, that is, the enormously strong doses of chlorine designed to prevent all afflictions from athlete's foot to VD. Entering the pool, particularly at the beginning of the season, was a hazardous exercise for one's eyes turned quite pink for some hours after leaving the water. A boy I remember, a remarkably strong swimmer and a fine diver, caused a terrific scandal by taking a girl to a local pleasure resort one night out near the Voortrekker monument and there, in the woods, was terrorised by a mysterious creature carrying a huge carved knife beaten from railroad steel, known as the 'Panga Man'. The Panga Man's capacity for sexual assault was unbridled and enthusiastic and he must have been very fit for he was said to be able to cover the several miles between attacks, which sometimes amounted to two or three in a night. Or, as was more likely, there were a number of Panga Men. They haunted the outer edges of our community. You might say that we occupied a position midway between Dr Verwoerd up in the Union Buildings on our right and the Panga Man in the dark woods, on our left. We told ourselves, in fact, that we occupied the middle ground, that we believed in parliamentary democracy and the power of peaceful protest.

128

As future events were to show, the first of these entities did not exist and the other had little effect.

As we enter the second-last week before the election a new tactic has become evident or perhaps I should say that an old tactic has been revived. In previous elections it has been customary, if not obligatory, for the Government to boost its vote by attacking foreign countries for interfering in our domestic affairs and the last few days have seen predictable fusillades against Britain and the US for failing to condemn what is called the communist onslaught against us, launched by Moscow's surrogate in Southern Africa, the African National Congress. But a new wrinkle has been added to this traditional sport; diplomatic representatives of most of our major trading partners have been summoned to the Foreign Ministry on what appears to be almost a daily basis and there ticked off like errant pupils up before the headmaster and sent away with instructions to tell their governments to mend their ways. Of course this sort of thing is always popular among South Africans of all political complexions but it was widely believed that this campaign was going to be altogether more sophisticated, that the National Party had really got beyond the old scaremongering and 'Black Danger' tactics of previous years. In fact nothing of the sort has occurred and we are now seeing the opposition parties joining the Government in attacking foreign meddling. I think I detect an element of panic in this, a feeling that things are beginning to go wrong, for after all this was supposed to be the election which would see the Government badly shaken, perhaps even seriously wounded. And now here is that self-same Government trotting out all its old familiar Shibboleths: the Black Danger, perfidious Albion, bullying Uncle Sam, and Reds under the beds. It is *beginning* to seem that the official opposition parties have decided after all that there is still capital to be gained from this sort of thing and they do not see why the Government should have it all its own way. The electorate is now in the depressing position of having to judge which of the two sides can be most beastly about the outside world.

Why is it that well-meaning people here are so depressingly pompous and predictable when they attack the regime? In the face of a Government order forbidding prayers for detainees Black and White churchmen get up in their pulpits and trumpet their promise to pray for whom they like and invite the Government to arrest them if it wishes. The temporal power has finally gone too far, they declare in ringing tones, it has taken to itself supernatural powers, and is now playing God. I really cannot think why anybody is supposed to be astounded or shocked by this. It has been common knowledge, since the present incumbents came to power, that Nationalist politicians believe in the absolute coincidence between tribal imperatives and the wishes of the divine spirit. In short, they have been playing God since they were elected. That is why they were elected in the first place. To accuse them of presumption is not a scandal – it is a compliment.

The source of White opposition towards the policies of the Nationalist Party is worth identifying; from the early 'fifties through to the mid 'seventies such opposition has come from groups within the English-speaking minority: churchmen, students, writers, politicians, editors, trades unionists. It is singular that no opposition groups to the left of the present Government have ever emerged among Afrikaners, though there are instances of individual opposition. But by and large the institutions of Afrikanerdom are there faithfully to represent the White tribe. Opposition has been a long, hard and thankless business but it has had some effects. However contemptuously the White Nationalist may ignore criticism he is not immune to it and the reason for this is probably because he does not feel it enough merely to be powerful, he wishes to be right as well and his reaction when under attack has generally been sullen resentment, followed by furious counter-attack. His critics are branded communists, subversives, traitors and, because the National Party has been exclusively identified with the State, attacks upon it are depicted as a betrayal of the country. Included among those branded as enemies of the country are English-language newspapers, the English universities, the churches, writers, lawyers, dissidents from every walk of life, housewives, businessmen, poets – all have felt the considerable force of Government displeasure: arrests, threats, bans, deportations, beatings, censorship and all the dreary, predictable yet effective measures so dear to Nationalist hearts.

It should also be said that the English-speaking dissenters have always been open to the charge of hypocrisy since they attack policies while continuing to benefit from the privileged status those policies confer; and also that they enjoy the luxury of attacking their political enemies without ever dirtying their hands in the business of government. And it is true that the posturing of some English liberals determined always to be pure, even if they cannot be powerful, is not an edifying sight. An instance of this is to be found in the reaction to the Government decision to ban prayers for detainees. The immediate outpouring of moral outrage is part of what I will call the Jericho Principle which holds that if only you make enough noise the walls of the apartheid citadel will come tumbling down. In the past decade, as the principal source of opposition began to pass from White to Black radicals, students, trades unions and political groupings, in the years following the Soweto riots of

1976, there is increasing evidence that the Jericho Principle is also alive and well and making much hot air among Black spokesmen.

Even so, the dissenting tradition among a small minority of English liberals is a long and honourable one and it should be understood that no comparable attack has ever come from Afrikaans churches, newspapers or academies and that, despite a good deal of loose talk about a growing mood of dissent among the Afrikaner intelligentsia, there is little sign of it to be found. Certainly there have always been exceptions to this dismal rule; and there are Afrikaans churchmen, writers and journalists who have turned their back on the tribe and gone into opposition, at considerable sacrifice, but their number remains tiny.

And of course on the other side there have been English-speakers who have thrown in their lot with the ruling Party. I recall a celebrated pair of politicians who defected to the Nationalists during the reign of Hendrik Verwoerd. These gentlemen rejoiced in the names of Trollope and Waring, which made them sound like a firm of estate agents. They were given uncontentious portfolios in the Government and upon these elevated positions they withstood the jeers and catcalls from the English community. When time in its fullness brought the departure of Trollope from the Government benches, a rather good joke went around the country (and there are very few good political jokes in this country). Rumour had it that Trollope's replacement was almost certain to be another English-speaker, a man named Horwood, at the time Principal of the University of Natal, who had long been a closet Nationalist and who then came out of the closet and declared himself to be what everybody had long known him to be, a devoted member of the National Party.

'Who would replace a Trollope?' the question went.

'Only a Horwood,' came the reply.

What purports to be reality is no more than a confabulation of joyless tricksters. As with all mountebanks, the travelling road show is essential to the business of hoodwinking the public. It is not surprising then that for half the year Pretoria is not actually here at all; Pretoria is to be found a thousand miles to the south, in Cape Town, where it has moved, lock, stock and barrel, with its miracle cures and its elixirs. In Cape Town three brand-new stages have been erected, each colour-coded for easier reference and it is upon these stages that the Government is attempting to perform its greatest illusion: the men who invented apartheid are promising to make it disappear before our very eyes.

On Easter Monday, groups in Pretoria celebrated Hitler's birthday with beer, sausages and right-wing literature. The German Embassy was invited to send a representative but declined. Hitler's birthday has always been celebrated in this country with rowdy parties on distant farms and in certain beer kellers in Johannesburg; it is on such sinister anniversaries that our remaining overseas connections are to be traced. In fact the whole business of international links is today a very shady and mysterious business. Our rare dealings in foreign affairs range from the unmentionable to the illicit. As more and more international companies withdraw from South Africa this trend can only continue and of course there are many here who welcome it with a spirit of fierce delight; they actually relish the coming of the siege and are already preparing to draw in the wagons. But, as people become more isolated, an air of furtiveness seems to hang over even the most innocent occupations, if indeed there are any innocent occupations left. People are undoubtedly very aware of their exposed position, they are jumpy, increasingly fearful of speaking aloud in public. There is only one real political question, and everyone knows it: what is to be done to accommodate the great Black majority who have no vote? Black political power is said to exist in the six legislative assemblies of the six non-independent states which are dotted about South Africa; to these are added the four 'independent' states, fruits of Dr Verwoerd's grand design for autonomous 'Bantustans', tribal reservations declared new countries, which carry the stamp of their manufacturer: 'Made in Pretoria'. Four decades of unchallenged power have reduced the country from a strong, rich and adventurous place in the early 'fifties (unwilling to face up to the Black majority in its midst, but not yet unable to do so) to a depressing patchwork of mini-statelets, obscure tribal fiefdoms distinguished only by their casinos and their soil erosion, large White cities desperately frightened and even larger Black townships angry, explosive and wretched; forty years of Nationalist rule has given us a continual state of emergency; from the long morning of granite apartheid we have passed into the afternoon of armoured cars, where almost absolute powers are invested in the Executive, where only the police are happy, and where the opposition English-language press has been instructed to collaborate in its own lobotomy.

Not surprisingly, the academic record of the hostel in my time was disastrous. I think every single boy in my class failed the final school examinations; there was something almost noble in the consistency of it all. I speak of those boys who remained to sit the finals, because there had been many casualties in the final months. Boys absconded, fell by the wayside, simply disappeared. Our most memorable losses took place on the morning after the school dance, when it became clear that several colleagues had failed to return at all. For boys to get in well after the one o'clock deadline was not unknown, but for boarders to remain out all night after a dance was unheard of, since the conclusions drawn were so sexually explicit and left to the hostel authorities no room for manoeuvre; at least half a dozen recreants were summarily asked to leave when they showed up after breakfast, red-eyed and unrepentant. This meant they were unable to sit the final examination (though in the light of the results, this was probably no bad thing). The culprits carried their lack of remorse to admirable extremes. They locked one of the housemasters in his room, flushed the keys down the toilet and left on a fleet of large black motor bikes, to the ringing cheers of the remaining hostel boys. I remember being quite overcome with emotion when we saw them off. Here were fellows who had been academically, socially and morally ruined, and yet they set off like conquering heroes, revving their bikes, acknowledging our cheers which quite drowned the cries of the unfortunate housemaster locked in his room. We could not have done anything for him, even if we had wished it, and it was some hours before the locksmith could prise open the door.

He was accompanied in his efforts by the prayers of the two Austrian nuns, one little and dark, the other plump, rosy, blue-eyed with a tremulous manner and a soft white down on her cheeks and upper lip, who were responsible for the cooking in our hostel. They spoke no English and knew nothing whatever about cooking but they were very strong in faith; to such an extent that when a cricket ball shattered a kitchen window depositing shards of broken glass in the great dish of potatoes awaiting frying, the nuns contented themselves by removing the larger and more lethal fragments and going ahead with the meal, firm in the belief that God would protect his own and served up a dinner of glass and potato with wonderful cheerfulness. This saintly fortitude in the face of adversity extended to the sick room where the rosy young nun ministered to bleeding, boils, stab wounds, and the punctures sported by a thin Italian boy named Carlo who had the temerity to beat the head of school at darts and had been used as a human target for his impudence. She would purse her downy lips, blink her china-blue eyes and prescribe a laxative, prayer, the avoidance of cigarettes and bed rest; and in most cases this cure was surprisingly successful.

I got two things from my days in the hostel which, together, amounted to far more than any mere success in examinations. I learnt to read the poetry of Ovid and Virgil in the original Latin, which was itself a rare gift in those surroundings. To be presented with the *Aeneid* and *Metamorphoses*, almost by accident, in the back streets of Pretoria is a gift beyond price. Even more valuable, and ultimately more crucial for me, was the lesson learnt from our embattled position as the whelps of Rome, the step-children of the Scarlet Woman encircled by the hoplites of Calvin. This had the effect of concentrating the mind on the difference between groups, as well as on the hateful, stultifying, lethally boring business of having to belong to a group in the first place. And, of course, groups in South Africa are obligatory. So our little band within the ramparts of the holy stockade that was our Catholic parish was obliged to experience the cutting edge of differentiation and found ways of resisting it, not by escaping it, because we could not do that, but rather by emphasising it. Just as the souls of the dead, the squeaking shades swirl around Aeneas in the Underworld, so we haunted the fresh-faced young Afrikaners, on the other side of the hedge, with their short hair and short pants and their even shorter tempers. Against the armies of Paul Kruger there stood the guerrilla forces of Elvis Presley. Since they wore khaki shorts, then what self-respecting boy would appear in public (and thus out of school uniform) in anything other than stovepipe trousers so tightly cut down that the calves bulged beneath the charcoal-grey cloth? Did they walk about barefoot emphasising how close they were to the soil of Mother Africa? Then never let one of us ever touch the ground in anything but blue suede or cowboy boots or gleaming leather shoes tipped at the heels and toes for especially noisy walking, ambulatory syncopation. Was their hair shaved cruelly short, back and sides? Then let your hair grow until it swamped your collar, grease it, tease it, comb it, spray it with grey streaks, push it into quiffs and flounces and Bill Haley kiss-curls and dress it proudly on street corners, in shop windows, on buses, in churches, on any public platform calculated to infuriate the opposition. If, as seems likely, the underlying idea of the racial separation that is so character-istically South African is based on the belief that life is a zoo, then we were the flamingoes in the lions' enclosure – and we revelled in it.

If I had to find one word to describe what I gained from those years in the hostel, a life which in its brief, painful compression I might compare with the position of the orange in the squeezer (it makes a brief, beautiful show but the fruit is really no match for the machine), then that word would be 'colour'. Now anywhere else colour is no more than an impression of tonal values, but in South Africa it is the world... and that world which, it seemed to me, had been under assault by those who wished to bleed it of all colour, to bleach it down to their own pallid specifications, to render it monochrome, had now offered me proof that things need not be like that at all. And so it was that out of a sense of gratitude to my surroundings, to the boisterous, fervent, frantic life behind the lines, and in an attempt to preserve the colour that I found there, for my own satisfaction and the pleasure of my friends, I began writing down some of these impressions. I could not bear that they should be forgotten: our ample and sorrowing English Rector so far from the Oratory, pink phantom at the far end of his smoky corridor; that boy who delighted us all by illuminating the dorm after dark with an amazing pyrotechnical display achieved with the most basic materials, a box of matches and his own intestinal gases; the rugby captain who declared that his girlfriend so loved him that, at his request, she would appear for tea wearing nothing but a fur coat, and proved it to the six witnesses drawn by lot who reeled at the flourish of fur and flesh with which she delivered the goods; or the boy so poor he burnt and ate charred matchsticks moistened with a little tomato ketchup; or the extraordinary creature who ate whatever others left and, for his ability to move across the dining tables devouring all in his path, became known as 'The Hoover', (the only boy not to flinch at the famous supper of French fries and glass shards, and even went back for more . . .). And I wrote of such things, not in prose, as one might suspect, but in that most dangerous medium of all, verse – pages of rhyming couplets. Dangerous because, to say the least, I was not living in a community of readers. In fact it would be true to say that many of my friends had trouble remembering not to move their lips when they read and a good number still pointed to each syllable as the brain ached with the strain of fitting sign to sound to meaning. I did so because verse was the medium which seemed to catch the immediacy of the experience most accurately and because, in my pages of rhyming couplets, I had something I could read aloud and so gauge for myself whether my listeners had caught some glimpse of themselves. And that was why I did it. It was not in the least a literary activity, it did not spring from my reading; the idea to write down such things was not taken from books which I consumed shelf by shelf. My sole ambition was to arrest the flow of time in image and rhyme, to re-create a scene instantly recognisable to my listeners or readers, and which seemed to me to flow directly out of the frantic hilarity of our lives, something too good to lose, too funny to forget. In turn, I was regarded by my public as an entertaining freak, someone with a gift of about the same order as the boy blessed with powers of unorthodox ignition who achieved such incandescent results with such modest means after lights-out in the dormitory.

Looking back, I realise that this was no bad training for a writer. Speculating on the origins of the novel, E.M. Forster imagines that it perhaps began when people first gathered in caves and someone told a story – if the tribe liked it, they asked for another the next night – if they didn't like it, they killed the story-teller. I took requests for more material as a good sign, coming as they did from boys in whom the word 'poetry' or even 'books' brought out the cave man. I was certainly very grateful to those of my friends who found a portrait of an old teacher, or an account of a flogging accurate enough to raise a smile. There is no more discerning critic than one who knows your material better than you do, no harsher judge of the missed accent, the needless modulation, the imperfect rhyme, the parading of sentiment in place of real emotion, of the spuriously poetical, the pretentious, and the silly. It was, in every sense, a useful school for a writer.

When news came through that like all my classmates, I had also failed my matriculation examination, there was considerable relief back at the hostel where the boys had perhaps suspected, because of my literary leanings, that I might have hesitated at the last hurdle and actually tried for a pass. A few weeks after the news broke I received a hand-made certificate which, in mock formal terms, embellished with cigarette stars and a seal made of the old school tie, congratulates me in painstaking posh script, which must have taken some hours of work (even the spelling is perfect), on having failed my finals and thus 'kept up the reputation of the hostel'.

But I knew that if I was ever to go to university then I would have to re-take the examination, which I did, a year later after a lethally dull stint in what is called a 'cram college' where the excitements of the hostel were sorely missed and the only ray of light was to be introduced to Shakespeare by a real devotee. He was the principal of the college, an extraordinary figure with a round gleaming face, a wardrobe of exceptionally beautiful Italian suits, a withered arm which he kept tucked inside his exquisite shirt front rather like Napoleon, and a taste for dizzyingly showy jewelry. He wore rings of rubies, garnets and diamonds on each of his fingers; I think he even wore one on his thumb. We caught frequent glimpses of this good arm, and the hand so loaded with treasure as if to comfort it for the loss of its mate, because his method of teaching was to walk up and down the classroom carrying a table-tennis bat which he used to drive home the beauties of Shakespearian verse into the heads of his students:

'Is this a dagger which I see before me,

The handle towards my hand?'

The table-tennis bat rebounded on the skull; not only the words themselves would be battered into the memory but this was his way of marking the iambic rhythm of the lines as well, which he spoke with a tenderness strikingly at odds with the bat... Years later I read in a newspaper that this man had been discovered to be a fraud and phoney. His degrees were a sham, his credentials faked and he was revealed as no more than a con man with a taste for good suits. But as far as I am concerned it does not matter a whit; they could expose his withered arm as a mere ploy to gain sympathy, for all I care. Sensitive Shakespearians are rare and those who can convey something of his power and excitement to a class of boys, many of whom had difficulty understanding Little Lulu comic books, deserve acclamation and a life pension.

Although passing my final examinations had nothing of the glamour of the earlier mass failure, it enabled me to go to University. But before I could do so, there loomed before me, as before every able-bodied White boy, the spectre of military training. In those days we did four years in all, twelve months at a stretch, followed by three years part-time. The uniformed boys I see around me in the streets of Pretoria today seem to be in it for what amounts to a life sentence. At any rate I went to the Navy. The choice was influenced by two factors: the Navy was in Cape Town and Cape Town was just about as far as you could be from Pretoria; and then, also, I had spent several years contemplating a great brick ship sailing through the veld directly in front of my hostel. In consequence, the start of 1962 saw me in Cape Town for the first time, dreaming of long cruises to exotic destinations.

Reform was a word frequently heard in Pretoria when I lived in the hostel. In those days it carried most unfortunate connotations. Reformatory was the place to which boys were sent who were too young for prison and too bad to be kept in the confines of a normal school. Many of my contemporaries fitted that description and were sent away to be 'reformed': it was notable that most boys on returning to the neighbourhood after a spell in the reformatory seemed far worse than they had been before they were sent away.

In South Africa, the men who actually run the country are also 'sent away' for six months in every year. They go down to Cape Town where the legislative assembly sits and where the much vaunted modifications to the apartheid system are to be most clearly observed. Cape Town might thus be called the Reformatory of South African politics.

Cape Town is the mother city, the Fairest Cape, the Tavern of the Seas, founded in 1652 by a Dutchman named Jan van Riebeeck, who led a party of the first White men to settle on the beautiful green peninsula, under the brooding, magnificent Table Mountain. At one end of town is a castle which the early settlers built to replace their fort. The fort was the first thing they built, and is indicative of the state of their thinking about the indigenous inhabitants of the Cape. At the top of the town is the parliament building, an elegant neo-classical edifice set in a garden. The legislators who run this country make great play of their attachment to parliamentary institutions. But the fact of the matter is that their hearts really lie in the castle down the road.

Cape Town a quarter of a century ago was striking, not only in its natural beauty, but for the manner in which the inhabitants of the city, Whites and Coloureds (which is to say the mixed race descendants of earlier settlers), met and mingled. To a Transvaler reared in the Black and White stringencies of the Highveld, this dilution of the usual racial severities, the relaxed jumble of White and Coloured neighbourhoods, the integration one saw on the buses, the camaraderie of the streets, all came as a revelation. At that time, many residential areas of the city were, to all intents and purposes, integrated, and in the centre of Cape Town was the historic settlement of District Six, with its mosques and painted houses where Coloureds had lived for centuries.

After my initial training, I spent most of my military service at Simonstown, the former British naval base at the end of the Peninsula. Of my impressions of that time in the Navy, one in particular is worth recalling. It came in one of those rare moments of frankness which arrive so suddenly and unexpectedly that for a moment you are not sure whether you can trust your ears. It happened one afternoon on the deck of a frigate tied up in Simonstown Harbour when the training officer abruptly broke off a talk on the naval forces of opposing countries to tell us with chilling brevity that all this was an absolute waste of time: the lessons in seamanship, the extravagant knots, the nights at sea in a hammock, the anti-submarine training, the liberty boats and all the arcane naval lore so painfully gathered; the useful lessons that you never threw up into the wind and never saluted in railway stations; all was an elaborate game, a charade...

'I really don't know why we bother with any of this,' our candid instructor remarked, 'because it won't do you guys a blind bit of good. You see , this is a very small navy, with a handful of ships. When the balloon goes up you won't get within a hundred miles of the ocean. You guys will be sitting on some railway station behind a pile of sandbags, in the middle of the veld, cradling your rifles, with a bullet up the spout and sweaty palms – because *that's* where the war will be, one day...'

This was a shocking piece of information. In the first place it was somewhat disconcerting to be told that twelve months of full-time training amounted to not much more than an elaborate game. But what concentrated the shock was the fact that this was something we ourselves had always secretly suspected; military training, at best, seemed an onerous chore, a form of tax applied by the Government, an indication to all of us that although we detested everything for which the administration stood, we might one day be required to go to war for apartheid... though in our heart of hearts we felt such an eventuality seemed unlikely, even absurd. We also, secretly, scoffed at the naval forces to which we were attached. After all, the Russians had submarines which could lie hundreds of miles off the coast and destroy our cities; hell, the Russians even had fishing trawlers which easily outran our flagship, a prewar cruiser called, somewhat optimistically, the *Good Hope* which chased the poaching Russians in vain, heaving through the swell off Cape Point, her rivets popping in the elderly steel plates like some ancient maiden aunt in pursuit of a lithe young cat burglar. But what we told ourselves was one thing, it was quite another to be informed in clear, cold tones that our naval training was an irrelevance, not because we could not hope to match outside aggression, but because the war we would one day have to fight would take place in quite another theatre altogether, it would happen back where we came from, in our own backyards.

Up until then the official line had been that the country was threatened by hostile foreign forces, who tended to be rather vaguely portrayed as the 'communist threat', and, more specifically, by hostile Black African states to our north

143

which were then coming painfully to independence. Suddenly, and rather rudely, we had been given the facts of life, and very disturbing they were too, for now the private thinking of those who made policy had been nakedly exposed; the enemy was not somewhere 'out there' to be encountered or not, one day, upon our borders in some conventional war – the enemy was with us here and now, the enemy was within.

To receive this revelation in Cape Town was particularly sobering. In this city Whites and Coloureds were so closely allied that telling the crucial difference in matters of skin pigmentation required an eye as finely attuned to the minutest variations in skin colour as, say, certain Nazis were said to possess when it came to detecting a 'typical' Jewish nose. It was a finesse we Transvalers, used to cruder racial divisions, did not possess. It was necessary to warn sailors going on shore leave of the dangers. Liberty parties were offered two tests for racial purity by the Petty Officer:

'Look at her nails, at the little half moon. On us it's white; on them it's blue. And if in doubt, ask to meet her folks...'

This was all very well when it came to facing the sexual offensive aimed at polluting our breeding stock. But such tests would hardly work in wartime and, as the indiscreet training officer had revealed to us, as far as those in command were concerned, it was wartime all the time. Furthermore, if the enemy was within, then he must be identified and removed. In this the exigencies of military strategy and the mechanics of apartheid converge, and their convergence is displayed with particular cruelty in Cape Town for it is here, where the two principal race groups have been closest for hundreds of years, that their parting was so much more savage. However, when I was first in Cape Town in the early 'sixties, the removals had not been pushed through with the kind of inflexibility that distinguished them in the Transvaal and Natal, but people were working on it.

When, four years later, in 1966, I returned to Cape Town,

the Coloureds were being forced out. Their central settlement, District Six, under Table Mountain was under considerable pressure, and thousands had been moved on to the windswept, desolate flat lands some miles from the mountain and the city. I lived in one of the little suburbs which had been purged of their Coloured inhabitants, smartened up and rented out as fine examples of old Cape Dutch architecture. Although the Coloureds had gone from the houses, it had not been possible also to change their places of employment which remained in the city of Cape Town to which they took the same routes each day, travelling by bus and train from the Cape Flats and they came pattering past their old houses morning and evening, dozens of them, like crowds of reproachful souls visiting the world they had left behind them, or which had left them behind.

I was back in Cape Town in 1966, after completing an initial degree at the University of Witwatersrand, in Johannesburg, and worked for a time as an editor at the Afrikaans publishing house and there I discovered how deeply the issue of the Coloureds touched Afrikaans Cape families. By this I do not mean to suggest that their predicament touched them, but rather that it seemed born in White Afrikaners to treat their Coloured cousins with affection tinged with anxiety. One of the reasons for the anxiety emerged when I learnt that the Coloureds were sometimes referred to as 'brown Afrikaners'. And it is the case that the Cape Afrikaner shares with the Coloured not only a language, but in some cases, common antecedents as well. There are no feuds fiercer than those among family members who fall out. Thus the only issue among Afrikaners was what they should do with the 'problem' of the Coloureds. What they had already done to them simply was not seen as an issue at all. That a government of Afrikaners down the road in the Houses of Assembly in Cape Town was applying policies which would tear to pieces the only example of racial amity still existing in South Africa and could do so without a single remonstration or objection by Cape Afrikaners, a cultivated, civilized and thoughtful people, threw a curious light on the inner workings of racial policy, known as apartheid. It is at heart, and in the beginning, a family matter, a device for quarantining dubious relatives, a dwelling on variations in colour so subtle the innocent eye cannot detect them – only later does it turn to the brutal simplicity of telling Black from White.

Back in Cape Town, in 1987, and upon the lap of that extraordinary slab-like, chopping block of a mountain, there is nothing but an open space where District Six used to be. It has been torn up by the roots and scattered to the wind which blows here with great force from the south east; the Cape Doctor, it is called. The place looks like a bomb site, but it was not bombs that did this, nor the wind; this devastation is the result of policy. It is said that there were various plans for developing the prime site in the heart of the city once it had been cleansed; it was thought that business interests would be enthusiastic about developing such extremely valuable real-estate, but for some reason, business has not touched it, so it moulders away quietly, like some forgotten battlefield with just one or two buildings still standing after the devastation. Talk has it that perhaps it will become the campus of a new technical college, but in the meantime it is left to the wind and the ghosts.

I hope they will never build on it, that these empty acres will be left for ever, just as they are; in the way that certain churches in Europe are left as they were when the bombs hit them during the last war, to remind us of what we have done to ourselves. I know of no more poignant, more evocative or more damning a monument to the way in which we have conducted our affairs than this gaping hole on the mountain-side, where people once lived.

There was once another doctor in Cape Town during my

second stay there in the middle 'sixties. Dr Verwoerd was doing his six months' sentence in the parliament building in the garden under Table Mountain. Sometimes I think of him as a visionary, sometimes as a mole, travelling beneath the surface of our lives; sometimes like a sapper, laying explosives – for it is the percussive effect of his policies laid long ago which are still powerful enough to blow up communities like District Six and we must, I suppose, at least acknowledge credit for the long-term planning that went into the concept of Grand Apartheid. And there are today growing numbers who deplore the fact that Dr Verwoerd was cruelly cut short in his endeavours by an assassin who succeeded where David Pratt failed.

'The first white man sailed into Table Bay . . . and you might say that the trouble began,' murmurs the charming guide who offers tours of the South African Parliament, in a moment of astounding, but honest, indiscretion, as she stands staring at the glass case in which is displayed a silver model of van Riebeeck's ship, *The Dromedaris*.

If you stand on tip-toes in the public gallery of the 'White' Chamber of Parliament in Cape Town you can almost see the spot where Dr Verwoerd fell, mortally wounded, when the assassin struck. It used to be said that it was possible, even at a distance, to see exactly where it happened, because the light green carpet, hand-woven in Donegal, is a slightly darker shade of green in that spot. The reason for the difference, the legend reported, lay in the fact that the section of carpet stained with blood had been removed and a new piece sewn into place. You may believe this story if you like, but then you may believe anything in South Africa. However, I can testify that from the public gallery it is very difficult to read the message on the carpet. The pleasant light green shade seems perfectly uniform.

But I do remember the incident with clarity. Dr Verwoerd was stabbed to death shortly after two o'clock on 6 September, 1966, as he sat on the Government front bench awaiting the start of the afternoon business. The man responsible was a half-Greek parliamentary messenger called Dimitrio Tsafendas, who walked across the floor of the House with a hunting knife concealed in his pocket and stabbed the Prime Minister four times. The assassination is one of the very rare instances when South African politics approaches the status of classic tragedy. More usually it resembles a violent, tear-stained farce. But in the single bloody encounter on a September afternoon great drama was played out: on one side was the most powerful man in the country, a gentle fanatic filled with a sense of divine mission, and an unshakable, bewildering belief in the tribal exclusivity of the White Afrikaners, the apostle of apartheid who believed in the absolute separation of different groups; and on the other side a swarthy, fat, ugly misfit with wiry hair, his life one long continual humiliation, rejected by his parents and his friends at school, who mocked his dark complexion and nick-named him 'Blackie', a lonely, tormented drifter who lived in a dozen countries, spoke eight languages and believed himself to be guided by instructions spoken by a snake coiled in his belly.

Verwoerd had been much in the news at the time. Just a week earlier he had banned a rugby tour of Japan by a team of students drawn from the White universities of Cape Town and Stellenbosch and a great controversy raged over the decision. The English-language press attacked it, while the Government papers and the State radio service not only supported it, but welcomed it. As reports of the stabbing began to reach us, my Afrikaans colleagues in the publishing house where I was working reacted first with horrified disbelief and then, at the news that Verwoerd was dead on arrival at hospital, with an outpouring of grief. As the only one in the place without tribal or familial connection to the dead man I felt rather like an infidel in a convent which had just received news of the death of a beloved Pope. We had, it is true, been near neighbours once but that hardly seemed an appropriate thing to mention. I cannot honestly say that I felt anything except astonishment at the utterly bizarre nature of the event. If anything I was rather embarrassed by the anguish of my Afrikaans co-workers and even more by my inability to offer even perfunctory sympathy in the face of their sorrow and disbelief, their grief; being without the least share of their mystical reverence for a man who seemed to me to have been more than anyone the baleful genius of a system of constitutional White supremacy, a man who permitted nothing to stand in the way of the historical imperatives of his tribe. I must confess, however, to feeling a sort of loss, tempered with a certain grudging admiration. He and I had been together, in a way, for a long time. After all, here was a man who had pledged himself body and soul to the most grotesque distortion of human values and had stopped at nothing in order to achieve his ends. His vision, however one looked at it, possessed a chilly grandeur, and to have died in so Caesarian a manner was somehow fitting; it made his life and death seem all of a piece. But then everything about my former neighbour from Parkview was on a grand scale.

I cannot help feeling that there has been rather a falling-off since then and that, in retrospect, the assassination of 1966 can be seen as something which genuinely altered the course of political history. After Verwoerd, the moral certainty went out of apartheid, fanaticism was replaced by expediency, the vision was gone from the grand plan for territorial segregation and government became an increasingly opportunistic play of power. When Verwoerd fell at the foot of the Speaker's chair, the granite years were over and the greasy hours were at hand. Balthazar John Vorster, who had a face somewhere between that of a bloodhound and a Renaissance cardinal with dubious predilections, succeeded the Doctor. His period of office was to end in public scandal, the abuse of Government funds, and, finally, in disgrace. B. J. Vorster is remembered now, when he is remembered at all, only by the large police station named in his honour.

Such is the smallness of the stage on which these things are played out and the tightness of the circles in which White politics move that the day of Verwoerd's assassination is linked to the present panoply of Government power. For as the Prime Minister lay dying on the Donegal carpet a Government MP turned furiously on an opposition member, Mrs Helen Suzman, and shouted at her that this calamity was the result of the policies of people like her and her liberal friends. The angry MP was Mr P. W. Botha, now the President. This incident is very revealing in a number of ways: it shows a capacity, when under severe strain, to blame everybody but oneself and it suggests an even less agreeable talent for making political capital out of a dying man. It also shows that characteristic mixture of intemperance and ruthlessness which continues to this day. Above all the profound inaccuracy of the comment is perhaps most revealing of all. For the truth of the matter is completely the opposite: life, as ever in South Africa, goes in contraries. If one were to go in for the business of establishing whose ideas were truly responsible for bringing the demented messenger to his victim that day, then I would imagine that the answer is very close to home. For who else produced the climate of prejudice and humiliation, of racial rejection, from which 'Blackie' Tsafendas suffered so horribly and who expressed it in its most pure and merciless form, if it was not the Prime Minister who fell beneath the rain of blows from the hunting knife?

The view from the public gallery today shows an empty debating chamber with the green leather benches awaiting the return of successful members after the election. The

Government majority is so huge that Nationalist members cannot all fit on their side of the house and must therefore be allowed to crowd onto the opposition benches across the gangway while the opposition is squeezed into a corner and from this embattled position must deliver their attacks upon a government so large, unshakable, so elephantine in its great grey girth, its leathery opinions, its long memory and its heavy feet, that it is most unlikely that the beast in question has ever felt more than a passing pin-prick from the Lilliputian forces which oppose it.

Just outside the chamber, side by side in unhappy camaraderie, hang portraits of Cecil Rhodes and Dr Jameson, peering gloomily through the door. Well might they despair, and long may they hang. In fact it might have saved a great deal of trouble had they been hung a lot earlier. I suspect this positioning of the hated pair is an Afrikaner joke; the two imperialists sentenced to watch for ever the unbridled power of the party they once worked so hard to destroy. It was the armed invasion by Dr Jameson into the South African Republic of Paul Kruger in 1896, supported by Rhodes, and connived at by the British Government, which ended in complete catastrophe for the invaders and destroyed, possibly for ever, any possibility of long-term trust between Afrikaans and English-speaking South Africans.

Dr Jameson set off to defeat Kruger with a force numbering 511 Europeans, 150 'natives', some machine guns, 3 artillery pieces, 640 horses and 158 mules. How the Boers managed to contain their laughter as they rounded up this forlorn posse and clapped them in jail, we will never know.

The raid almost certainly made the war of 1899 inevitable and as the poet William Plomer has said, out of that foolish war 'an alp of unforgiveness grew'. The Irish philanderer, Frank Harris, resting briefly from his amours, so moistly remembered in *My Life and Loves*, visited South Africa shortly after the Jameson Raid, determined to get at the truth of the matter, quite convinced that there had been a British cover-up and that Rhodes was in it up to his ears. An interesting meeting is recorded between Harris and Rhodes on the slopes of Table Mountain during which the Irishman told Rhodes precisely how he felt about the misadventure. If God, said Harris, had once chosen the Jews for his special people, then it showed considerable wisdom, because the Jews were an intelligent and energetic people. But if, as Rhodes was always suggesting, God had now chosen the English as his favourites, then surely it showed that He was in his dotage? I believe that Dr Jameson was for his time, what Mr Pratt is for ours.

Down the corridor is the second chamber, reserved for members of the Coloured House of Representatives with its eighty-five members, elected under the new Tricameral Constitution. Though not facing re-election themselves they are awaiting the results of the all-White elections before returning to the House. Their chamber has red leather benches (in fact I recognise it as being the old Senate Chamber). The benches are in a state of complete disarray, scattered all over the place, some upside down, others lying on their sides. Perhaps there has been a vigorous session, members coming to blows? But no, not at all, the charmingly indiscreet guide explains – the 'Coloured' chamber is being redecorated. And where is the third chamber for the Indian MPs, the forty members known as the House of Delegates? That is somewhere over the road, she gestures vaguely, still in the process of construction.

So each group has its own place and under the new Constitution manages its own affairs, a phrase which under the tricameral Parliament is pregnant with meaning, for 'own affairs' means everything related to matters of racial identity, or call it ethnic integrity, or cultural solidarity, in fact call it whatever you like, only please don't call it apartheid. On questions relating to 'own affairs' each House is 'sovereign': however, the Constitution requires that the three chambers should come together to legislate on 'general affairs'. Should confusion arise as to where 'own affairs' end and 'general affairs' begin, then the matter is referred to the President, who acts as referee. All matters not described as 'own affairs' become 'general affairs'.

Leaving the House of Assembly and walking through the pleasant Cape Town streets I encounter a large band of singing, dancing people. At first I think it must be some kind of a street party because of the note of celebration and good humour quite evident among the crowd. The singing is particularly beautiful and resonates among the skyscrapers in downtown Cape Town. But when I stop and ask what they are doing it turns out that these are supporters of a number of men currently on trial, charged with belonging to the African National Congress. It is altogether a most extraordinary protest because the beauty and the vigour of the singing and the sheer note of exhilaration suggest a spirit which nothing can suppress, far more awesome than any display of violence – for who can stand against singers? What is to be done when your victims take to dancing in the streets?

The prayer of the White electorate is rather similar to St Augustine's prevarications on the subject of chastity: 'O Lord make me pure – but not yet.'

But when? This year, next year, some time, never? And yet the word reform is perhaps the most often used in this election contest. Reform, declares the President, Mr P. W. Botha, runs through the history of the National Party like a golden thread. At first I think I have misheard him when he says this because he speaks the words without a blush or a smile. I have come to Cape Town to listen to the President address a rally of the ruling party. The Party is responsible, he continues, for every significant piece of reform the country has ever known, everything from votes for women to the new tricameral Parliament. He says so; I watch his lips move as he says so. He speaks the words at a big election meeting in the town hall of Stellenbosch. It is a pretty, placid, sun-splashed, whitewashed university town outside Cape Town, set among oaks and vineyards that stretch away to the smoky blue mountains in the distance. Stellenbosch is sometimes called, with that crusading ignorance which infects overseas reporters when they turn their attention to South Africa, the Oxford of South Africa. There is of course no resemblance whatsoever. Stellenbosch University, like all other comparable Afrikaans bodies, exists to support and extend the role of the people, Party and the Government. By now these three entities are pretty well coterminous. Stellenbosch University has produced a string of Prime Ministers including Smuts, Hertzog and Malan. Hendrik Verwoerd was Professor of Applied Psychology here, which gives fair indication of the practical application of the academic pursuits of such places. It is a tradition that South African Prime Ministers become Rectors of the University and tonight the President has taken the stage in the Stellenbosch town hall to talk about the golden thread. The meeting is very well attended. There are two reasons for this. Stellenbosch is a centre of interest in the campaign because the Independent candidate, former Ambassador to London Dr Denis Worrall, is standing in a local seat against the leader of the National Party in the Cape. The other reason why the hall is packed tonight is probably more interesting. It is because the doors were opened early to Party supporters who now fill the front of the hall and applaud every syllable with defiant enthusiasm. Some half hour after the faithful have been seated, the general public is permitted to enter and take up the rear of the hall and the gallery. Posses of security men and plainclothes policemen with walkie-talkies march up and down the aisles. The hall is decked with the South African flag in a bewildering variety of shapes and sizes; it hangs from the ceiling and spreads on the wall and drapes behind the stage in gigantic splashes of blue, white and orange. And this symphony of patriotic hues is made even more thunderous by the fact that these are the party colours of the National Party which has, quite literally, wrapped itself in the flag. My old problem with the vivid orange makes me feel slightly queasy.

It is interesting to compare the varying styles of Prime Ministers since 1948. Each had his own very particular public mannerisms. I do not remember the first of the Nationalist Prime Ministers, Dr Malan, but those who knew him declare him to have been the most charming and probably the most shrewd of them all. But I can remember being taken as a child in Pretoria to a party address by his successor Mr Strydom, the Lion of Waterberg, and I recall his characteristic habit of holding up a stiff right arm and waving it when wishing to emphasise a point. Then there was Dr Verwoerd, that St Paul of segregation, the theoretician of the system of militant segregation we call apartheid, the man whom doubt never troubled, unrepentant ideologue for a form of discrimination which he more than any other gave shape to and coherence and which established the 'sixties as the penitential years when a fanatical espousal of something called *Baasskap* (or 'Bosshood') was the philosophy of the future. He spoke in a surprisingly high-pitched voice and his eyes were dreamy; they had an other-worldly gleam to them which I also saw in the watery blue eyes of the poor, dead English Rector of my school boarding-house. Verwoerd was a forceful but rather colourless speaker. It needs perhaps to be remarked that all questions of philosophy and politics in South Africa, as with all matters of history, and as we have seen recently, even questions of prayer, eventually become the business of the police and the Army. Such was the legacy of Verwoerd. In the days of Malan and Strydom when politics were very volatile, pitched battles at election meetings were not infrequent, and fists and blood were the sport of the day. Under Verwoerd such things became less common and his public addresses were imbued with the sort of solemnity one associates with a formal papal homily. Under his successor, John Vorster, there were those who imagined that things were beginning to loosen up; as far as I could tell this misconception was based predominantly on the fact that John Vorster played golf with English businessmen. At political meetings he was extremely aggressive and awkward questions from the floor were met by threats of violence from supporters and, in one celebrated case, the Prime Minister promised a persistent questioner a short sharp visit from the security police, which duly took place, as promised, a few days later.

These are amusing tales of old times. What we have now is a leader who actually personifies all the power of the land. That of course is something which previous Prime Ministers held as well, though less firmly and they were obliged for constitutional reasons to go through the motions of repudiating absolute power by deferring, in former times, to the Governor-General, in the days before this country became a republic. Later on, the Head of State became a symbolic and rather curious figure called the State President who wore a sash and carried a top hat and was accompanied upon all ceremonial occasions by the State President's guard dressed in Gilbert and Sullivan uniforms, dizzy with fronds, fringes, flashes and epaulettes. However, the present leader of the National Party is now a kind of supreme pontiff; he has subsumed the ceremonial character of the former State President and now embodies in himself the twin offices of Prime Minister and Head of State, and holds more power in his hands than any leader since Paul Kruger.

The meeting opens with a prayer from an excitable young Dominie, followed by a short speech of introduction from a man who declares himself devoted to the President and bids us welcome the leader, describing him as the man we love. The Party faithful in the front rows cheer wildly. There are a few muffled catcalls from the back of the hall and the police patrolling the aisles grip their walkie-talkies and look stern. The man we love now enters from the back of the hall surrounded by a young honour guard carrying flags. When he takes his place on the platform it is possible to see that this is a leader who undoubtedly feels the substance of his office, he has taken on a kind of regal colour, a Roman *gravitas* and he possesses an impressive sense of his own dignity, any lack of appreciation of which he finds distasteful and painful. He rises to his feet, gazes sternly into the audience and begins to talk of the golden thread of reform. It will be undertaken, he says, in a spirit of 'renewal'; he is busy with reform but he warns that it must not be 'reform just for the sake of reform'. He is prepared, he says, for negotiation but not for surrender. There is obedient applause from the front half of the hall. He believes in the freedom of the press. There is laughter from the hecklers at the back. Black people in South Africa are better off than anywhere else in the world. It was he who made the country self-sufficient in arms and it was he who faced the problem when the country had only a week's supply of oil left and he talks of a National Council on which Black leaders will one day sit. They will be given the opportunity to come forward, and Black communities will be given the chance of electing their own leaders. He repudiates the charge that no Black leaders will talk to the Government, he and his colleagues talk to hundreds, discussions take place every day. He appeals to everyone to make a success of the building his Government is erecting. A heckler interjects: 'As long as it's for Whites'. The hecklers do not present much of a problem, they are faint voices from the back of the hall. More interesting is the young questioner who, at the end of the meeting, stands up and asks the President whether he intends to retire at the height of his fame or to soldier on? You can tell by the tremor that runs through the seats at the front of the hall that an act of *lèse-majesté* has been committed. The round, hard and polished person of the President begins to glow visibly, the lips curve and set hard and the finger begins to wag: the President is, in short, hopping mad. The dignitaries on the stage, men in expensive suits, assume expressions of distress and regret. The President turns from red to a rather dull brown and he flies at the questioner, pronouncing him juvenile, uncivil and mischievous. He tells him to learn some manners, to go home and study the procedures of behaviour at public meetings. I have the feeling that if he could have gone on to add that he intended tossing him to the crocodiles at the first opportunity he would undoubtedly have done so. The urge to cry 'Off with his head!' must be almost irresistible. But then the display of temper is unremarkable. This is the choleric, fiery, intemperate man who wheeled on Helen Suzman on the day that Hendrik Verwoerd lay dying on the carpet. This is the man whom, as Minister of Defence, they used to call 'Pete the Weapon'. And before him is just the sort of young man who ought to be taught a lesson. He rounds on the questioner calling him *'n jong mannetjie*, a young, little man – a fine example of the Afrikaans diminutive used for insulting purposes:

'I was elected to serve five years and I'm determined to see them out.' The forefinger stabs the air. 'And I can tell you if I go on feeling the way I do tonight, you'll have to put up with me for a lot longer than that!'

My goodness how the faithful cheer. Why, it's almost like old times.

The other important political meeting held in Stellenbosch is presided over by Denis Worrall. He is also full of talk of change, of a new sense of direction and a new political dream. He has said that he detects 'a fluidity' in the country. He believes that party loyalties are very 'loose'. Millions of South

Africans of all political parties and persuasions are looking for a new direction, for 'vision', for 'light at the end of the tunnel'. Precisely what these phrases mean is far from clear. For some weeks now I have been going about the country looking here and there for this 'vision', and I must confess to being unable to find it. But it is said to be out there, by many observers, by Dr Worrall and his fellow Independents, by the English press, both here and abroad, by liberal politicians and businessmen. There is a widespread belief that this election will see an end to the log-jam of South African politics. Visible among these new directions is something called the *indaba*. It is merely a Zulu word that means to talk, a pow-wow, a conference of chiefs. This *indaba* is taking place in the province of Natal and Dr Worrall has confessed to an enormous interest in it. That is why today he has on the platform with him, Dr Oscar Dhlomo, the Secretary-General of the conservative Zulu organisation known as Inkatha. Dr Dhlomo reads a speech which was to have been delivered by his boss, Chief Buthelezi, the head of the Zulu 'homeland' government of KwaZulu. The line taken by Buthelesi is a reaffirmation of his belief in a multi-party Western democracy, in sovereign government with full adult franchise, and the politics of negotiation. He recognises the difficulties of bringing people of different cultural backgrounds together but speaks of common goals and hints at a future alliance between like-minded groups. He calls the present Government a national and historical catastrophe and warns of conflict if reform does not come soon. This, says the Chief, is a White election fought on a Black issue. He makes several gracious gestures of support towards the three Independent candidates.

Dr Worrall's reply is a remarkable blend of assertion and desperation; there are frequent expressions of gratitude towards the Black speaker, Dr Dhlomo, who is thanked for his presence on the platform, for the message from his leader, and for just about everything including the colour of his eyes. None of this is particularly persuasive or compelling. Perhaps most damaging is the inability, or the refusal, of Denis Worrall to specify his programme, or to say where the differences between himself and the National Party really lie. As one of the men who designed the three-chamber Parliament, the Theatre of the Absurd beneath Table Mountain in Cape Town, a more specific plan of action might have been in order, instead of this strategic vagueness. But the audience in the hall are young and enthusiastic about the speeches. They are buoyed up by the fact that twenty-seven academics from this University have just resigned from the ruling National Party.

Back in what I have increasingly to think of as the 'real world' the news is grim. Troops have taken up positions on the railway stations; South African forces have raided Zambia, blown up a number of houses and five people have been killed. Yet all these developments take place, as it were, offstage. None will be permitted to interfere with the election in two weeks' time.

People who once spoke out loud quite fearlessly now drop their voices in public; in very odd contrast to this reticence people will blurt out the most curious things to complete strangers. A wild-eyed man stops me in a supermarket:

'Did you know that Italy has had forty governments since the war? We've had one. I don't know which is worse.'

Fear is accompanied by a somewhat aggressive urge to explain things, to put them in 'perspective'. Deaths in the Black townships, you will be told, do not seem particularly notable when you remember that 140 people died in the annual carnage on the roads over the Easter weekend. But this is surely a very curious 'perspective'? Everywhere there is this curious mixture of aggression and anxiety, of bravado and panic, a desire to accept the most flagrant contradictions is essential. A government which holds many thousands in detention declares that it is firmly against the practice; the declaration that the policy of the forced removal of Black people and their resettlement miles away from their original homes is at an end is accompanied by press reports of the forced removal of a squatter camp. Besides the incontrovertible fact that power remains more firmly than ever in the hands of the White minority who have held it since 1948, all the talk is of 'change' and 'power sharing' and 'negotiation'. What all this discussion of such abstruse concepts as group rights, minority protection, own affairs or ethnic autonomy amounts to is not so much a change in the political structures of the country as an extension of the vocabulary in which these things are discussed.

What is interesting is the way in which what one might call the politics of the barricade is being increasingly reflected in the architecture of the cities, in the pill-box or bunker style of many commercial buildings and, most fetchingly, in a city such as Johannesburg, once known for its very striking houses, which now increasingly is becoming the capital of beautiful walls: crenellated, tessellated, stepped, curved, concave and convex, set with iron grilles, hung with carriage lamps, adorned with burglar alarm warnings, 'Beware of the Dog' notices, topped with barbed wire, or spikes or broken glass, mounted with searchlights, video cameras, infra-red lights, sensors, detectors, bells, buzzers, and patrolled by armed sentries. And today we have news that a stretch of electrified fence, some several hundred kilometres in length on the Mozambique border, is now fully operational and must be regarded as highly dangerous. Not long ago a concrete fence some three and a half miles long was erected on the outskirts of Soweto. It has been dubbed by Soweto residents 'the Berlin Wall'. But still the tumult in the country at large continues and the news, filleted into the tiniest slivers, is spoon-fed to the White electorate behind their walls, in baby-sized bites: Black workers plan massive stay-aways and strikes; barricades go up in Soweto; grenades are thrown in the Cape peninsula; a man is burnt to death in Durban, after having petrol poured over him – and all of this in one day. The railway strike grows more violent, sixteen thousand railworkers are fired; six strikers are shot dead, the union headquarters is surrounded and all found inside the building are arrested. Trains burn. And how do people deal with unpalatable news when it comes to call? They behave, I suggest, rather as the woman did who was charged in Johannesburg a short while ago with witchcraft. On being confronted by two policemen who had come to arrest her after a series of reports from discontented customers that her magic did not work, she threatened to turn the arresting officers into frogs. South Africa today is the country of the Frog Witch.

Instances of 'White Magic' abound. A lack of discrimination in the use of words becomes obligatory and a good deal of effort goes into the perverse transformation of meanings which no longer carry their customary weight. This is why a word like 'international' is so charged with significance, it is not simply a word any longer, it is a weapon in the war against the rest of the world. Thus we have just recently enjoyed what is described as an 'international' tennis tournament; this sort of contest increasingly means playing teams from Paraguay, Taiwan and Israel. Paraguay is one of our old favourites, since it is one of the few countries to which South African political dignitaries have been invited on official visits and their progress was recorded at home in large pictures showing our leaders embracing their leaders on beflagged platforms, exchanging large medals and bestowing cumbersome titles. If there is one thing more galling than the loss of old friends it is the rather gamey aroma given off by the new ones who have come to take their places.

If the talking has ground to a halt in Cape Town, it goes on in the province of Natal, over a thousand miles away. Several people urge me to go to Natal to seek enlightenment. This is odd because in former times we visited the sub-tropical province for sunshine and its beaches – never for enlightenment. It was called, not unkindly, 'banana land'.

All the talk in Natal these days is of the *indaba*. This talk has been going on here for months amongst different racial groups and the reasons for this pressing discussion are sharp and immediate. Natal is the most densely settled of the South African provinces and the violent scenes here in the past few years have increased in savagery, with bombs on the front, riots and even fist fights on the beaches.

As always one has to look at the figures.

The Black population of Natal, which is made up predominantly of Zulus, numbers some 5,232,135; there are also 706,691 Indians; the Whites here are predominantly English-speaking and number 586,018; and there are also 95,479 Coloureds. After eight months of discussions, representatives of these different groups astonished everyone, perhaps even themselves, by coming up with a solution. It is a form of power-sharing arrangement which proposes a two-chamber legislature; the first chamber would have one hundred seats elected on the basis of one man–one vote and there would also be a second chamber with fifty seats comprising representatives of the various racial groups. It is a system absolutely bristling with checks and balances and immensely complicated, but it addresses what is seen by many as the great question in South Africa today. This is: how do you acknowledge Black aspirations for majority rule while conceding legitimate White fears of domination? There are, of course, some who would say this is no question at all. They say that if the lion tamer would put down his whip the lions would not eat him. But fear is the reality and thus the solution proposed by the *indaba* offers one way round the problem. The model would produce a majority party, which is to say a *Black* majority party, and a series of minority parties formed from the White, Coloured and Indian groups. And while there would be a President, chosen by a process of democratic, universal franchise, ministers would be appointed from each of the minority parties or groups or – whisper it not – races. In other words, you get around the problem of a free and open system of voting in which the winner takes all by substituting a system in which the winner takes a great deal while the others take a little bit here and there.

The achievement of the *indaba* has been to make clear that the participants accept the inevitability of a Black leader, and that is something new. Also accepted is the necessity for all people to be able to vote. On the other hand, that old South African obsession with thinking in groups, minorities and skin colour will be entrenched in the constitution; but it is an achievement, hedged about though it is. A sensible, modest proposal which inches towards the inevitable. Yet even this is still too much for the people in charge. The first reaction of the White government has been to reject it out of hand. Black leaders on the left have been equally quick to dismiss it as an attempt by White business interests and Black reactionaries to stave off the inevitable revolution. The Government resorts to frog-witch terminology, talking of its opposition to 'majoritarianism' and the lack of 'constitutional checks and balances', and of its preference for 'multi-group protection' and it suggests that the *indaba* proposals do not take sufficient notice of 'group divergence', and all the other gobbledegook which, in this country, has become a method of avoiding change. Linguistic system-building is replacing action; the Government does not merely control the police here, it also holds the sacred book of incantations which it has written and only it knows how to pronounce. There has been some fudging since the first brusque outright rejection of the *indaba* by the leader of the National Party here in Natal. They have begun to hedge their bets, at least until after the election. The Government now declares itself to be in favour of the idea in principle, but against it in practice. It will not be the first time opponents have been broken on the rack of Government contradictions.

The trouble with the *indaba* proposals is not in the substance of their suggestions, but most probably in the fact that they amount once again to yet more talk. And this is not talking, but fighting, country. None the less, enormous hopes repose upon the ideas unveiled by the *indaba* conference. A solid vote for the opposition parties in the province of Natal on May 6th will show that people support the kind of power-sharing envisaged in the *indaba*.

Be it also said that the Government has declared itself unequivocally, frequently and angrily against any split, crack or even the remotest sign of something resembling cement fatigue in the walls it has built so painstakingly between the different races. The notion of separate groups is the rock upon which all Government policy is founded. Lest there be any mistake about this, the President has declared only this week, in a BBC interview, that there will never be a Black president in South Africa and that the principle of Group Areas will not be abandoned. Consider the implications of this statement: it was once illegal in this country for people of different races to sleep together. They may now do so, since the Immorality Act was scrapped and, one presumes, the entire posses of policemen once detailed to haunt the favourite spots of courting couples with torches and notebooks have been disbanded. They may have to be redeployed. Because while you are quite entitled to go to bed with somebody of a different colour these days, what you cannot do is to swim in their sea. So maybe they have taken the constables out of the bedrooms and put them on the beaches?

A serious business, these beaches. When a Coloured political leader wished to assert his independence of the Government and to show that, although he served in the token Parliament in Cape Town he was a free spirit – what did he do? Did he go to prison? No, he took a swim. He led his followers, like John the Baptist, into the sea waters reserved for bathers of the White group and he knew what he was doing; for in a country where the petty demarcation of territory assumes sacred status, this was true defiance! Defiance it may have been, but he was neither John the Baptist nor Martin Luther King and this is South Africa and not Alabama. Such was the fierceness of the Government's reaction that the wretched swimmer was obliged to apologise to the President and promise not to do it again.

It is said that there is a man in Durban who deserves attention. He goes about with a saw visiting beaches which adorn the semi-tropical city, curving and golden-white miles of sand and surf behind which the great hotels jostle and soar. Whenever this man comes across a notice confining some strip of land to a particular race group, he saws it down. There are many beaches and all of them are zoned by colour and so his job is a busy one. The predominantly English council, though it opposes Government policies, is responsible for erecting the signs and takes a dim view of this activity. In fact it takes the man to court, fines him, and threatens him. But the fellow is unrepentant. He deserves a medal. It is the lovely simplicity of his programme which is so rare, its freedom from talk. This man is, I suspect, someone of whom President Kruger would have approved. 'You have the notices', he would seem to say, 'but I have the saw.' One man, one saw, and one dead notice. But he's got a long way to go, mind you – the signs are everywhere.

Looking out of my hotel window I find it is the very

calmness of things which is at once so dislocating and so disturbing; it is as if the violence of this country, which is now becoming endemic, has a way of lurking on the edges of my imagination, keeping just out of sight, only occasionally erupting into the centre of one's field of vision; generally it happens just off camera, in the room next door, down the road. Below, I see the Indian Ocean, blue and rather intimate, so much more cordial than the grey-green swell of the Atlantic Ocean off Cape Town. Today the waves are breaking some distance from the shore and, after this brief interruption to their shoreward flow, running forward in a great wedge of foaming, creamy surf that slides hissing up the beach. Further out, the water is all frills and froth, riding on a big swell. On the beaches the sunbathers lie face down like the wounded after some battle and white-coated waiters scurry between them, visiting each of them like medics. Directly in front of me is the White beach. Next to it is the Indian beach and a little further along is the Black beach. Same sand, same sea, but in fact a series of battlefields. For this is a war and these are the beaches that will have to be stormed if there is ever to be peace.

Blood has flowed to ensure these territories will be preserved. There have been clashes on these beaches when people from one group invaded the other; running battles in swimming costumes, fists among the suntan oil and the beach-balls, violence among the blond boys with their surf boards, and the life savers flexing their muscles. On some Natal beaches there are to be seen large silent creatures taking a stroll along the sand, not the Walrus and the Carpenter, but the Beach Patrol, religious volunteers, sensitive men who believe that God created separate beaches for His creatures and that anybody transgressing His law shall be reported to the police or given a thick ear for their impertinence, or both. It is not just that such actions contravene the law which confines separate groups to their own areas, it is that to many

Nationalists this law is based upon holy provisions for the divine protection of the tribe. Calling the police in such circumstances is not simply a legal requirement, because this is not merely a secular matter. One goes to the police station as one would to the Church, because police stations are, after all, way stations upon the road to Paradise. In the Catholic faith it is believed the Pope is God's representative on earth; in the faith to which most White Africans adhere, that role is increasingly assigned to the police.

In former years, I remember, it was anything up to a ten-hour trip from Pretoria down to the south coast of Natal, always starting before dawn. It seemed to me that real journeys always began in the dark, stopping at Balfour for petrol and arriving in the sweltering heat of the Natal seaside around four in the afternoon. We went, not to Durban, but to a little place down the coast where a number of these seaside villages show their English influence: Margate, Ramsgate, St Michael's on Sea – a small resort near Amanzimtoti. It never amounted to much in those days, a hamlet, a few hotels and some holiday flats. You smelt the sea before you saw it, that curious Natal aroma of salt, sugar-cane, luxuriant decay and the faint, distant but unmistakable whiff of sewage.

In the 'fifties, seaside holidays were clearly regulated. All holidaymakers were White, the waiters were Indian and any Black people to be seen were curio sellers, nannies, floor-scrubbers and urchins. The road along the south coast meandered between banks of sugar-cane which hugged the hillsides like a green fur: it had this wonderfully supple way of moving in the wind which pressed down on it, flattening it and making it shine. As you drove through the rolling cane-fields, baking in the humidity of high summer, you had the feeling that the whole countryside was somehow alive, like some sleeping animal, and if you watched it carefully you would see it breathing.

Amanzimtoti still lies there, set among the green hair of the hillsides, with the great blinding blue of the sea in front of it. But times have changed. It is now a holiday metropolis among the small villages on the coast, a place where all the steak-houses look like churches and vicious fighting has taken place on the beaches and bombs have exploded in the shopping centres. Entering the town a large sign warns you that local businessmen are invited to a meeting 'to pray for South Africa'. The bowlers are out on the greens but the beaches are deserted for this is autumn, mile upon mile of empty sand. The place has that sad, out-of-season look. It's difficult to believe that not long ago troops and police were brought in to separate the combatants clashing amongst the sun umbrellas and deckchairs. The Jumbo Fun World, which is neither large nor much fun, swelters among its rubbery black slicks of trampolines, its single slide and its deserted fairground booths. Black urchins at the side of the road hold up fresh, illegal crayfish. A man in a grey rabbit suit jumps up and down with his woolly head bobbing and his ears shaking and exhorts you to visit the Blue Waters Road House and filling station where waiters, despairing of clientele, are sitting in the shade. Immensely ugly, extraordinarily tall blocks of holiday flats dominate the village. Walking along the empty beaches it is difficult to tell where White beach ends and Black begins. You need to be able to read the notices. And this is curious, when you think about it, because about sixty per cent of people in this country are illiterate.

Most of the people specifically excluded from such facilities are unable to read the signs that exclude them. One has to deduce from this that, in a sense, the notices advertising segregation or, if you like, the notices forbidding mixing, are not there so much to warn off Black interlopers, as to reassure White citizens, White readers. And to that degree apartheid culture presumes a literate population. But in fact reading levels among Whites, to judge by the alarming sloppiness of most newspaper comment, together with the syntactical looseness of most political discourse, suggest that words in their written form are not actually very important to anybody and that the real language of the country is a succession of barks, growls and yells. The true texts, or literatures of this country, are to be read in gunshots, walls and fences. It is sounds that matter, and signs and symbols.

Everyone, perhaps, has their own story about the mystical powers accorded to the police. Mine is set here on the South Coast.

Twenty years ago I used to holiday in a little seaside village called Ramsgate, named in memory of a famous English resort and about as far removed from the original as one could imagine, a beautiful, humid, tousled settlement set on a ridge among fields of sugar-cane and wattle, and the sinuous, serpent-like beach scrub that knits the neck of the sand dunes into a protective ridge. Half a mile of perfect beach, a little bridge across a lagoon which is to be found in most of these resorts, a tongue of fresh water lapping at the beach as if straining to cross the few yards of sand which separate it from the painted blue of the Indian Ocean.

Upon these lagoons are paddle boats for the holidaymakers and it was in a midnight raid that these paddle boats were rustled by a party of my friends, all of them former naval colleagues, who set off in their purloined flotilla on a voyage in the moonlight. But the owner who slept nearby his beloved boats was woken by the singing and laughter and corralled the lot of them, rounding them up, I seem to recall, in his motor boat like stray steers. And having captured them, he sent for the police.

But there was among the raiders one fellow who had managed to escape and the shivering party on the shore was amazed when, a little while later, their friend returned in

170

naval cap and hastily assembled uniform claiming to be the very same police for whom the owner had sent, and carried off the prisoners, promising that they would be severely dealt with.

Now the point of this story is that the naval cap looks not in the least like the blue cap of the police nor does a hastily cobbled-together outfit of jeans and jersey remotely resemble the police uniform... but the suggestion was enough; in this country of the frog witch such is the magical power attached to the notion of the police that my friend had only to claim to be a policeman and he became one...

Back in Durban, I pay a visit to the bar, two doors away from my hotel, which was blown up by a bomb not so long ago. The bomber was captured, tried and has just been sentenced to death. The bar has been refurbished and is full of customers once again. When the death sentence was announced the roar of approval from the packed bar could be heard down the street. Now that is where the heart of politics lies! And this is the way to proceed generally if one is to learn anything; don't look, rather listen; believe nothing; when approached by people who wish either to explain the situation or tell you they prefer to talk sense, hide or run; be most careful, above all, of anyone who gives the impression of normality.

Watch how even the seemingly ordinary translates into something new and alarming. A couple of men advance on a stranger with that curiously cheerful truculence common now, and they speak to him rather gruffly, hedging him in, pushing him up against the wall. No, this is not a mugging that we are watching – this is a political interview, on television.

This is fighting country and perhaps the battles on the beaches and the bombs in the shopping centres and the riots in the townships serve only to remind the people of the cities that there are forces at work here against which a good suntan lotion, a pair of dark glasses and a beach umbrella, are insufficient protection. The province of Natal was, after all, once a Boer territory, a fact not often recalled here. When British troops arrived in the 1820s the Boers resisted fiercely but eventually bowed to the inevitable, and pulled out. But their claim to the province runs deep. They spilt a lot of blood fighting the British and the Zulus. And there are places up in Northern Natal which testify to their claim, they have names which recall the old ideals of liberty: *Vryheid* (freedom), and *Weenen* (the place of weeping).

Northern Natal, in particular, saw heavy fighting during both Boer Wars. It is a landscape scattered with memorials, graveyards, battlefields; the names evoke famous battles, victories, sieges: Ladysmith, Colenso, Majuba. Perhaps the most sacred site is Blood River, where the Boers, under Andries Pretorius leading a commando of fewer than five hundred men and sixty wagons, won a famous victory over fifteen thousand Zulu warriors under the command of the Zulu Chief Dingaan's most experienced generals. The place is worth a visit because it is without any question one of the most haunting sights in all of Southern Africa and one that lies close to the heart of realities here; without seeing it you cannot understand the Voortrekker Monument, you cannot understand the attitude of Afrikaners towards Blacks, you cannot, for that matter, understand the attitude of Blacks towards Afrikaners, or of South Africa towards the outside world. You cannot know the true meaning of the word *laager*. Nor can you comprehend the degree to which the fictitious undermines all straight readings of South African history.

The battlefield of Blood River is about a four-hour drive from Durban, through the old battlefields of the Boer War, up towards Vryheid, in the green and grassy uplands of Northern Natal, and it is not an easy place to find. Tiny notices point the way, or do not, and towards the end of the trip there lies a further hour and a half of jolting over bumpy, stony, dirt roads before you hit the place itself. The monument stands in an immense open space and all around it stretch the empty, gentle grasslands. It is nothing less than a full-size re-creation, in bronze, of the sixty ox wagons drawn up in their great fighting circle, or *laager*, upon the spot where, early on Sunday morning, 16 December 1838, the morning mist lifted after a cloudy night and the Boers gathered within their *laager*, situated with great strategic ingenuity so as to be protected on two sides by the Blood River and a great ditch or *donga* running off it, confronted the massed ranks of the Zulu impis which had moved up into position during the night. The Boers were armed with muzzle-loading rifles and three cannon; and they were, moreover, very brave and extremely accurate marksmen. With these weapons they inflicted the most terrible damage. By midday, three thousand Zulus were dead and not a single Boer life had been lost. It was a famous victory, though it was won by men with guns against warriors armed only with spears, sticks and cowhide shields. However, it is a fact that Zulu armies, with these same weapons, were to inflict upon the British army in 1879 one of the worst defeats in British military history, when they encircled a complete army and wiped it out.

The river is said to have run red with blood. It was seen by the Boers as a miracle and proof of divine intervention on their behalf. It signified God's pact with His people who had promised Him their remembrance for ever if He gave them this victory. This was a religious crusade, commemorated in the Church of the Vow in Pietermaritzburg and of course in the sun striking the stone on 16 December each year in the great granite mausoleum on a hill near Pretoria, the Voortrekker Monument (now closed for 'repairs'). And it is commemorated most deeply and irrevocably in the consciousness of the Afrikaner people.

It is a very strange sight: a legend cast in bronze, these great brown wagons set in the huge circle among rolling countryside. The place today is absolutely deserted, tremendously desolate and the only sound is the wind. The wagons, perfect in every detail, lack only for people, guns, tumult. Opened in 1973, built at enormous cost, it caused something of a scandal, but then that has been the way with most of the sacred monuments to the Afrikaner faith. On 16 December each year, a public holiday, the Day of the Vow, the site becomes sacred ground again and neo-religious ceremonies which pass themselves off as political rallies are held here, on this great, empty, grassy space, so utterly and yet characteristically deceptive in its peace, both a graveyard and a battle station, a monument and a warning.

When armoured cars and soldiers roll into the Black townships today it is on a mission sanctified by monuments such as these which give notice of the Boers' resolve to stand their ground. There is quite possibly an unpalatable lesson here. It has been usual, even fashionable, in recent years, to imagine that unarmed Black people in the townships could effect some crucial revolution by hurling themselves against guns used by determined men. There is something both frightening yet entirely admirable in the faith of the people who oppose the Government and this is to be found amongst all of them, Black and White. It is as if they say to themselves: 'If only our faith is great enough, we will be saved; the soldiers' bullets will be turned to water and the hated enemy will be driven into the sea'. Such acts of faith have a long tradition. It should be pointed out that the Boers gathered within the *laager* on 16 December, 1838 believed much the same thing. This being the case, one might formulate the following proposition: that faith is an admirable thing, but faith with bullets is better.

As I leave Blood River, a small Black boy dressed in sacks appears from nowhere and offers me an ox fashioned from black clay. It is about three inches by two, heavy in the hand and beautifully shaped, a curiously gentle and entirely unexpected gift in this place of the dead. We look at each other. A White man, a Black boy, an ox of clay and the wind whistling through the wheel spokes of the bronze ox wagons. The ox is fragile and needs careful handling. The wagons are expected to endure for centuries.

And what of countering dreams? Dreams that stand against bullets? A form of resistance that believes in both peace and in practical action? Well, there was once such an attempt made, by no less a person than Mahatma Gandhi, who may be said to have learnt much about the nature of human conflict in his twenty years in South Africa. You can see the results of Gandhi's faith in a little place just outside Durban, out of sight of the golden beaches and the big hotels. It is to be found about ten miles north east of Durban, among the sprawling estates reserved for Blacks and Indians, people designated to live, as it were, behind the front lines, a shanty town on a low hill. Here the gently rolling green countryside, hazy with heat, spreads out in every direction. The houses range from the vividly palatial to the meanest, most squalid little shacks, poor hovels of mud and paper, tin and old sacking. Generally speaking, the Indian estates are better off and the Black areas vary between the tolerable and the disgraceful. Out this way you find the Phoenix Settlement, in the heart of one of the very poorest areas. Entering Phoenix you face the blank, incurious stares of the Black people who occupy the shanties and lean-tos on the hillside; you proceed down a dusty dip, across a filthy and stagnant stream, up a deeply rutted and precipitous track to the brow of a little hill where there stands a collection of buildings which are all that now remain of what was once a considerable and powerful dream. The Phoenix Settlement was founded in 1903 by Gandhi and established upon the stalwart Victorian ideals of self-help, education, hygiene, further strengthened by an interleaving of the Gandhian virtues of cooperation and self-sufficiency. The buildings are wrecks; they have been burnt out in violent rioting which took place in and around the Phoenix Settlement in 1985. The main building which housed a printing press has been reduced to its gable and the date of its founding, and for the rest it is a gaping wound. Next door is the library, or at least a building which once housed the library and which this Sunday morning is being used for a church service, the hymns echoing noisily in the empty hall. The books once kept here were burnt in the troubles and the few that were saved have been taken away, although I can see what looks like the remains of an old printing press leaning up against one wall. All but one of the buildings in the settlement have been damaged or destroyed. Only the clinic remains. In this bristling, cheerful place a number of extremely efficient Black Sisters are dealing with long lines of mothers and their babies. The women queue, or they sit on benches in the central hall, and on one of these benches, waiting like any other patient for treatment, there is a curiously pale, albino bust of Gandhi. It sits upon a chair staring blindly into the distance. A smart new ambulance flies up and down the narrow rutted track ferrying patients to the clinic.

In the riots which blazed through these Indian areas in 1985, the very poor suffered most. Phoenix is described on the maps as an Indian area, but this small hill on which it stands and from which one gets a distant view of the skyscrapers of Durban, is a Black slum; the patients with their babies waiting for treatment in the clinic are not Indian but Black and yet, of course, this is an Indian settlement, how could it be otherwise with the name of Gandhi up there on the gable? A few years ago it was attacked and gutted by angry Blacks. Racial violence directed by Blacks against Indians is a nightmare here; people remember the riots at Cato Manor in 1949. But there is something else to be observed; it is the deplorable South African habit of preferring to attack your allies rather than your enemies. It is perhaps necessary, in times of violent change, to be seen to spit on the graves of your dead enemies, but it is particularly poignant when you desecrate the graves of your former friends. Phoenix was founded by the apostle of non-violence and has been put to the torch by marauding Blacks for reasons which are difficult to ascertain but probably have something to do with the fact that relationships generally between the Indian and Black populations in Natal have always been dangerously mixed. There are undoubted grievances amongst Black people against the Indian shop-keeping class and these are easy to exploit. Only a day or so ago it was announced that a delegation of Indian students from the local, all-Indian segregated University college has flown to Lusaka for consultations with the ANC about their future. It makes sense. And this, despite the claims that the Black opposition in this country recognises all non-Whites as fellow sufferers beneath the skin. Walking around the ruined settlement of Phoenix I have to wonder whether it will ever rise from the ashes and I realise once again how unutterably complex, savage and foolish are South African affairs. When Gandhi returned to India after the end of the First World War he had perfected the strategies of passive resistance which he was to apply with such effect and his departure was our loss and India's gain. But then, by comparison with the deep, traditional intractabilities of South African racial affairs, and given the lack of confidence of the British in their administration of India, that country would have presented far greater opportunities to the former Johannesburg

177

attorney. I sometimes think that if he had stayed and attempted the struggle here, South Africa would have broken his heart.

And yet, and yet . . . on the wall of the broken, gaping, blackened printing house building where the grass is growing through the floor and birds fly through the windows, someone has written one word on the wall: 'Sorry'.

We're now a week away from the election on 6 May and I want to get back to Johannesburg. Cape Town and Durban may propose, but the Transvaal disposes. So how do you travel from Durban to Johannesburg? Well, you take a plane or a train – or, if you know there is a rail strike on, you take a train. Just because there is a strike does not mean for a moment that the trains are not running. This is, after all, South Africa. The Durban to Jo'burg run is an old favourite of mine, and besides, you get to talk to people on trains, you also get fed and you can watch the green hills in Natal turn blue as the train pulls slowly uphill.

On trains these days you sense the recession that grips the country; trains are increasingly the way that poorer Whites and Blacks travel, those who cannot afford to go by car or plane. There used to be a touch of glamour to the train, a little romance, but not any more. Glamour was one of the distinguishing features of the privileged lifestyle of increasing numbers of White South Africans; it hung around their lives like a rather gamey perfume, like the smell of cured hides in a country store, rank and meaty; or whisky on a pretty woman's breath. It is not so much in evidence these days. Time was when I imagined the day would come when all White people would drive Ferraris. No more. The chances are that they are likely to be driving little Japanese saloons. Toyota has just announced that its millionth vehicle has come off the production line. How did the Japanese do it? No, more to the point, how did the Japanese *put up* with it? For a very special arrangement was made in order to accommodate visiting Japanese within the ruling White minority. The deal was done years ago and involved a question of pig-iron, I seem to recall. We had a lot which they wanted to buy and they had all sorts of things they wanted to sell. The question was, how did you stop Japanese trading delegations from being arrested for sitting in a Whites-only hotel? Well, you declared them to be not Japanese at all but 'Honorary Whites'.

And the people who can't even afford Toyotas? They are under pressure. They are also the sort of people who probably wouldn't recognise an Honorary White if he offered them a glass of *sake*. They are the Whites on this train: they are indeed the sort of people for whom apartheid was invented. Half of them are in uniform, soldiers reporting to base or taking leave. The rest of the passengers seem to be working for the railways. One may deduce from this that the passenger services in some parts of the country exist for reasons of State security, or to give people who work for the system a cheap ride.

It is a twelve-hour trip, overnight, out of Durban at six and into Park Station, Johannesburg, about the same time the following morning. We leave dead on time and behind us now the battlefield beaches and the big hotels fade from sight. Out we go, past the hillside settlement Gandhi built where the burnt-out buildings open to the sky, and starlight falls on the stone floor. Out past the Boer War battlefields of Northern Natal and the certain peace of the military cemeteries, past the bronze ox wagons of Blood River, cooling and contracting in the chill evening mists of autumn. One well-lit room in the black veld, this dining car crowded with soldiers, as we grind our way uphill towards the Transvaal highveld. A man in uniform in the dining car is the spitting image of the leader of the Afrikaner Resistance Movement, Eugene

Terre'Blanche. I am sure I recognise the beard, the brooding eyebrows and the sensitive, somewhat saturnine face. Perhaps I am mistaken, perhaps I am beginning to see things. But then again I know that he happens to be speaking at a big election meeting in Johannesburg in a few days' time. I sit down for dinner opposite a horticulturalist who travels about the country supervising the large stretches of land owned by the South African railways. He agrees that the soldier is Terre'Blanche, or his double, but he doesn't seem particularly surprised or disturbed. He merely says: 'If you'd seen the amount of damage that our development has done to the flora and fauna of this country, you'd be horrified. The only consolation is the ability of various species to survive against the odds, you always get these hardy individuals who kick back. Surviving is their revenge.' From this it is difficult to tell whether he approves of Terre'Blanche and his movement and sees them as botanical specimens thriving against the odds. This man is one of the few I have met who seems to have managed to have escaped the excruciating and obsessive world of South African politics by finding other battlefields; people no longer interest him; he goes round the country fighting for plants. He identifies the lilies I saw floating on the pond in Melrose House, Pretoria, as being what be calls 'Cape Blues', *Nymphaea Capensis*, Nymphs of the Cape. He describes his discovery of secret fields of the *Strelitzia Reginae*, called the Crane Flower, with its delicate beak and flaming orange hair. He is a happy man.

The light from the dining-car windows is thrown several yards into the darkened veld and shows the grass sliding by like a river. The diners are doubly reflected in the thick glass of the carriage. The horticulturalist is very informative about the seaside village I've just visited, Amanzimtoti. He mourns the passing of the natural vegetation along the coastline, ripped out when the mammoth blocks of holiday flats and the hotels were built. But he tells me that the earth has a way of

180

retaliation. It seems that the sewage facilities cannot cope with the added pressure of thousands of holidaymakers. Effluent passes in its raw state directly out into the surf, which is after all the chief attraction for the tourists, and there it is met, he tells me with grim satisfaction, by the wastes discharged from passing ships.

'I wouldn't swim anywhere within ten miles of that place,' he smiled quietly. 'Do you know what it means? Amanzim-toti? It's a Zulu word – it means "sweet waters". You can't beat that, can you?'

'It doesn't bear thinking about,' I say.

'Nothing bears thinking about. But sometimes things just happen like that. It cheers you up.'

At about five in the morning the train pulls into a station and stops, and in the first moments after a night of creaking and grinding across the Drakensberg Mountains into the Transvaal, the sudden surging silence is so deafening that I wake immediately. I hear footsteps, slow at first, then getting faster as if someone were trotting along the platform. I roll out of my bunk and raise the blinds. I can make out a number of people on the station, in the pre-dawn gloom. They seem to be wearing capes across their shoulders. Then the trotting feet come nearer and I recognise a soldier, huddling under a grey blanket to keep warm, his rifle swinging from his shoulder. In the icy grey light I can just make out the name at the far end of the station: this is Balfour. I feel faint and pull my head in. At five o'clock in the morning there are soldiers on Balfour Station, trotting up and down to keep warm, White boys running. From this point on until we reach Johannesburg all the stations are occupied by troops in combat dress, and police in blue fatigues; they carry guns, whips, truncheons, gas masks, walkie-talkies and before the rush-hour begins they outnumber the White passengers. Doubtless this is in reaction to the rail strike; it demonstrates a capacity for immediate armed mobile response; the army wish to show that they have the appetite and the energy, the guns and the determination to impose upon the country the discipline of an armed camp. Most of the White population will be carrying arms soon, and those who do not will be carrying walkie-talkies. What would my grandfather think? There are soldiers on Balfour Station. My indiscreet naval training officer warned us about this, and his words were prophetic.

III

GOOD MORNING, LEMMINGS!

*(Election Day greeting
on a Johannesburg wall)*

JOHANNESBURG, GOLDEN CITY, just a hundred years old, from the very start rampant, from dusty tent-city, to mining camp, to gold-rush town, now richer and bigger than any other city in Southern Africa, the place that tried to lynch Paul Kruger and dreamed of rebellion in collusion with that perfect model of military incompetence, Dr Jameson, and his doomed raid against the Pretoria government in 1895. Just nine years old, and this upstart settlement tries to overthrow Kruger! Still brash, ebullient, but increasingly troubled and confused; city of walls and watchdogs, where the Rottweiler is king, 'instant armed response' vans patrolling the suburbs, where the mine dumps surrounding the city, towering flat-topped memorials to enormous riches, their sides the texture and colour of baked pie crust, are being reprocessed to reclaim any golden particles which escaped the first time, and where, from the roof of one of the skyscrapers that dominate the central city you may get a glimpse, on a good day when the smog clears, of Johannesburg's sister city, Soweto, out beyond the mine dumps to the south west.

Out of sight but never out of mind for long. Black workers are demanding a holiday on 1 May – May Day. Strikes and stay-aways are planned for 6 May, when the White people go to the polls, the day, a Sowetan tells me, 'the shit's going to hit the fan'. This sounds pretty impressive and is designed to make my flesh creep. In my experience, when the phenomenon described does occur in this country, you generally find that somebody has moved the fan.

May 1st, and the demand by Black workers for a holiday has been granted to pre-empt a mass stay-away. But it is not called May Day. The government has granted the holiday – and called it 'Republic Day'. It is not what you do, it is what you call it that counts. The ghost of Dr Verwoerd gives another grin.

In five days' time the country goes to the polls and the real election of 1987 takes place. That is what the newspapers, radio and television claim. Increasingly one finds deception in love with the straightforward approach. In truth, only the count of days is accurate. A party dedicated to the antediluvian, conceived in reaction, built on division is presenting itself as a force for unity and progress. Why are people not to be seen paralysed with mirth on street corners? The official dispensers of the government line have been going through the motions of pretending that nothing could be more normal than a frightened confused group of White voters preparing to give their backing, yet again, to a government drawn from the Party which invented apartheid, while three-quarters of the population, who are not to be consulted, look on in dismay or derision.

So it is better not to talk to anyone, and to read no papers. It is far too late for that. Above all, I try to avoid official reports on television which is remarkable in the fawning servility with which it underscores, supports and promotes the policies of the ruling party. South African broadcasting services have always been a state monopoly. Announcers display a kind of ghastly vivacity as they chatter about the histories of various constituencies, and representatives of the various political parties confer furtively in the carefully coded language which has replaced normal speech. They talk of 'negotiation', 'security' and 'power sharing'. In the studio, under interrogation, candidates blink uneasily. The woolliness of the questioning is matched by the vagueness of the responses; and in any event very little time is allowed for either. This is no mere attempt to disguise the essential fraudulence of the electoral system by dressing it up in the trappings of democracy, no one is pretending that the emperor has new clothes. It is widely understood that matters have gone a lot further than that – the emperor is dead, this is not an election, it is a wake, and yet among the White population it is felt that somehow the corpse must be made to put in a lively appearance; thus politics as practised on television may be said to belong to the mortuary arts. The state-run radio faces a similar challenge to make the dead speak, but it possesses a few unique features which had not been introduced when I lived here. The formerly 'straight' services now carry advertising and these advertisements suffer from what one might call sentimental rot. The most popular selling line these days, for everything from financial services to dog food, is to pledge your whole-hearted commitment to something called 'caring'. Supermarkets use the concept a good deal, presumably hoping that you will believe your megastore has your interests tenderly at heart when it sells you six eggs or a loaf of bread. Talking to each other, listening to each other, getting together ... Manufacturers of motor cars wallow in it and building societies swear by it. Commercial messages drip sympathy and concern from every syllable.

The newspapers conceal other traps and surprises. If the Afrikaans papers are the poodles of apartheid, the White-run English papers, generally in favour of the opposition parties, have problems of their own. At the heart of the problem is a grave, possibly fatal, contradiction: they deplore on their front pages and in editorials the effect of government policies, while the rest of the paper is given up to celebrating a standard of living for their White readers which these policies secure. It is hardly surprising then that English-language newspapers have always been regarded with anger and contempt by the ruling party. But, at least until the present fierce censorship laws came into force recently, the main achievement of the English press has been precisely its ability to anger and dismay the government by attacking policies at every turn. The effect has been rather as if they occupied the cheap seats at the circus and spent a lot of their time jeering and cracking nuts while the fat men of apartheid flew through the air, defying not only the law of gravity, but the frequent prophecies of doom. In the past one was grateful for their irreverent commentary. With the new regulations requiring newspapers to censor themselves, the English papers have a vacant, lobotomised air.

A hike in the gold price acts like a euphoric drug. It has risen over fifty dollars in the past month, oblivious to bombs, strikes and political uncertainty. Then, too, trade figures are up and the value of the currency, for some time now badly depressed, has recovered somewhat. This has led to a mood of defiant jubilation. Then there are selected news stories from abroad, for nothing is more calculated to lift the spirits of White South Africans than news of foreign catastrophes. Ethnic confrontation is much favoured for headline treatment: let Sikhs in the Punjab revolt or Tamils shoot Buddhist monks in Sri Lanka, and the sense of satisfaction is palpable. This reaction is actively encouraged by the media who are happy to put about the notion, when communal conflict takes an ugly turn in various other countries in the world, that the world would be much happier if it embraced policies more like ours. This feeling has always been at the basis of any foreign policy which we may have possessed. It can be summed up in two words: *Tu quoque*, or 'Same to you with knobs on!' That we so depend on this very specialised brand of *Schadenfreude* indicates how deeply we must now dig for consolation.

A fairly common bumper sticker around town reads: 'Life's a bitch, and then you die', which captures the mood of the times. But today I saw a variation which suggests that cheerfulness keeps breaking through: 'Life's a bitch – and then you marry one . . .'

The Government is running a clever, two-tier campaign. White man speaks with forked tongue. In the country areas much concerned with problems of security, and where bombs and landmines have exploded and where the right hopes to make gains, the Nationalists are talking tough. In the cities, among affluent, White, English-speaking voters, they are underplaying security and stressing reform. I think they must have run some pretty good market research to develop their campaign message. Their procedure is as follows: first catch your voter and thoroughly frighten him into believing that a vote for the liberal opposition is a vote for chaos and then put an arm around his shoulders and tell him: 'Baby, you're safe with us.'

A deputy Government minister speaking in Durban, a stronghold of the Progressive opposition, talks of the advance achieved by this government, pointing out that only four apartheid laws remain on the statute books. These are: the

Group Areas Act, which we first glimpsed in the location on the other side of the hill outside Balfour; the Separate Amenities Act, which is what keeps the beaches colour-coded and which the valiant man with the saw, down in Durban, is attempting to demolish single-handed; the Slums Act, which deals with problems often directly attributable to the above two laws; and the Population Registration Act, in the working of which the deep surreality of South African life is exposed. This last is one of those laws which words fail to describe and figures speak most loudly, offering in their calm, arithmetical precision a means of contemplating the lunatic without becoming severely unhinged. For it is perhaps not widely appreciated that not only are skin tones the only realities in South Africa, but it is possible to change colour with permission from a special government department. This miracle occurred many times in 1986. But let the figures for the year, given by the Minister for Home Affairs, speak for themselves:

   9 Whites became Coloured
560 Coloureds turned White
   2 Whites became Malay
   2 Blacks became Malay
 87 Coloureds turned Indian
  9 Indians went White
666 Blacks declared Coloured
 61 Indians went Malay
 15 Malays turned Indian
  5 Blacks reclassified Asians
 10 Blacks became Indians
 12 Coloureds declared Chinese
  2 Blacks reclassified Asians
  2 Coloureds became Indians
  7 Chinese became Whites
 40 Coloureds went Black

   67 Indians went Coloured
    4 Coloureds became Griquas
    2 Griquas reclassified Black
    1 Griqua declared White
   26 Coloureds became Malay
No Blacks turned White

Do those responsible for this system feel giddy when they contemplate it? Certainly not. Contrary to expectation claims to arcane powers do not invite scepticism, they are a source of strength. This is, after all, the world of the Frog Witch, where, if she wishes hard enough, the policemen will turn into toads. *That* trick is easily done, compared with the magic performed by the Minister for Home Affairs.

As the election gathers head and races towards polling day on May 6th, with its foregone conclusion, clues to what is really happening are found in unorthodox places. It is only when you are able to convert the so-called facts of political life into the useful symbols, metaphorical correlatives, that you are rewarded by a revealing glimpse of the way things are. The application of logic, reason, sense, does not lead one closer to, but further away from, the truth of affairs which, in this reverse world, must be sought behind the scenes, beneath the figures, out of the glare of publicity, far from the scene of the crime. The racial arrangements in South Africa might be backed by guns and tanks and all the visible signs of armed power, but their true basis is to be sought in dreams, wishes, metaphors, necromancy, illusion.

There is a man living in a lion's cage in a small private zoo some miles from Pretoria. The lions are rough, tough specimens from the Eastern Transvaal with names like Big Boy; there are altogether six males and two females. To complicate matters one lioness is pregnant and the other is just coming into season. The sign on the front gate of the zoo reads; 'Lion Sit-In'. Though the prices charged are steep, a long line of the curious filing through the turnstiles are all eager, it seems, to pay to see the lunatic in the cage.

He is dressed in a khaki outfit and a bush hat and sits at a flimsy table, his back to the wall of the cage, drinking tea with some delicacy from a china cup while a line of visitors gawp at him through the bars. The volunteer's ambition is to spend forty days and nights in the cage, thereby breaking the record set by the biblical Daniel in the lions' den. He has been here for several weeks and looks as if he could use a bath. A note on the bars explains that he is hoping to raise money to buy two gorillas for the zoo, because the zoo's last gorilla, Kaiser, passed away very sadly a week before, of brain cancer.

On looking around me, I decide that Kaiser is well out of it. The sand floor of the cage is baked hard by the sun and by the continual padding to and fro of eight large animals in this small place. The cage is dirty, ugly and depressing. The man has a stick with which to protect himself and, if things turn really sour, he can use his chair. His food is handed to him through the bars and he must sleep in the lions' night-quarters, a dark little enclosure set into the back wall of the cage.

Daniel has a roving eye and he gives the distinct impression that he imagines his ordeal will enhance his attractiveness and that sitting out his time in the lions' den is going to pull girls in a big way. A pretty blonde in white jeans, hanging on to her husband's arm, squeals when a lion strolls up to the table where the man sits. The dare-devil behind the bars immediately invites her to join him in the lions' sleeping-quarters that evening.

'I'd rather have you snoring in my ear than these babies.'

The girl blushes, her husband grins uncomfortably.

'They steal my mattress,' he tells the audience outside the bars. 'I was writing a book, but they came along and grabbed the paper. I've got this two-way radio for communication, but they chewed it up.'

'When is it worst?' someone asks.

'Nights,' comes the prompt reply. He winks at the blonde. 'You see they get fed late afternoon and that makes them a bit frisky. And when they mate –' he points to one of the lionesses, 'she's in season and they go for her in a big way. That's very dangerous. It's the males that worry me. Maybe they'll see me as competition for the female, then it's over-cadovers.' He takes a sip of tea and grins roguishly, 'If you get my drift.'

We fall silent as we try to get his drift. The lions are gathered at the far end of the cage and seem pretty much intent on ignoring their uninvited guest. The pregnant lioness is clearly quite mad and she obsessively pads up and down the cage front. It's hardly surprising that the animals should go insane in these horrifying cramped conditions because this is really no zoo, it is a concentration camp for animals.

The lions, by comparison with some of the other species, are quite well off for space and light. A troop of monkeys crowd a nearby cage no more than a large cupboard. Very big birds like vultures and eagles suffer terribly, fluttering heavily in the few square feet of air space allowed them in their tall, narrow wire cage. An otter basks on a rock surrounded by a stagnant, milky green pool of filthy water. There are also lots of snakes around here, kept in small glass cells. Two green mambas coil about each other in a display of menacing affection. The green of the mamba is the colour of grass after good rains, it is an innocent, leafy green but it has an alarming tinge to it which warns you not to think of apples or gardens when the mamba is about. The green mamba has a very small head as if it would belie the toxicity of its poison which brings sure death in a very short time unless an anti-serum is administered. Looking at the green mamba I get the impression that this is a highly lethal snake of few brains. Strolling spectators tap the glass and giggle in fascinated repulsion. The creatures walking about here are without any doubt far more frightening than anything to be found in the cages.

The lions get up from their corner from time to time and walk towards the man, throwing him curious glances while he waves his stick in their direction and backs his chair up against the stone wall behind him. The crowd along the fence press forward when this happens. The lions back off and he leans back in his chair, takes another sip of tea and smiles rakishly at a red-head who has just joined the onlookers.

'Are you nervous?' she asks him.

He replaces his cup and nods. 'All the time. Maybe you'd like to come in here and hold my hand?'

The crowd titters. We all share the same unspoken thoughts: will he be eaten before his forty days are up? Or are the lions simply too bored to be bothered? These are not circus lions, they are young, strong and wild. But perhaps they possess another, unsuspected, leonine strategy for over-coming their enemy, if he is their enemy, this Lothario of the lions' den. At any rate he seems to represent the position of the White man in Southern Africa today. Or say, at least, the position of the Whites in Government. Can they hold the ring? And why does the liberal opposition pretend to be anything more than a gaggle of onlookers, prepared to hold the ring-master's hand, possibly, but unwilling to join him in the cage?

Well, perhaps. But this is to be taken in by the scene before me, by the sleight of hand which so beguiles the onlookers crowding the cage front. For of course the man is *not* a prisoner in the cage, the truth is precisely the opposite – it is the lions who are behind bars and the man may leave whenever he chooses.

Finally, the secret is out. In the last days of the campaign all pretence has been dropped regarding the true nature of the moderate opposition parties. Government strategists have decided to use the election to send a message to the forces 'out there', the men with guns and bombs as well as to those increasingly angry, violent, but as yet unarmed people in the Black townships. Having marginalised the liberal opposition the National Party has an even crueller fate in store for them. It has been running a series of huge press ads suggesting that a vote for the Progressives is a vote for the African National Congress. Now there is a smart ploy! The reaction of the Progressive Party has been cries of pain and complaints of a vicious smear campaign. In this last they are wrong, I feel. This is not a smear campaign; it is, if you like, a very brutal joke. In a sense you may say that having locked the opposition out of the cage, the Government is now setting about convincing the White spectators who shiver for the fate of the romantic tea drinker, that there are people among them who secretly support the lions. Naturally, the PFP is protesting bitterly. Such conduct, their spokesmen complain, makes the ANC the silent antagonist of this election and assigns to it a role which it does not deserve. I am afraid the Progressive Party has missed the point because the government recognises a real opposition when it sees one – just as old President Kruger would have recognised it. Well-meaning critics may protest as much as they like but, as Kruger pointed out long ago, they have no guns and this Government will talk seriously only to those with guns. It is being put about by the independent candidates, by the Progressives and by other

Government opponents, that the time has come for the Nationalist Afrikaner to sit down and talk to those now fighting a guerrilla campaign against the White regime. What nobody appears to have noticed is that, in a sense, they have already taken the first step towards doing so by recognising the other side is serious about power, and when historians look back in future years it may seem that the first meaningful dialogue began with this election campaign. Such contenders begin by showing each other their guns.

Tonight the television news covers the unveiling of a new helicopter gunship for the South African Defence Force. It is a wicked-looking machine and its arrival is greeted with considerable pleasure by the President, who is in attendance. These appropriate images are carefully chosen. The President was once known as 'Pete the Weapon' when, as former Minister of Defence, he was responsible for building up this country's armament industry to its present impressive standard. Advances are so spectacular, as he reminded us in his speech in Stellenbosch, that far from being dependent on imports of weapons, we now export them. He is proud of this achievement in the face of the arms embargo applied by Western nations. Once again, the resourcefulness of the Boer has been underestimated. This helicopter, one might say, is the child of that arms embargo and the man responsible for bringing it into the world is on hand to see it arrive. No wonder he beams with all the proud paternal joy of a father in the maternity ward.

A moment of light relief. The Moderator of the Dutch Reformed Church, the body which supplied the textual foundation upon which the fortress of apartheid was built, has just announced that it is quite conceivable that he may one day agree to act as a go-between in future discussions to be held by

this Government and the African National Congress. This is
rather like Herod suggesting that he be put in charge of a
children's home.

The brutality, as well as the deftness, of the government
smears against the Progressive opposition, which have about
them a kind of inspired, monumental inaccuracy, are best
demonstrated by a glance at the Progressive Federal Party's
election manifesto which promises a 'better, safer, new South
Africa'. For reasons best known to itself it commits itself to
bread-and-butter issues and promises to fight inflation, create
jobs, care for pensioners, protect against crime, and plan for a
better education for all. Rather low on the list come such
promises as concern those dangerous, difficult and undefined
terms: security, reform, negotiations. On paper, perhaps
there is a case to be made for this sort of homely, prosaic
politics: inflation is up in the twenty per cent bracket; there
are over five million people unemployed; the economy is in
recession; the currency has halved in value, so it is reasonable
to suppose that the Government will be vulnerable on these
issues. This is indeed the language of common sense ... and
maybe that is why it sounds so crazy.

Imagine I am a voter in the forthcoming elections and I
choose an opposition candidate from the leafy northern
suburbs of Johannesburg. I read his campaign literature
adorned in the red, white and blue colours of the Progressive
Federal Party and I find myself addressed in the following
terms: my candidate tells me that his Party seeks to encourage
the 'emergence of reform-minded independents'; he predicts
a 'groundswell of people ready to bury past differences and
seek a new direction for South Africa'. On the standing and
status of the Government, he says: 'The Nats have failed
totally to produce the political and economic changes we

desperately need. Indeed they have divided this nation, created insecurity about our future, inflicted a great deal of hardship upon us and caused untold suffering for so many'. Then he invites re-election on the basis of his record, and lists his achievements. And what are these? At the top of the list is the proud claim that he has negotiated with the Minister of Law and Order to provide a temporary police station in my suburb and he has ensured additional police will be available to deal with the ever-increasing crime level in the area. Next, he has convinced the Minister of Communications to build new post offices in the area; also he has been his party's spokesman on the Bureau of Information and, finally, he has kept open the lines of communication between his party and leading members of the Black community.

Fine words, and of course it is probably unfair, even unwise, to examine too scrupulously in an election what politicians actually say. But I shall do so all the same. 'Untold suffering for so many'? What is that but an allusion to racial questions? Though it would not do to say so. 'Economic hardship'? What this means is that riots in the townships have been met by police and army action and this has depressed the currency and hurt business. 'Divided the nation'? But there is no normal sense in which you can speak of a nation to be divided. There is *no* nation, there is only a conglomerate of antagonistic groups. The promotion of antagonism between races is the major premiss of apartheid. This talk of 'the nation' is the most regrettable and revealing of the phrases used, for it demonstrates the bankruptcy of the liberal opposition. It is nothing more than a clangorous statement of the obvious; after all, what have the past forty years been *for* – if not for division? Why has this country been fractured, Balkanised, scrambled into an omelette of tribal states, casinostans, White cities, Black townships, grey areas, Indian reserves and Coloured suburbs? And while it is true that the National Party is the organisation which exalted the differences between peoples into a civil religion, it is also true that they built upon what they found, upon what they inherited from the earlier, predominantly English-speaking, and more liberal, governments which preceded them: on the South Africa Act of 1909, passed by the British Government, which stopped Blacks from sitting in Parliament; and on the first Native Lands Act of 1913, which began the business of putting Blacks into their own 'homelands' and laid the basis of a political system which later claimed eighty-seven per cent of the available land in South Africa for Whites and gave the remaining thirteen per cent to other groups. If the Nationalists have instituted policies of division while they have been in office, then so, of course, would the opposition parties were they by some monumental miracle to come to power. For all the parties in this election are united in fear – fear is the basis upon which White politics proceeds. There is much to suggest that if the White, English-speaking voter in this country finds anything more alarming than the prospect of yet another term of office for the Afrikaner Nationalist Government, it is *not* having them in office for another term. However much we might disapprove of its racial policies, we believe we sleep securely in the knowledge of the brutal efficiency of its police.

What then are we left with in my candidate's election manifesto? What of the approaches to the 'Black community'? Not even this promise will stand up to scrutiny, it is simply a terminological island in an ocean of babble. It begs all the questions: Which Blacks? What community? There remain only reported sightings of a mysterious 'groundswell of reform-minded opinion'. That then is all we have left to look to; this is the last and best hope of the Progressive White opposition who, in reversal of Peguy's dictum, may be said to begin in politics and end in mysticism. The results on May 6th will determine whether the dream has any substance to it.

I go to a Progressive Party meeting to hear the veteran MP

Helen Suzman speaking in her constituency of Houghton. The meeting takes place in a school hall crowded with well-groomed, affluent supporters. There is no carnival of South African flags here, just a little one, draped over the speaker's table on the stage. Most of the people in the audience must be neighbours because they call each other by name and jostle for seats which soon run out; someone has underestimated the demand. The Chairman gets up to introduce Mrs Suzman, the television cameras at the foot of the stage poke their noses forward like feeding birds and the bright lights blaze. It is only now, when we see his lips moving, that we realise the Chairman is well into his opening address. 'No sound!' people shout. The Chairman taps his mike; the woman beside me covers her eyes and curses quietly. A ripple of unease mixed with embarrassment runs through the audience. Eventually sound is restored and the main speaker comes up to the lectern. A very drunk supporter encourages her, with a shout from the back of the hall; 'They must have cut your current, Helen, but they'll never switch you off!' This compliment is meant to help but unfortunately the platform cannot hear and takes this to be some form of heckling and appears even more ill at ease. It is a relief to us all when Suzman begins speaking.

She makes a cool, elegant, pointed, very witty speech which delights her supporters, though I get the feeling that most people have not come for political enlightenment but in a gesture of solidarity, rather as members of a family might come together to support one of their number who has been through a bad time. But the house is full and she expresses appreciation. It's just like old times, I hear somebody say. It seems that many of the young people who once supported the Progressive Party have drifted away. There is talk of spoiling voting papers, or boycotting the election entirely and Mrs Suzman makes an impassioned plea to them to reconsider these negative inclinations and support her party. There is no doubt that she is going to hold her seat and much wry amusement is extracted from the presumption of her opponent, a Nationalist Party candidate named Pagan. She promises to see him off. She also refers to a photograph which appeared in an American magazine and shows her embracing the wife of the imprisoned Black nationalist leader Nelson Mandela. It has been suggested, she jokes, that the picture will cost her five thousand votes. She dismisses this out of hand and says she does not regret the embrace for a moment. The crowd applauds enthusiastically. Mrs Suzman is a doughty campaigner. She is now the longest sitting member of Parliament and was, for many years, the sole Progressive member in the house. Her manner is assured, ironic, accomplished and the audience stamps on the floor and claps at every opportunity. But although she cheers them up enormously I have the strong feeling that the people around me are far from easy about things, in fact I imagine that if they could put their arms around each other they would do so. There is something rather sad about this gathering, the little table on the stage, the faulty mike, the drunken supporter at the back of the hall, the expensively dressed men and women. It takes me some time to work out what it is that depresses me but eventually, unwillingly, I feel it, or rather I smell it; for over this hall here tonight there hangs the scent of failure, and fear. The White liberal opposition in this country might be compared with the more distant particles of the tail of a comet and they have about as much chance of influencing the giant, icy head rushing into the unknown.

The photograph of Helen Suzman and Winnie Mandela, first seen in *Time* magazine, has caused such a sensation that Government newspapers blow it up and feature it on their front pages. It is a delightful picture showing a pair of middle-aged women embracing one another, clearly good friends, cheerful and relaxed in each other's company. That it should symbolize the deliverance of South Africa into the arms of communism is a measure of the strange climate of this election campaign. Forty years of unchallenged power and the Nationalists are waving the picture like a flag to frighten the voters. It is more curious still that there is every chance that the voters, accustomed as they are to the proper reaction when the appropriate pressure points are squeezed, will be duly frightened. I must say it is enormously tiresome to be told that the election is a matter of polls, percentages, voters' intentions and groundswells of liberal opinion, when of course it is, as it has always been, a matter of people putting on masks and jumping out of the cupboards to terrify the voters.

In 1963 I went to the University of the Witwatersrand, in Johannesburg, in the manner of most young white South Africans, expecting to move into the academic stratosphere, the disjunction between school and college being so great that few made the transition without considerable discomfort. It could be said that whereas most young people going up to university had been very lightly prepared for the rigours ahead, in my case there had been no preparation whatever, it being an article of faith among the Brothers who taught us that most of us were marked for the gallows, some for sainthood, all of us for an early death. The core subjects of my school curriculum, if you ignored the more mundane business of reading, writing and arithmetic (which we generally tried to do), being rugby, religious instruction, Latin and death. Eschatology was the theme of my schooldays, the study of the four last things, death, judgement, heaven and hell. It was not, surprisingly, a specially morbid preoccupation and it had the effect of toughening the troops, which is what we thought we were, Catholic soldiers patrolling our trenches and it developed in us a spirit of grim levity which, I suppose, arose from our siege conditions and was, as well, made more sharp and fiery by that special Irish quality which mixes mourning and revelry and which is summed up in the custom of the wake, where it is quite possible to hold a rather jolly party in the presence of the deceased.

It had its darker side and we felt its shadow most when we were very young, when bedtime came, when I was literally unable to close my eyes lest I die in my sleep, lest death come like a thief in the night, a prediction confidently, even optimistically made for us by our teachers who, it is true, also taught us to pray for a good death before retiring, but this charm did nothing to calm a sweating, terrified child pacing his room alone in the early hours convinced that tonight was indeed the night. Yet somehow we grew to endure it, grew even to be able to make light of it, grew finally, I suppose, even to be strangely fond of this spectre always by our side, and developed a line of feverish banter all our own, hot, sticky, morbid. After all, we had been taught that it was not death that was so important – persistent perhaps, jealous, crafty and ever-ready, certainly, but in itself a matter of little importance, certainly nothing compared to the loss of the immortal soul ... I remember that Picasso said somewhere that death was the only mistress who never left him, and I thought it a rather charming thought. In my case I think it true to say that death was the first girl-friend I ever had ...

Going to university was therefore something of a disappointment to begin with because it seemed so incorrigibly lightweight and one was therefore obliged to choose subjects which did something to lend dignity to the experience.

So I chose genetics, because it seemed appropriate to study the operation of Mendel's laws of dominant and recessive genes within swiftly breeding populations of fruit-flies, so beautiful and so stringent in their operation and in the observable, predictable, ratios of mutations and the wonderful, paradoxical contrast between the iron commands of the genes and the seemingly inexhaustible possibilities of their variations: new colours, stubby wings, redesigned eyes – all of this so reminiscent of, and yet so far from, the breeding taboos of the ruling tribe.

To this I added moral philosophy and I was lucky to be introduced to the German existentialists, to Karl Jaspers and Martin Heidegger in particular, with their enquiries into the lonely, vital nature of freedom and existence, and their perturbing questions about the meaning of being. It was a philosophy particularly suited to wartime and the situation of the individual *in extremis*, a survey of predicaments both troubling but disturbingly familiar. And their philosophical investigations into the nature of freedom, choice, authenticity, though their reference points were widely different from ours, at least offered an intellectual stringency otherwise lacking in a campus dedicated by and large to marriage, mining, motor cars, engineering and dentistry. Of course the German existentialists, though valuable, also served to emphasise the contradiction we faced as a White minority increasingly pushed to the margin. The problem was that though our reference points were always European, it was African reality which we faced. But at least these readings forced me to contemplate the brute fact of our nonentity in philosophical, intellectual terms.

It accorded with something I suppose many of us already suspected. Indeed one of the reasons why South African writing in English so frequently deals with looming catastrophe is perhaps acknowledgement of our very tenuous position, at any rate insecurity is a recurring theme in our literature: the footprint in the rose beds; the looming threat of the border; the spectres beyond the camp-fire; rumours of the massing barbarians... Yet while my studies in German philosophy were useful, they also allowed fear to be focussed elsewhere, rather than brought home. Ironically, there was a further factor which prevented us from facing our diminishing importance, for what stopped us from facing unpalatable political facts was precisely our involvement in politics. Although going up to university might, at first, have seemed a little pallid beside my earlier schooling midway between hellfire and eternity, Witwatersrand University, being perhaps the greatest liberal teaching institution in the country, had something to put in place of death; it offered instead the heady delights of crusading politics: the march, demonstration, sit-in and protest meeting.

These of course were widespread phenomena in the liberal universities across the world in the 'sixties. But when I look back now to that time I am struck not by the volatility of our political tempers but by the extraordinary modesty of our demands. We clamoured for racial tolerance and enlightenment, freedom of movement and ideas, the right to pursue academic studies at the place of one's choice, irrespective of colour or creed, an end to detention without trial, to bannings and house arrest, and we dedicated ourselves proudly to the paramountcy of the rule of law and to the principles of constitutional democracy.

But more chastening still is the realisation that these goals, sought with the utmost fervour and in the unshakable belief that, in time, those in power would be obliged by the sheer moral weight of our case to yield to our arguments, are as far away as ever. In the twenty-five years that have passed since I first went to the University of Witwatersrand not a single one of these battles has been won.

Perhaps the really important question posed by the forthcoming election is directed at those of us so convinced of the moral strength of our cause and so determined that reasonable suasion, moral pressure, legal argument, peaceful procedures would eventually win through. Now we are being asked to reconsider the possibility that we were wrong.

Christian Revivalism is in the air. Tent cities sprout from the veld just as they did a century ago when the gold-diggers came to town. Only now they are digging for salvation. Upon a prominent and substantial building, a sign proclaims: 'The Invisible Church of God Meets Here'. Born-again Christians sport the outline of a fish in the windows of their cars. Sceptics have come up with an answer – in their car windows, the gentle fish is pursued by a hungry black shark.

Two days left before the election. Today Mrs Mandela visits the University of the Witwatersrand at the invitation of the Black Students Association and crowds are expected to turn out to see her. The campus is located in the pleasant, wealthy northern suburbs of Johannesburg, from where it draws the bulk of its large English-speaking student population. In the 'sixties Wits was without any question a circle of light and a tower of hope, chief among its virtues being its role as the university most deeply detested by the Government for its recalcitrant belief in liberal ideas. Almost daily, it seemed, students formed on the lawns bordering the main thorough-fare, Jan Smuts Avenue, and marched into town, banners flying, placards waving. Among the thousands of students on campus a small number of Blacks somehow remained, despite every endeavour by the Government to decant them into tribal colleges in distant places. Those were the days of the premierships of Hendrik Verwoerd, followed by John Vorster, the great exponent of detention without trial. 1963 saw the introduction of the Ninety Day Detention Act. In 1965 it was raised to one hundred and eighty days. In 1967 time limits were dropped and although people stopped counting the days, it was still possible to keep a tally of those detained. In 1982 this sad arithmetic went out of the window and people stopped counting altogether as unrecorded numbers of people simply disappeared for unknown periods of time.

Looking back now, it seems as if the early 'sixties were curiously innocent times; certainly many of the marches, protests and the campus meetings had about them an air of carnival. There was about student dissent, which in those days was predominantly White-led, a curious defiant gaiety. The association of students for purposes of political protest was as much a cultural, even a theatrical event, as it was to demonstrate political disaffection. Perhaps this was due to the fact that many students at the liberal universities, frustrated by the ponderous quality of life, which seemed as much part of Government policy as its racial programme, went about inventing their own forms of entertainment. They had little option, for most of the time the Government seemed intent on banning everything that moved. They banned *Who's Afraid of Virginia Woolf?*, and *Mother Courage*; they banned Robert Kennedy, they banned speakers invited to address students on Academic Freedom, which was then the great issue on campus, they banned speakers of colour and speakers as white as driven snow, without discriminating between them. They banned film shows and jazz festivals, poetry readings and political meetings. They banned marches, protests and demonstrations; they banned films and posters. They banned Karl Marx and Lady Chatterley; they banned student leaders, lecturers and books of every description; they banned slogans on T-shirts, and designs on packs of women's stockings; they banned pop groups and priests, they even banned learned botanical expositions upon the rich variety of South African grasses because the author's politics were unacceptable; they expelled White professors who slept with women of other races and bishops who wrote books, and bishops who did not, and they seeded the campus with spies and informers. One had the feeling that not only did they object to the political expressions of Wits University but they deeply rejected and resented even more the sight of students enjoying themselves.

And since there were on campus numbers of students who enjoyed nothing more than finding ways of discomforting the regime the whole atmosphere had about it a heady exhilaration.

Looking back, I suppose there was something rather poignant about the countless lunch-time meetings which I attended in the Great Hall, when we were addressed by vocal and enthusiastic teenage leaders of the Students Representative Council; it was only at such meetings, to which students crowded in their hundreds, that you were likely to see people of different races sitting next to one another. Speakers had a habit, I recall, of repeating themselves: invariably quoting Abraham Lincoln to the effect that 'For evil to succeed it is enough that good men remain silent...' Without doubt there was a self-congratulatory element in all this, a thorough enjoyment of rocking the boat and an intense desire to kick against the status quo. If Wits was against anything, it was against people being silenced. And this was a proposition widely endorsed, enthusiastically, naïvely perhaps, but it had widespread support even in the outer regions of those academic faculties where politics were considered, privately at least, to be pointless or a most colossal bore. There is not much doubt that the political leaders of the time constituted a very small minority within the University. Yet the message of defiance carried throughout the student body, even as far as the engineers who arrived in their shorts and their thick woollen khaki socks displaying a defiant prickle of blackjacks; and the medics and dental students in their white lab-coats – they were very proud of their white coats and wore them everywhere. Even the commerce students came, in their ties and silk shirts, trying to look as if they really ought to have been somewhere else and longed for the day when they would take up well-paid positions somewhere in the city and not have to be embarrassed by these associations with arts students and political weirdos in their pink shirts and winkle-picker shoes. But they came, all the same; they marched, demonstrated, were arrested and waited for their parents to pay the bail or fine. And, at the end of the day, we genuinely believed that something had been done. It is possible, I suppose, that these were really no more than exercises in mass hysteria, in self-delusion, but it did not seem so at the time. Anybody who actually opened his eyes and looked hard would have noticed that these meetings caused a great deal of refuse; and when the Black cleaners moved in afterwards collecting lunch wrappers among the seats and half-finished sandwiches, some might have realised that the fragments alone which rich students left behind them would no doubt have fed a large crèche. But I do not believe we opened our eyes particularly widely.

The University has always been hemmed in; it is surrounded on three sides, by a brewery building, by the old Show Grounds sacred to the memory of Mr Pratt, by extensive parking lots, and by funeral parlours. Of these establishments I notice Doves is still here. 'Storks brought you into the world, let Doves take you out...' the old joke went. Then there is Avbobs, a name which, for reasons I have never quite been able to ascertain, carries in it a hint of sinister menace. Despite being so close to the city the campus was once a green, airy place with lawns, walks, terraces descending gracefully from the neoclassical Great Hall with its Corinthian columns down to the library and swimming pool. But no more. Since it found itself unable to grow outwards it began growing inwards and today the air has become virtually unbreathable among the great square sturdy towers which have obliterated all but the last few green yards of lawn. Seen from the outside, and perhaps that is the only way to see it for there really is no inside left, the great bunkers frown down on you. Wits is no longer a place that you approach but one which you enter through the very few means of access which still survive. You thread your way among the fortress faculties. Once inside, you find an angry, disturbed place where the Black students, still a minority but a fiercely militant and exclusive grouping today, are making the running with the White liberal students running behind them as hard as they can just trying to keep up. Viva ANC! declare the spray-painted graffiti on the sides of buildings. 'One Person, One Vote in a Unitary South Africa' declare the posters. 'Votes for All, Jobs for All'.

I stand on the steps leading up to the Corinthian columns of the Great Hall, which today are varicose with steel scaffolding, and notice high above the metal tubes clamped around the columns there hangs a large sign, warning: 'Danger – Men Working Overhead'. I look up – but there is no one on the platform overhead. I have the distinct feeling that danger persists, all the same. The autumn weather has been particularly beautiful and there is a fine, dry, crisp clarity about the air which gives the sky a perfectly uniform blue colour as it arches enormously overhead, it seems to sail above ordinary human aspirations, nothing offends its serene indifference.

Times have changed: the brewery has vacated the building across the road and the expensive variety of the parking lots is not what it was. Those rich fields which once displayed rows of Volvos and souped-up Italian esoterica are depleted. Even many of the old stand-bys are going, like General Motors, and rumour has it that Ford is to follow as disinvestment, boycotts and plain fear among foreign manufacturers takes hold. The market appears to have been left to the Germans and our 'Honorary White' partners, the Japanese. However, the funeral parlours continue to flourish. In fact I suspect they enjoy a continual high season. The mood on campus, too, has changed. There is these days a growing clamour against unpopular speakers, among them many liberals. The University authorities have added their weight to the boycott by refusing permission for all political gatherings during the weeks in the run-up to the election on the grounds that these may prove to be provocative. There was a time when this University existed to be provocative and there is something very painful in the spectacle of a great liberal institution banning its own. We used to leave that sort of thing to the Government; they were so good at it. But then it is a very curious thing about dissenting South Africans, in opposition and on the left; they seem unable or unwilling to direct their fire where it is most needed, it is as if they cannot come to grips with their enemies, and prefer to savage their friends.

Today's lunch-time address by Winnie Mandela has projected a further note of tension into an already very jumpy campus. With the election just a few days away, no one knows how the University authorities will react to what looks like, after all, a political speech, though this goes against current regulations. The reaction of the Government is unknown. Perhaps the most fruitful source of tension and animosity lies within the student body itself. A trip to the canteen will show you that not only are prices as high as ever but the race groups split these days into separate tables; Black students, that is African and Indian students predominantly, keep to their own areas, and so do Whites. It is striking to note how this voluntary apartheid prevails. The ghost of Hendrik Verwoerd would chuckle to see the Wits University canteen twenty years on. Alas, poor Hendrik, I knew him well . . . and perhaps he knew us rather well, too.

As the meeting is still some hours away I leave the campus and cross the road, passing the small pretty statue of buck drinking, which stands in the middle of the traffic island opposite the main gates, a favourite place for demonstrations for as long as I can remember. It was here that the brave women of the Black Sash used to gather, dressed in black, heads bowed over their placards, quite silent, mourning the death of freedom. They did look at times, to the stranger, as if they were protesting against animal cruelty. Demonstrators standing out here in the old days were a constant target for abuse from passing motorists who delighted in suggestions ranging from the banal 'Why don't you get your hair cut?' to the traditional 'Go back to Ghana!' People gathered here because Wits leaned a great benevolent shadow out across Jan Smuts Avenue and seemed to afford protection to small and solitary groups.

My destination is the café which stands beside the University bookshop. The place is called Pop's and it is a student institution. In the early 'sixties, when a good number of people preferred, above serious academic pursuits, parlour games, motor cars and sexual adventure, this place with its massed ranks of pinball machines filling the front room of Pop's tea room was a heavy draw. I see the pinball machines have gone, replaced now by space invaders and electronic rifle ranges, but there is still no shortage of paying customers.

Upstairs, in the back room, where I sit over a cup of coffee I get a clear view across the road to the University. Parked outside the coffee-room window is a police van, one of the yellow Range Rovers that they drive around here, its windows covered with steel mesh, dogs panting in the back, and three policemen in the front seat waiting patiently by the kerbside. The young officer nearest the window is sipping pineapple juice through a straw. The men in the van and the dogs are probably the forward contingent for the trouble that is expected today on the campus.

The original owner and founder of this establishment, the old man, Pop himself, whom I can remember shuffling around behind his counter keeping one eye on the pinball wizards and the other on customers calling for coffee, seems to have passed on to that great café in the sky. It was on Pop's counter where, fresh out of school, I can recall seeing my first banned book. It was called *An Act of Immorality* and the shaky column of these novels towered beside the till. I imagine that Pop, whose English was never more than minimal, had no idea what the book was about, and the pinball players were not much given to reading, so I do not think it was an act of defiance but rather by accident that he stocked this contraband. The title was an allusion to what used to be called love across the colour bar, a sensational topic that drove people mad, and to jail and sometimes even to suicide. There was no more explosive issue than interracial sex. The merest mention of it electrified books, films or plays, and never got past the censors. The book was expensive and I began saving. When I went back with the money, the illicit pile was gone. Someone had had words with Pop. Maybe some Greek-speaking policeman had put him wise. But if Pop is gone, I see the place is still in family hands, and they have still not learned much about South Africa. The lady behind the counter, seeing me fumble with my change, asks if I am a foreigner. Before I can answer she smiles brilliantly, waving her hand at the University across the road:

'Lovely country!'

Out of the corner of my eye I watch the police van begin pulling away from the kerb. The meeting is scheduled for twelve-thirty and the student numbers are growing outside the Union Building where it is to take place. Several television crews are beginning to take up their positions. A rumour begins to spread that the government has just officially declared the meeting illegal. But the crowds continue to swell and now, for the first time, I see the police feeding on to the campus. Through the narrow alleys running between the squat faculty buildings they come, wearing helmets with visors, blue fatigues and sporty caps, carrying truncheons, guns and whips. The atmosphere grows tense. A week ago, on the campus of the other great English-speaking academy, the University of Cape Town, the police opened fire on demonstrating students with birdshot. Many students were tear-gassed and whipped with the quirts, or *sjamboks*, which the police now carry as a matter of routine. It is believed to be the first time the police opened fire with live

ammunition on a White South African university campus.
Another boundary crossed.

On the Wits campus the lawns below the Great Hall form a
natural amphitheatre in which well over a thousand students
are milling about, the number growing all the time as if the
arrival of the police has acted like a magnet. They soon
prevent one television crew from filming but others continue.
Further detachments move in, jostling them and grabbing
their cameras. It is evident that the police are quite good at
this. There are now thousands of students milling about and I
can see what looks to me like stones being thrown. I leave the
lawn and walk up the steps of the Great Hall which gives me
an elevated view over the scene of the battle. The police are
shouting warnings at students, some of whom continue to
throw things. Suddenly policemen are running at groups of
demonstrators and firing canisters of tear gas. I spot the young
officer whom I watched earlier sipping pineapple juice
through a straw. You can tell that he is gainfully employed, I
would not be surprised if the pursuit of protesting students is
probably high on the training schedule at police college. Of
course this was always the way, it is a kind of traditional
sport, but now everything is serious. There are no more sit-
down protests, a handful of students dragged away, token
arrests, cheers, jeers and funny songs. Now sticks and stones
are used, whips, guns, tear gas. Any feelings of nostalgia,
which the early stages of this demonstration evoked, have
disappeared. This is *not* like old times. Perhaps there is
something in the view that this kind of meeting, this perverted
contact by means of assault, is the last form of communication
available in this country. As if by hitting people you can, in a
curious way, somehow stay in touch.

The students are now running in all directions and the
police club some of those who fall and continue to attack the
television crews. The alleys between the buildings provide
means of escape and students run up the stairs and congregate

on the second and third floors, even on the roofs of some of the buildings. There they line up like spectators at a bullfight. I am reminded of the young men running before the bulls at Pamplona, an event which always starts off with the young men full of fire and boldness, but as the bulls come more dangerously close, the challengers in their haste to escape clamber over the barricades. I do not go anywhere. Perhaps because I am standing still the police run past me, though the tear gas makes my eyes water and it is difficult to get a clear view of what is going on, but I do glimpse a rather touching scene where a group of teaching staff, professors in their gowns, a number of them elderly men and women, march on to the battlefield and attempt to form a line between police and students. There they stand, looking faintly clerical. The young cops stare at them with an odd look in their eyes; it is familiar, but somehow I cannot identify it. Then they fire more tear gas and the dons stumble away coughing and weeping. Most of the area on the lawns is clear now, except for the police, and the people who have fallen over, and the TV people who have trouble moving their equipment. On the balconies and corridors students stand shouting insults from their high, safe vantage points. I suppose that sort of thing must be satisfying to a degree but of course it amounts to an admission of defeat. Good intentions, even bold actions, have given way before the incontrovertible advantage possessed by well-armed, extremely determined and disciplined men. I am sure I have not been touched because I stayed still. I think there is some kind of Pavlovian instinct in these policemen. I imagine it is rather like facing wild animals in the bush. Whatever you do, don't run.

A bewildering variety of impressions occur almost simultaneously: how young the policemen are: short hair, healthy complexions, eager young faces beneath the visors, guns and truncheons banging on their hips; athletic in their blue fatigues, out for a bit of sport; many look no more than 17 or 18. And how much they enjoy their work! Job satisfaction is no problem here. These boys have been raised for this. A curious feeling of nostalgia – this is almost like old times. Except of course it's nothing like old times. Then we went out and met them in ritual confrontations which were no more than elaborate ballets in which the responses of students and police were carefully choreographed, the red-faced officer with a megaphone, fifty or sixty students carefully arranged on the ground, and then a few token arrests. But now they come looking for us. No distinctions anymore between White and Black students, both are beaten with equal ferocity. Strange new democracy. And who cares now? Who is looking? None of this may be reported under the emergency regulations – as the TV crews are finding to their cost. Arrests are being made. Extraordinary pain, ferocious anger and tear gas tears from the faces of the Black students. Quite suddenly I realise that I am watching a kind of dumb show, a charade, this isn't the real thing at all, it's a kind of very rough rehearsal for a far more violent confrontation expected, even *longed for*, by both sides. But that's the worst of it. What police and students really want is not to go around banging heads or shouting insults or running away; what they want, eagerly, horribly – is a real showdown. They want to start shooting, they are full of hatred and wish to kill each other.

Now I remember why the looks on the faces of the policemen confronted by the orderly line of the academics, well-meaning, gentle, lining up in their black gowns in the sunshine, was all so familiar, and so sad. This was how the Calvinists of Pretoria looked at our priests and nuns when they stepped out in their clerical uniforms, looked at them as if they were Martians, a look which combined faint surprise, scorn and pity. This polite, apologetic insinuation of peaceful democrats into the heart of the riot only serves to reveal their irrelevance, a thin, dark line of learned fossils.

The terrifying anger of the Black students is new, it is to

them that the initiative for action has passed. They are quite literally making the running. There is no more talk about good men 'speaking up', no dreams that democratic protest will alter the course of events. That is finished, dead. The present Government, through its police and its soldiers, is at war with the rest of the country. It may talk, it may posture, promise, pretend, it may 'consult', it may announce 'reforms', but it seems to me to have lost even the last threads of legitimacy and nothing it does can disguise that. It represents nothing more than naked power. I would not be surprised if this has come as a relief to a number of its supporters no longer having to pretend to moral scruples; there is an impatience of all that, again on both sides, a feeling of 'let's get it over'.

The unbridled use of power is many things; it is ugly of course, but it can be impressive, and even familiar when you recognise what you are looking at, and perhaps when it happens often enough people awake to the true comparisons which we must now, I suppose, become accustomed to drawing between this Government and the sorts of regimes we never dreamed ours would resemble: tin-pot dictators and the dialectic of tanks. I see some wit has already begun to spread the message. Across the road from the University, stencilled on the wall, in the form of a mock newspaper poster, is the stark headline:

'P.W. FLEES TO PARAGUAY!'

It's rather funny. But smiles are accompanied by shivers – funny things sound less and less like jokes. 'Lovely country...'

An advertisement in my newspaper today calls on voters who might be out of the Helderberg constituency to return, if at all possible, this coming Wednesday to vote for Denis Worrall. Beside it, an advertisement offers property in Australia and New Zealand. And next to that is an ad for a book of explicit

Love Positions. In the column above, American lawyers, with names like Tannenbaum, offer consultations on the finer points of US immigration law. Next door, someone anxiously advertises 'Barbara, come home. I love and miss you.' Perhaps Barbara was one of those who listened to Mr Tannenbaum? No wonder people prefer to keep their eyes closed, wish to be kept in the dark. South Africa is a place where grotesquely disparate elements are found in horrible, homely juxta-position. Open your eyes and your head flies apart.

Inevitably, I am told that there is nothing to be learnt about South African politics in cities and towns, that I should go to the country, down to the *Platteland*, quite literally the 'flat land'. And that is what I do, taking the highway east from Johannesburg. 'We ought to be talking to each other', says an enormous billboard, a hopeless, poignant, pathetic message. Mine dumps dominate the country around the Reef. Peculiar things, extraordinarily beautiful some of them, in a shaggy crusty way; half grass, flat topped, eroded, fenced of course, everything is fenced. The older dumps even have trees growing on them and they are scored with grooves and striations. The colour of the mine sand is fascinating, ranging from bronze to a faint, pale, whitish yellow, the colour of beach sand. In some cases the colour is close to the golden hue of the metal which makes this area so fabulously rich. In fact, the 'sand' is really pulped rock, blasted out of the earth miles underground and crushed as fine as chalk dust and plunged in cyanide to extract the fragments of gold. Because the rains have been good these man-made mountains make a pretence towards softness in their temporary greening. They rear enormously on the side of the road, showing their golden skins through their rather scabrous, grassy hides. Outside Benoni, there is perhaps the most extraordinary mine dump I have ever seen. It is a wild mountain, the kind of thing Turner sketched in his wanderings in Switzerland. The colour of the sand ranges from icy white to a kind of dirty, liverish yellow, streaked with black and brown. One side of the dump, probably the weather side, is completely denuded, almost nakedly obscene. The other side is a swarming, tangled mass of grey-green fierce-looking trees. Signs of the wealth that has come from the diggings here are, of course, everywhere to be seen and now and then you do get glimpses of old deserted workings, the dead equipment strewn about the veld, but it is the mine-dumps themselves that are the real landmarks, the only bit of history we have, the only reason for being here, since gold was discovered in 1886. If future archaeologists wish to pick over the remains of this country one day, it will be the dumps that fascinate them, though even they are beginning to disappear now as the high gold price encourages a second sifting of these auriferous hills for any treasure which escaped the first examination. But if any remain, or are overlooked, they will tell historians of the future where our interests really lay, that we cared a lot more about what was to be found under the ground than we did about the people who lived above it. People, in our society, are for throwing away and we have thrown them away in considerable numbers. All we will leave behind are our sand heaps.

I stop in a small town in the *Platteland* called, appropriately, Middelburg. In the local pub where I lunch there is a sign which reads: 'Gay Whales Against Apartheid'. Amusing stuff, particularly in this part of the country which is a stronghold of the new White Right who are expected to make further gains in the forthcoming election. This particular note of dissent is remarkable since it was only the other day that a candidate of the Herstigte Nasionale Party called on homosexuals not to vote for him because, he promised, when his Party comes to power he intends acting against them. He plans to prevent South Africa from becoming a homosexual colony.

If the White Right do not court the homosexual vote they are clearly after support in the lower ranks of army and police. Rumour has it that soldiers in various units are being advised to vote for the Conservative Party. I foresee further 'marches of gratitude' on unsuspecting police stations, if poll predictions prove reliable. The South American model again comes to mind. It is not that we are likely ever to have a junta here because there is no great politicisation of the military. The higher ranks of the Defence Force are already integrated into the Government and closely allied to its programmes. Instead, what one is seeing is increasing military consolidation within governmental power structures. If there is ever to be trouble from army or police, directed against the present regime, it is more likely to come from elements below the rank of colonel. The interlocking structure of military and civil administration is well summed up in a poster put out by those attempting to end conscription in this country. All young White men over the age of sixteen must serve two years full-time in the Defence Force and an indeterminate period thereafter. Posters appeared one morning around Johannesburg, a few days ago; their message was beautifully expressed:

THE TROUBLE WITH THIS GENERAL ELECTION IS
WE DON'T KNOW WHICH GENERAL WE'RE ELECTING

The increasing militarisation of civilian life is a further factor, as the farmer with whom I stay in the *Platteland* explains to me. Listening to him I think that this place increasingly resembles ancient Sparta. As with the Spartans, the way things are going most of the population will one day be in the army, or in the security services, attempting to hold down the helot population.

If you are farming further up north, on the borders of the country, my farmer friend tells me, each morning you will see the army out sweeping the roads for mines and you are conscious of the air of an armed camp. 'Lovely roads they've got up there,' he said. 'Too good for motor cars. I reckon they build them like that so one day they can land planes on them.'

The situation is better, though not dissimilar, here in this rich, flat, maize-farming country. The difficulties of security, the threats of land mines, robberies and general air of uncertainty and anxiety are to be found everywhere. There is nothing to be seen, of course; you can travel for perhaps fifteen to twenty miles in any direction and hear only the sound of the wind moving through the dried-out maize standing in the fields. It sounds so like a river at first, you think you are close to water. The soft susurration you hear as you walk the dirt road is wind playing gently through the brittle desiccated leaves of the maize plants – they call them *mielies* – standing in the fields like emaciated scarecrows, rattling their chains. Into this immense, exhilarating, vacant space stretch the fields of mummified stalks, like the vast terra cotta armies buried with the ancient Chinese emperors. On the distant horizon are three smoking chimneys which belong to the power station; twenty miles away I can see another five or six. The call of the doves is quite deafening. This is rich, fertile land, seemingly in the middle of nowhere, but in South Africa these days even in the middle of nowhere you find yourself looking over your shoulder. The sun is going down now, and it is very beautiful, delicately descending behind a copse of blue gum trees. The light and colour radiating out from behind the sun is a deep yellow tinged with indigo, pink and grey and these colours spread by imperceptible degrees into the faint haze of cloud that is beginning to build along the horizon and which mixes with the smoke blown in the other direction from the power station. The smoke and cloud mix and become purple and green, and, nearer the sun, the colours thicken into a vibrant glow which makes the actual disc of the sun appear to increase in size. As you watch the yellow disc it suddenly, quite literally, like a coin slipping into a slot machine, drops out of sight and all that is left behind is a glow like firelight on a wall, a last touch of gold on the faint wispy clouds drifting on the horizon. Darkness comes quickly.

There are two forms of violence which add to the air of anxiety which hangs over this place, seemingly so peaceful and remote. There are continual strikes in the nearby coal mine and it is necessary to place the power stations under heavy guard. All able-bodied White men in the area are liable for military service, whether they have done their army training or not. All are to be retrained and made to serve for a couple of days each month. My friend talks of the grim near panic a few months before when land mines were exploding and the owners of this rich, prosperous farmland found themselves having to erect security fences, to ride shotgun on the bus that takes their kids to school. The farmers around here are predominantly Afrikaans-speaking and their politics move further and further to the right; once they would have been natural supporters of the governing National Party but now their votes are more likely to go to the Conservatives and to the HNP, for whom my friend reserves his particular scorn. He calls them hypocrites, people who talk in terms of the old Verwoerdian dream of separate homelands, lavatories and lifestyles for Blacks and Whites, while running successful liquor shops in the Black townships down the road.

'What will smash them will be the day when Black people begin to exercise their economic power,' the farmer says. 'Black businessmen have started chasing the Black market, and Black customers are learning to boycott White businesses they don't like. That sort of thing really hurts.'

But he warns against general assumptions based on particular occurrences. He cites, as an example of the pliable nature of questions of morality when they run head-on into the demands of comfort and profit, a story of what happened when American film distributors insisted that cinemas throughout South Africa be de-segregated or they would allow no further films to be released. Integration went ahead in response to pressure from the American companies, but things are not ever as easy as that in this country. One White housewife was heard to hope aloud that the de-segregation of cinemas would proceed as quickly as possible because she looked forward to the day when she would be able to send her children to the movies with their Black nanny. It would relieve her of the chore.

As fears about security grow, one parallel with what is happening here is a constantly reiterated theme for conversation. It can be summed up in one word: 'Rhodesia'. With monthly military service now a prospect, with the intention of arming and training every able-bodied White man in the country, old and young, it seems increasingly that the authorities are facing up to a shooting war. My friend tells a story:

'A new bunch of recruits are being taught how to avoid terrorist attacks on their houses. The method which their instructing officer advises is as follows: Go to your front window and look out into your garden. If you see a tree behind which a terrorist may hide, cut it down. If there's a shrub blocking your vision, yank it out. Same goes for a rock or a clump of grass – remove them. That's your task for today. Go home and act on it.' My friend laughs ruefully and shakes his head. 'Imagine the implications if this advice is followed on a large scale, we'd have a desert stretching away in every direction.'

But this is his place, he intends to stay. The only thing that will make him reconsider would be the introduction of the Rhodesian method of conscription.

'During the worst days of the civil war this is what it got to up there – six weeks on, six weeks off. When that happens here, I go.'

The Rhodesian experience is underlined by a number of immigrants who moved down south after independence came to Zimbabwe. My friend refers to them as the 'Whenwees', a name derived from their apparent habit of prefacing all items of conversation with the line, 'When we were in Rhodesia . . .' Now that this part of the country is beginning to suffer from the Rhodesian disease, farmers have a new name for the settlers; they call them 'Sowetos' – it is short for 'So where to now?'

I suppose the fact of the matter, and it is to be seen even here in the middle of *Platteland*, in Middelburg itself, is that the granite structures of apartheid are crumbling and no one is going to be able to put them back together again. The genie is out of the bottle. Though Middelburg is dominated by the Afrikaner far right, who believe in segregation and domination, the process of slow erosion has gone too far now to be stopped. If an Indian businessman, for example, wishes to own a business in the heart of Middelburg which is, strictly speaking, an all-White town, he simply appoints a White nominee who fronts the operation. This procedure is widely practised across the country. In other words, if you are rich, and discreet, it does not matter how Black you are because the rules can be bent, the authorities will turn a blind eye. While laws remain to enforce residential and commercial segrega- tion, in practice non-Whites move increasingly into White areas. The aim of the far right is to reverse this tide but, for some curious reason, they have never allowed their principles to interfere with their desire to make money. A government official, a supporter of the old-style supremacists, who has some power on the council will, for example, prevent Black businesses from opening in the town itself while running a thriving liquor outfit in a Black area nearby. Exploiting people has never been wrong in this country, it is living with them that brings the objections. The choice facing voters in the *Platteland* is between classical apartheid on the Verwoerd- ian model and cautious reforms of the present Government, what one might call apartheid with a human face.

If it is true to say of South Africa today that within heavily policed tranquillity you have an undeclared war, then it is also true that in the midst of plenty you have near-starvation. A growing army of unemployed wander the roads. Not a day goes by without the arrival on these farms of filthy, exhausted, starving people looking for work. My farmer friend grows anguished when he talks of them. 'They haven't eaten, they haven't washed, they've slept in the mielie fields, they have been walking for days, and they're desperate.'

In the end it is these people, the great silent, underfed army, growing all the time, who pose a far greater threat to the order than the deliberate military incursions of guerrillas, or the fire and fury of the great Black townships. This is my friend's feeling and he is probably right. Estimates suggest that by the year 2000, should jobs be lost at the present rate, anything up to ten million people, almost all of them Black, will be unemployed in South Africa. The Black population is growing at a rate five times faster than that of the White, who at present are outnumbered five to one. By the middle of the next century this disproportion will have risen to seventeen to one. And, economically, times are hard, even prosperous farmers are feeling the pinch and when White men feel the pinch, Black people starve. The constant stream of work-seekers, the hungry, malnourished, the desperate who arrive at his door in such numbers, distress and trouble him deeply. He has nothing he can offer them. He warns that unless the Government addresses this problem no number of guns will ever be enough. Undoubtedly, the Government has also seen the demographic projections, it knows that the population of the country by the year 2040 will be around eighty million, the vast majority of those Black people. Now it understands that the old systems and regimens will simply not do any longer and so it is casting about for ways and means of changing them. Thus in forty years it has moved from 'baasskap' (literally 'bosshood'), to 'separate development', to 'pluralism', to dreams of 'overarching bridges' – and the words are running out.

Indeed there are some brave spirits who will tell you that the Government is genuinely undergoing modification and deserves credit for beginning to wake from the old racial nightmare. But this is nonsense; if not a lie, then, at best it is a consoling fiction because this Government is itself the greatest barrier against any sort of meaningful change. It is too much to expect that the men who invented apartheid could begin to understand how it should be dismantled. The people in charge are not attempting a new programme; what they are seeking is a new language which will not only enable them to describe in more favourable terms those old apartheid laws they have jettisoned, but to put a more acceptable gloss on laws such as the Group Areas Act and the Separate Amenities Act which the Government is determined to retain. Consider the dilemma: the Afrikaner cannot effect meaningful change without ceding power to another group. This regime is on record as declaring that it will never cede that power, yet it seeks change. In other words, it is after the impossible and I have very little doubt that when the impossible lives up to its name, things will very quickly revert to customary methods of repression. Nowhere is the dilemma of the present regime more keenly appreciated than among its opponents on the far right.

To Johannesburg – to press an ear to the heart of the White right. Tonight the leader of the *Afrikaner Weerstand Beweging* will address his followers in the City Hall; a chance too good to miss. The Afrikaner Resistance Movement has been described as neo-Fascist; the words are used shyly, spoken softly and almost with a blush; they are a source of some wonder, like a rare jewel or a costly gift; no one is quite sure what they mean but they sound expensive. Do they conjure up visions of black shirts, brown shirts or grey shirts? Well, beige really – in the shirt department, or rust and orange. The predominant colour outside the Johannesburg city hall tonight is orange. The evening has a positively citrus tinge. These people are our very own Orangemen and they make a cult of the colour, the livid shade central to the South African flag which has always made me feel unsettled. The official journal of the AWB (or ARM) is *Orange Perspective*. Free copies are available. The hurrying faithful who come from great distances, carrying babies, blankets, sandwiches, are aglow – tonight they hear their leader and Führer, poet, playwright, former policeman and presidential bodyguard (unrelated, I feel sure, to the man who fainted when poor Pratt took aim at Dr Verwoerd). He is the famous Eugene Terre'Blanche, or Mr White Earth.

The hawkers of literature outside the hall are children in khaki shirts, some no more than nine or ten, with sweet smiles and no change. And the books they offer are expensive, passionate little inspirational tracts adorned with white horses bursting to life on the cover, leaping out of the heart of an orange South Africa, its coastline fringed in white. Titles are direct: 'White Man, Where is Your Freedom?' and 'White Man, Where is Your Homeland?' The work of a number of hands, these little books are couched in the language of prayer and inspiration: 'May this book make the flame of freedom burn high and strong in every reader . . .' A message from the editor. And the sacred text upon which the Afrikaner Resistance Movement hangs both its hopes and its guns is succinct: 'Freedom'. Freedom for the White man in his own homeland in Southern Africa, freedom for the Boer Nation.

Eugene Terre'Blanche is dismissed by knowing White South Africans as an irrelevance, worse still, as an embarrassment. They laugh at him and his followers in their uniforms, their Boer War slogans and their deep desire to return to the past. If there is any laughter to be found in South Africa I have always believed that it is not to be missed. But that is not why I have come tonight. I want to see whether Eugene Terre'Blanche is indeed the fellow traveller on the train from Durban to Johannesburg. I also want to see the Boer fighting force in action, because what makes the Afrikaner Resistance Movement so interesting is that since the National Party came to power in 1948, it is the first White group prepared to oppose them unequivocally, openly and fiercely.

The other association which bore some resemblance was the Torch Commando, formed after the 1948 elections and which so enlivened my childhood mornings when I found their symbols plastered on the letter-boxes down Henry Avenue. By all accounts, it was also a vivacious organisation. About a quarter of a million ex-servicemen provided a rich recruiting ground, particularly since the men returning from the war were, to say the least, somewhat touchy about the fact that while they had been out fighting the Germans, many Afrikaner Nationalists had been sitting at home knitting socks for Hitler. But although the Torch Commando generated considerable excitement at the time and had a certain genuine defiance about it that must have disturbed the recently elected Nationalist Government, it was not long before the forces of 'pragmatism' and 'responsibility' prevailed and the torch flickered and died. Besides, I was too young to see the Torch Commando. I was always in bed when they called.

Not until the formation of the Afrikaner Resistance Movement had this government faced such a serious challenge from a section of the White population and it is ironic that it should come from their own kind and that the programme of Eugene Terre'Blanche is one which envisages, openly and eagerly, the restoration of precisely the sort of racial structure which has made the National Party top dog – and in so doing has plunged the country into the tragedy it now endures.

228

Terre'Blanche and his people read their history, their heroes are powerful and, not surprisingly, all dead – Paul Kruger, Strydom, Verwoerd. They remember Kruger's contemptuous dismissal of the foreign *uitlanders* who wasted their time protesting to him when they had no guns. The Afrikaner Resistance Movement is fully aware of the possibilities of protesting when you do have guns. It is difficult not to admire the appropriate bluntness of this strategy.

On approaching the Johannesburg City Hall, a venerable, rather dowdy edifice in the centre of town, the first thing to strike me is the sight of a tall Black man urinating beside a post box. The postal strike continues and it occurs to me that this is perhaps intended as a gesture of defiance. Or does it reflect his opinion of the meeting tonight? Fortunately the derisory urinator is not within sight of the storm troopers patrolling the approaches to the city hall. The uniform of the ARM makes them look rather like cadets, or recent army recruits, who have not been very well kitted out. The uniforms are ill-fitting, baggy, cheap. All display the badge of their movement, the circle of three sevens, toe to toe. Once inside the hall I am aware of a number of very large, burly men in leather jackets, greased hair, tight pants, lounging strategically and keeping a sharp eye on all those entering. There is about these guys an air of real menace. They wear large gold rings and crack their knuckles and stare right through you. These are not the kinds of supporters you usually encounter at party political meetings, but then this is no ordinary party. In the gents lavatory a flag carrier, with hair like whipped black cream, is having trouble adjusting his swastika, which resembles somewhat the flag of the Isle of Man. It is also the biblical symbol for perfection; an adversarial symbol, three sevens are, it seems, set against the three sixes, for it is disclosed in *Revelations* that three sixes is the mark of the Beast. What we have in the Afrikaner Resistance Movement, therefore, is the struggle of the sevens against the sixes (not for nothing does numerology send men mad). The man in the gents is now happy with the hang of the flag, brushes it carefully as if he were smoothing lint off a good suit, straightens up and saunters back into the lobby to take up his place in the honour guard awaiting the arrival of the leader.

Inside the hall the colours are red, white and black. This is Nuremberg designed at Woolworths. Enormous banners hang from the ceiling and behind the speakers' platform on the stage are displayed the flags of the old Transvaal and Orange Free State Boer republics. Song sheets await us on our seats as well as a copy of the 'Manifesto of the Afrikaner Boer'. The hall is already three-quarters full and there is an air of intense excitement among the audience, many of them young and rather poor. There are lots of children who cannot be more than ten and eleven, wearing the drab brown uniform of the movement. The Manifesto is a homely affair. It looks as if it has been designed on the kitchen table but its language is succinct and uncompromising. It promises the resistance of the Afrikaner Boer against the present Government's plans for a multi-racial South Africa, with its inevitable culmination in a Black presidency; it gives notice that it rejects all reform and any degree of 'power sharing' (one of the catchwords of the National Party in this election); it rejects forcible integration; it pledges its thanks to the police and to the army for their valiant services in this time of trouble and it promises that these forces will continue to enjoy the gratitude and support of the Resistance Movement. Now of course 'gratitude' is an extremely powerful code word in South Africa. It has been used for years as a very subtle threat, heard perhaps in its most familiar guise in the ritual thanks bestowed by innumerable appointees of the Government over the years, to the Government which appointed them. 'We thank the Minister,' is not merely an expression of gratitude, therefore, but a veiled threat to deal severely with anyone who feels that the policies of an Afrikaner Nationalist Government are anything other than a cause for unconfined joy. What is interesting is the employment of the gratitude weapon in the hands of the far right. The Manifesto is shot through with such threats, masquerading as declarations of intent. It rejects angrily the conspiracy, by the Americans in particular, by foreign influences and Big Money, to force the Afrikaner to cooperate in the extinction of his own identity and it ends with a short prayer from the leader himself who declares it to be his daily office to ask from God the strength that will enable all of us here tonight to lay our offering upon the altar of the people. Upon the stage now, before the organ, a man in a green blazer strikes up the first of the evening's tunes, all old songs, tried and tested, uplifting and sentimental. We begin with the traditional Boer song, 'Sarie Marais'. We go on to sing songs which tell of long lost love, of little houses in the veld, of a glimpse of brown eyes, loyalty in battle, the death of comrades, and the dream of a homeland protected by God. As the song cycle progresses it takes on a semi-religious connotation, with sentimental standards like 'Ou Boere Plaas' (Old Farmstead), and we give a spirited rendition of the 'Song of Young South Africa', which appears to have been adopted as the anthem of the movement. The palpable spirit of yearning to be found in many Afrikaans folk tunes, the persistent refrain of dreams of home shot through with unrequited longing for a safe refuge, clearly moves the audience very greatly. The singing continues for a good half hour. Behind me I hear a man telling his neighbour of a farmer he met up on the northern borders who has given an appropriate response to a journalist, when asked how he would respond to the installation of a Black government. The farmer has replied that, in this eventuality, he will kill his wife, his children and himself. This declaration, heard through the strains of the Boeremusiek, evokes in me a feeling of the most curious nostalgia; what I am hearing is a concert made of the old, warped music of my childhood. Standing in

231

this hall tonight I know where I am. This is, after all, where I began.

The excitement thickens as the top brass of the movement take up their places at the table on the platform. There are outbreaks of spontaneous applause, despite the fact that the man testing the microphone has discovered that there are amplification problems with the sound system, a gift, he tells us, of an anonymous friend. Further joyous applause. Then suddenly people are jumping to their feet and clapping and behind me, walking up the aisle, is the leader himself, flanked by his storm-troopers, they in their brown uniforms, he in a grey three-piece suit, a flower in his buttonhole, smiling and waving to left and right. All around me people are stamping and roaring, waving their banners and flags and chanting '*Ah Vey Bay! Ah Vey Bay!*' In front of me there are two young girls, I suppose in their late teens, almost hysterical with excitement, clutching each other, and crying: 'Here he comes – the big boss! The leader of leaders!' The organ swells and the entire place is on its feet now, whistling and stamping and cheering as the leader of leaders makes his way up to the platform.

Media interest in a movement, which official reckoning declares to be of no consequence, is very great. The cameras of several American networks are here and throngs of press reporters are penned into one area to the left of the podium where they mill around, rather as one imagines the groundlings must have done during Elizabethan plays, eating oranges and cracking nuts. They talk, grin and point throughout the proceedings and give every impression of being a kind of privileged class. I suppose that is what they are, a new clerisy who may come and go as they like, attend private meetings and speak at public discussions, consulted, quoted, read, a privileged cast revered and reviled for the same reasons as their clerical forbears, that reason being essentially close links to the sources of power. The media, I suppose, is a new universal church. However, rather like the old clergy, it can also fall from grace. While the chairman of the evening's proceedings makes clear that he welcomes both local and foreign media to the meeting he gives the representatives of a well-known Afrikaans newspaper, presumably one which has made severe criticisms of the Resistance Movement, exactly five minutes to leave the hall. One or two people slip away, whether they are the guilty people concerned or merely nervous journalists, unused to being threatened from the platform, I do not know. But members of the audience make plain with cheers and whistles their satisfaction with this summary excommunication.

The format of the meeting is exactly the same as that of the governing National Party which I attended in the Cape. We begin with prayers, led by a young Dominie, almost demented with the passion and the justice of his cause. A long, rambling, spittle-flecked, pop-eyed harangue, a peroration which leaves the speaker exhausted and damp-eyed and the audience, or perhaps I should say the congregation, ecstatic.

And now the man himself, the leader of leaders, boss of bosses who has been sitting quietly on the platform nodding agreement at various points during the Dominie's sermon. Terre'Blanche is a shortish, rather portly figure with a dark skin tinged with grey, a short beard and neat auburn hair, altogether a haunting, slightly dreamy but substantial presence – and without any doubt the same man with whom I travelled on the train from Durban to Johannesburg. He steps up to the lectern and two men in dark suits take up position behind him, facing outwards, eyes watchful. A further detachment of uniformed storm-troopers lines the back of the stage. The dark-suited gents turn slightly outwards and stand at ease, eyes watchful; they are clearly the personal bodyguard. The audience is on its feet, stamping, waving flags, and the chanting begins again: '*Ah Vey Bay! Ah Vey Bay!*'

Terre'Blanche smiles, and begins quietly. He tells the story of a little girl, a refugee from the horrors of the civil war at the time of independence of the Belgian Congo back in 1960, a tiny waif who has flown out to safety and who, when the plane landed at Jan Smuts – can we picture her? – standing on the aircraft steps in her torn dress, began asking in bewilderment where she was. And on being told that she was in South Africa, she declared her gratitude for her preservation, thanked the land of apartheid for her salvation...

It is a thoroughly mawkish opening but as far as the audience is concerned, it seems to be highly valued. It is expertly done – the death of Little Nell, South African style. Phrasing and timing are carefully gauged and I am reminded that this man has poetic aspirations. It is whispered that he is a failed artist, that he wears platform shoes to compensate for his short stature, that he is a clown, a joke. Quite possibly this is all true, but when he is up on the platform he actually seems to grow, to get taller and broader as he speaks. I suppose it must be the voice that works the magic, adding dignity and lustre to the banality of the opening comments. All around me I see people are moving forward to the edges of their seats, drawn to the voice which is rich, brown, strong and possesses a considerable melodic range. He has a musician's sense of intonation. If one knows anything of Afrikaans (essential, for not a syllable of English is spoken all evening), there is the discovery that the man speaks the language quite beautifully.

He is without doubt one of the most powerful and poetic speakers I have ever heard in South Africa, a natural orator, capable of playing upon his audience like a virtuoso. His art is a mixture of the broad, rich siren song of homeland, struggle, and undying loyalty, interlaced with the most specific and uncompromising threats of violence and it is difficult to know which of the two strands is more appealing to his excitable followers, the music or the blood. His message is blunt; his people are not prepared to become the 'White slaves of Africa'. Though they do not seek conflict and while the Afrikaner Resistance Movement is not made up of men of violence, by the same token he warns the unseen enemy beyond the city hall: 'We are not frightened of you. Oppose us and we will wipe you away ...' The delirious audience greet these promises with wild affirmatory cries of 'Yes! We will!' Altogether they spend a good deal of time on their feet and I reckon there must be anything up to three thousand people crammed into the hall, packed into the aisles, jostling in the upstairs gallery for a view of their hero.

Terre'Blanche describes the creeping evils of racial integration and accuses the government of selling the Afrikaner people into bondage. The Boer people have won their right to a country in this part of Africa; and they have drawn its borders with the bodies of their wives and children. The people have a right to this sacred soil nourished by the blood of the twenty-seven thousand women and children who died in British concentration camps during the Boer War.

But his greatest scorn is reserved for the present national Afrikaner Government and for its leader whom he has referred to on other occasions as – 'This old milk cow who has run dry'. He ridicules the present tricameral constitutional arrangement of separate legislative houses for Whites, Coloureds and Indians, and he refers to a celebrated swim taken by the leader of the Coloured House, from a Whites-only beach, for which attempted protest the daring bather was reprimanded by the President and forced to apologise. The audience hoot with laughter. Terre'Blanche spits his contempt: 'And this is the Government that says it will absorb Coloureds into itself. How does a President, who cannot even allow the leader of the Coloureds to swim in the same sea as himself, go on to tell us that he may sit at the same table?'

He speaks for perhaps fifty minutes, lacing his detestation of the present administration with continual promises that the

Resistance Movement will defend its followers, its children and the sacred Boer Nation with all the force required. Pledges of support are made to the police – the gratitude weapon is enthusiastically waved. It is a theme of his address; ARM is the policeman's friend, and, given the rumours, never discussed and of course never admitted that fertile recruiting grounds are to be found among the lower ranks of the constabulary, one can see the thinking behind this. He has a message for the police. When they need support, ARM will provide it. For too long now they have been forced to fight the agitators in the Black townships, the instigators of the violence which shakes the country, with their hands tied behind their backs. He wants them to know that they have his sympathy and support. An equally devotional attitude is expressed towards the Army, for which he has a special message: he urges members of the Defence Force to remember their oaths of loyalty; they have sworn to remain true to South Africa, and he calls upon them never to allow those oaths to be watered down or diluted. The clear implication, understood by all, is that the Army's first duty is to the preservation of the security of the ruling White tribe, not to stand by as the walls of apartheid are dismantled; not to allow themselves to be used by the present rotten administration as an instrument with which to put down resistance among loyal White patriots. And he makes a promise: should the need arise, the AWB will be ready to play their part in supporting the Defence Force.

Next he turns to economics which have the great virtue of being poisonously and sinuously simple, deeply appealing and, as far as his hearers are concerned, utterly convincing. Ninety-nine per cent of the country's income is generated by White people and yet two-thirds of it is spent by the government on Black people. Sixty-six cents out of every hundred are lost to those who generate the wealth. Cries of

'Scandal!' from the floor. Terre'Blanche promises that the ARM will put an end to that.

And now we come to the heart of the matter: the movement are not asking for much, they ask only for a small country for a small Boer nation. This emphasis on smallness is quite interesting and it filters through into the actual language he uses. Afrikaans (like Austrian German) has always been a language that lends itself to the use of diminutives which allow one to stress intimacy, family ties and affection – and there are diminutives in great evidence tonight. What he is asking for, Terre'Blanche declares, is quite straightforward: he demands the return to the Afrikaner nation of the old Boer republics, the Transvaal Republic of Paul Kruger, the Orange Free State, and Northern Natal; these last named are the lands sacred to the memory of those Voortrekkers massacred by Dingaan and the Zulus. All three areas constitute sacred territory for which the Boer Nation gave its blood. And the rest of the country? The rest of the country can go to hell. He does not want the Cape and he does not want the rest of Natal. He does not want South Africa. All he wants is a White homeland for the little Boer Nation. The orange books of the movement are full of this dream of a homeland. A small beginning has already been made and names have been suggested: there is 'Orangia' and 'Southland'. A group called the Union of Orange Workers has formed the White Homeland Action Committee. ARM literature is full of these plans, as well as warnings, that members must be ready for sacrifice, and for warfare, for what is called the Fourth Freedom War.

And what will be done with the Blacks? He deals with them briefly. They will have their own self-governing homelands and stay there, separate and exclusive. He asks for the Boer Nation only what all other nations ask for

237

themselves, territorial integrity, a land of its own. And what will be done, for instance, with the Indians? Well, it was the English, was it not, who imported them to work as indentured labourers in the cane-fields of Natal? Well then, let the English have them back, every single one of them. He calls the Indians *Koelietjies* – little coolies – an example of the diminutive being used not as an endearment, but as an insult. The way he hits just the right note of contempt sends the hall into paroxysms of pleasure.

Now he turns to one of the great enemies; the state-controlled radio and television service, the government's brainwashing machine, he calls it. He demands the right to a debate with a spokesman from the Government side, anyone they like. His request is ferociously modest (a brief shark's smile). All he asks is ten minutes. The crowd erupts – 'Ten minutes! Ten minutes!' The cry is deafening. Terre'Blanche holds up his hands and silence falls. He shakes his head in mock repentance. 'No, no,' he says gently, 'that's too much. I don't even ask ten minutes, give me just five ...' He holds up five fingers. 'Just five!' His followers are now almost hysterical and keep jumping to their feet and applauding with their hands held high above their heads and when they do this the denim jackets and leather jerkins many of them wear fly upwards and tucked into the waistbands I see the revolvers. I cannot imagine how many guns there are in this hall tonight, but if you ran a metal detector over it it would ring like all the bells of St Paul's. I am sure the majority of the people here are carrying some sort of offensive weapon. And then I realise that is what this movement is for; the ARM was born to encourage people to carry guns.

It is quite clear why the Government will not allow this man within several miles of any broadcasting studio or television station. There is not a minister, functionary, spokesman within Government ranks who even begins to match the magnetic power of his personality or the potent seduction of his oratory. Eugene Terre'Blanche is, without doubt, a dangerous man, a demagogue and a sentimental neo-Fascist. He is also the most vituperative, insolent, arrogant and effective opposition speaker I have ever witnessed.

But the election looms and there is still a question to be addressed – how to vote? Terre'Blanche will not tip a particular party because the audience know where the two acceptable parliamentary forces stand, the Conservative Party and the HNP. But, direct and original as ever, he poses a starker choice: White voters will have to decide between the AWB or the ANC; the future of South Africa lies with one or the other. Now, no matter what one thinks of Terre'Blanche's economics, his geography, his history or even his politics, this strikes me as profoundly accurate. Of course it is possible that I have been sitting in this hall far too long tonight and the man's spell is even more powerful than I suspected, but I have to say that this crude and simple challenge seems to me to be nothing less than the truth.

The people leave the hall as if from some great revivalist meeting, refreshed, exulted, happy and they toss money into the black plastic buckets shaken by uniformed storm-troopers who prowl the exits as we leave. In the main, the supporters of Terre'Blanche are poor, frightened lower-middle-class and working-class people feeling the pinch at this time of deep economic recession and great political uncertainty. They are not, it has to be said, a very impressive lot as they stream from the doors with their babies, their tatty khaki uniforms, their silly swastikas, their leather jackets and their guns. If anything will bring Terre'Blanche down it is not that he is ridiculous, it is rather that he has so much more class and so many more ambitions than his followers who are a very motley crew. Really I cannot help feeling that Terre'Blanche deserves better.

The English press is endeavouring to cheer up its readers by reporting on racial animosities in countries abroad. It is ironic, declares some demented correspondent, that just as South Africa is beginning to lower the racial barriers, reports from London indicate that a new period of racial hostility has begun.

What is one to say to this sort of thing? This desperate clutching at straws, this inanity, these desperate lies we tell ourselves? The report appears in a newspaper in a city which lies next door to Soweto, the giant Black township of which Johannesburg sees nothing and knows nothing. This report appears in a city so fiercely segregated, so rich and exclusive, that it can turn its eyes away from the millions of people crammed into the ugly, dusty, reeking ghetto in its own backyard and yet detect at a range of six thousand miles increased racial tension in London.

I must remind myself that this example of brain-popping impudence is an everyday affair.

I have been thinking about President P.W. Botha's outburst all those years ago, on September 6th, 1966, in the Cape Town Parliament when Hendrik Verwoerd lay bleeding and dying on the green carpet, the victim of the demented Greek messenger Tsafendas; 'It's you! It was you liberals who did this! We're going to get you now!' Wild words, intemperate, inaccurate, characteristic and accompanied, I have no doubt, by the wagging finger. But in another way, I suppose, a kind of tribute to the power which a government leader imagined was wielded by the liberals and their friends. I doubt that such a perverse compliment will ever be paid to them again. The liberal parliamentary opposition in this country has long ceased to make anybody angry; I am afraid they inspire instead feelings of rueful regret and deep embarrassment.

South Africa does not exist as a place, it is only the expression of policy; it is not a country, it is a *condition*. It is the result of forty years of social engineering in which it has been hacked about and reshaped according to a wild ambitious dream that maintained that it was only by building fences between groups with differently coloured skins that you could make the Black people free and the Afrikaner people safe. Since the nightfall of 1948 we have not been living in a country, but in someone else's dream, a forty-year sleep, heavily policed, and from which we could not awaken without permission. Now, people are beginning to wake up and find that four decades have passed and Black people are not free and the Afrikaner is still not safe.

Some White people still visit Soweto, that huge sprawling city of perhaps two and a half million people, lying just eighteen kilometres from Johannesburg. A White person may slip in secretly, at the invitation and under the protection of friendly local residents; or he may visit in some professional capacity, that is to say, as a supplier of services or goods – I have a White friend who sells kitchens there. After all, even in Soweto people must cook, though it has to be said that there are many, many people in Soweto to whom the idea of a kitchen is no more than a distant dream. But perhaps the most usual way for a White man to enter Soweto is to do so in an armoured car, wearing a uniform and carrying weapons, since the townships have been, for some years now, occupied camps. My visits are both private and public. I go in alone but I also use a little-known method, and that is to take a tour. For against all expectations, coach tours of Soweto run regularly and there is, if you like, something sensible, even if somewhat unexpected, in the idea of getting a bus to see what is after all a giant city comprising twenty-six loosely related but different townships, the nearest of which, Orlando East, is a mere eighteen kilometres from Johannesburg, while the furthest is forty kilometres away. Soweto is an acronym for South Western Townships.

These tours have run for years now. Once they were arranged and controlled by the White authorities and used as a form of propaganda by means of which curious foreign visitors were to be shown the enlightened ways of the White man and his dealings with his Black work force in their vast dormitory town, and to prove that, contrary to hostile foreign reports, Soweto was not a festering shanty town whose inhabitants dwelt in sullen discontent. This ambition presumes, as so often happens in South Africa, either an inordinate confidence on the part of the White propagandists in their own powers of persuasion, or, which is probably more likely, a firm belief that foreign tourists were innocents abroad – there to be taken for a ride. Then, as now, and I fear for some considerable time to come, the merest passing acquaintance with Soweto proves that it is indeed, in many of its sections and suburbs, a festering shanty town in which its inhabitants dwell in simmering anger, frustration and discontent. But it is not, as some might imagine, a slum on a South American model, or, even, on the African model, that is to say, an accretion of hovels beside the downtown skyscrapers. It is a vast conglomeration of tiny brick, or breeze-block dwellings, stretching away from the eye up over the low hills and far into the distance covering an area of one hundred square kilometres, and through the heart of this Johannesburg's shadow sister city, the tour continues to run regularly and safely. And far from being duped, the foreigners who take the tour see things to which South Africans remain blind.

In the old days, when I took the tour, the guides were snappy little White men, usually decanted from the lower branches of the South African Railways, who used to point out in tones of undisguised self-congratulation the single house of the fabulously wealthy witch doctor, or distant views of the power station, glimpses of the football stadium and other declarations expected to gull and seduce the innocent foreign visitor. For even then, it was mostly foreign visitors who took the tour, though it has always been open to White South Africans. But then why should they take a tour of Soweto? In the old days it simply was not done. Today, in the current unrest, it is out of the question for the inhabitants of the White city next door. Soweto is a place of guns, rampaging mobs, fires and hatred. This is the reason given why nobody goes there now. Today the White con-men are gone and the tour is in Black hands. The passengers on the bus are all foreigners: Germans, Americans, Australians. The clear intention of the guide is to explain to us, in tones of unmistakable and quite horrifying candour, what Soweto really is and why this visit is a journey into the heart of South Africa.

It is sometimes thought that Soweto came into being as a direct result of the Afrikaner revolution of 1948 and the exaltation of formalised racial segregation into a civil creed. In fact the place grew out of the early discovery of gold in 1886. Gold was the father of Soweto, together with a need for separate lavatories, or what used to be called 'reasons of hygiene'; this twin theme is to be found everywhere in South African history and culture. When the dizzying richness of the reef of gold upon which the Witwatersrand stood began to reveal itself, a tent town sprang up on the empty veld, growing with an alarming vigour and a lavish intermingling of races which made President Paul Kruger despair, and condemn with horror this new Babylon of the veld with its fearful racial fluidity, where Black labourers lived among the gold-crazy emigrant diggers, without regard for the laws of God, or, worse still, the laws of the Transvaal Republic! However, it was not disapproval that put an end to this golden bestiality; it was the arrival, in 1904, of bubonic plague which led to demands that the Blacks be moved as far away as possible from the golden Babylon. And it is from this time that Johannesburg went White, as we say in South Africa, by night, and drew in by day its required quotas of Black labour from the dormitory suburbs and townships of which Soweto is possibly the best known.

The little box houses blur into the veld and darken upon the further horizons. They run from the eye in every direction making it impossible to focus on anything; there is no centre, no great buildings or special landmarks to hold the eye; there is just this extraordinary, untidy, unstoppable spread. This is the place of four thousand taxis, of rows and rows of buses so frequently boycotted or stoned that they are lined up behind barbed wire, of stations where the trains burn and where the soldiers patrol. While it is forbidden to photograph military vehicles or the soldiers or the police, it is difficult for the visitors on the bus to know where to point their cameras, because everywhere you look there are uniforms.

Perhaps it is not known that such is the passion for dividing peoples according to their colour and culture that the policy applies even here in the heart of Soweto. Away over to your left, that smudge on the horizon, is the Indian township. And over there to your right, if you look hard, you will see a group of houses that seem to all intents and purposes like the others, but in fact belong to the Coloureds; separate housing developments within the separate development which is Soweto.

Electrification came recently to the township and is spoken of, in Johannesburg, with considerable pride as a great advance. What you will see are electric lamp standards, pencil-like structures fifty to sixty feet high with a flowering of powerful lights. They stride across the Soweto township like Triffids. It is a curious business, this electrification, particularly when you consider how long it took to get here and its present manifestation in the form of these towering, anorexic mushrooms; because there has been a power station in Soweto for decades, its brown cooling towers smoking steamily. But the thing is, you see, that this station was never intended to supply power to Soweto, which stretches away beneath the huge cooling towers like some medieval village at the foot of a great château. This station supplies power to Johannesburg.

Electrification was only one of Soweto's many problems. The place is, in fact, a constellation of problems, the chief of which is the deplorable housing. Most of these little boxes are no more than two rooms and many have been extended with corrugated iron and now, instead of sleeping three or four, they sleep six or more. Some of the older houses have garages, but these garages are not for cars. In Soweto garages are for people and this is why the estimate of the population, at about two and a half million, is almost certainly on the low side, for anything that provides some cover will be sub-let to people desperate for a roof over their heads. The truth is nobody could possibly know how many people live here, in fact I am sure they don't want to know. Life is difficult enough – why look for trouble? There are roosters strutting up and down the pavements pecking at morsels. A dog scavenges on a rubbish heap. Heaps of garbage, stinking and smoking, are every-where to be seen, a symptom of the rent strike which has been going on for months and which adds to the general air of malaise which hangs over the township. People have decided they will no longer pay for inferior services, or live under a Town Council which, they feel sure, speaks only with its master's voice.

It is precisely in this rebelliousness that the spirit of Soweto shows, a defiant struggle against the odds which allows it to create islands of achievement where otherwise there might be only anger and despair. Consider the sheltered workshop for the disabled where crippled seamstresses ply their delicate trade. Here are banners whose colours heat up from emerald green to magenta, brightening a big, cool room. Here is the place of gold thread, of fat tufted swags, ruffles and brocade, where patient, silent, shy women tack and stitch sacred words, crosses, eucharists, vines, sheep and doves on embroidered altar cloths. Here are the formal purple and black draperies of a burial society; and cassocks and cottas for altar boys in fire-engine red and icy white, all frills, flounces and effusions of lace at the neck and sleeves ... A pleasant, industrious workshop whirring with old Singer sewing machines and clacking foot-pedals; up in the corner upon the wall beside a poster advertising bicycles, showing a blonde all smiles and fleshy profusion, there hangs another poster from the *Librairie Romantique* advertising *Poesies de Victor Hugo* in which a pretty reader, her book fallen to her lap, is staring dreamily out of the window yearning perhaps for some handsome aristocrat to collect her in his carriage and to drive her down the Bois de Boulogne. Beneath these wonderfully inappropriate images Black ladies prick out their sacred satins and silks. Next door, in a series of sheds, crippled men hand-knot nets and hammocks, and weave place mats, in vivid colours. The sign on the back of a weaver's wheelchair reads: 'Where to, Soweto?'

Sheltered employment though it may be, for these disabled people it is at least a job, and that is increasingly rare with unemployment in Soweto running at over fifty per cent. One of the responses to this are small-scale and in some cases rather beautiful forms of private enterprise. You will see the cobbler out in the morning sun beneath the palm tree, cross-legged on the ground, stitching away; or women who stop and display their fruits arranging them in fan-shapes, with the precision of surgical instruments; or, on a street corner, what they call here a 'boutique' of second-hand clothes spread upon the grass as if put out to dry. The resilience of the response which finds a way around despair is at once the most striking, and shaming, illustration of the extraordinary spirit of the people here.

The rich are always with us, even in Soweto, and are to be found in the suburb dubbed by the locals 'Beverly Hills', an exclusive development of modern, expensive, large houses. Here is the home of the Archbishop of Cape Town, Desmond Tutu; and that crenellated wonder over there is owned by a famous soccer player. Here is the house, or should I say the castle, of the only man in Soweto who drives a Maserati. The attitude of most people towards this tiny colony of high-fliers is interesting; the rich are not resented. The feeling seems to be that if you've got it, flaunt it, because that is one way of showing that you're every bit as good as the White man. And how is he going to know, unless you tell him? Soweto salutes its famous sons and daughters, expecting them to live in the style to which most of its people are not accustomed.

The garbage is piled high outside the renamed Mandela High School. The schools are known by their broken windows, and by the attempts to change their names; clumsy daubs on the walls announce their new status as 'Socialist Universities' or 'People's Academies'. Here is the Morris Isaacson High School, where the student riots in Soweto began on 16 June 1976. The children, of course, are the real powers, and it is not difficult to understand why when you realise that half of the Black population of South Africa is under fifteen. The future implications are profound. Daubed and smashed though they may be, the schools are at least functioning again after long strikes.

That is more than can be said for the beer-halls, enormous drinking sheds, which were sacked during the height of the troubles by children objecting to their fathers' boozy ways, declaring that the government-sponsored sophoric of the beer halls dulled the political edge of the older generation. Drinking now takes place in the shebeens, ordinary houses licensed to sell liquor, or sometimes not licensed: the capacity evolved for defying the law in all its labyrinthian complexity is well developed in Soweto. At the top of Sisulu Street, a smashed, deserted beer-hall gapes in the bright sunshine.

And here is perhaps the most famous landmark of all, the house of Winnie and Nelson Mandela, one of the very few to possess large and beautiful trees because, by and large, Soweto is a bare, treeless place. Although the bus slows down, photographs are not permitted at the request of Mrs Mandela because, as the guide delicately explains, she never knows who her enemies are. Two intense young men standing guard outside the house turn their backs when they see the cameras. Obviously it is not only among government security forces that men are camera shy.

Here now is a place of skulls, doves of peace, giant green tortoises made of cement, tin men, death masks, fetishes, straw hats and ululating women dancing in a stone circle. This extraordinary and unbelievable settlement in the middle of modern angry, grubby, rampant, vibrant, super-cool Soweto is intended to be an island of tradition, of straw huts and native gods. It is in fact a sad, shabby, fraudulent little tourist trap, a fantastic mixture of fakery and authentic knick-knacks. As if sensing the disbelief that most of the visitors will feel, a prominent sign at the front gate reads: 'All fools, liars, sceptics, atheists must please keep out...' It is a good sign, though; they should paint it at the entrance to this country.

And now here is a tower you may climb and at the top, where carved Zimbabwe birds sit in a stone circle, you can look out across the sprawling mass of Soweto and begin to comprehend the size of the place, as well as the hopelessness of the venture which decreed that you could keep millions of people hidden away in a labour reservoir, to be tapped and pumped into the White city over the hill, the skyscrapers of which may be dimly glimpsed in the distance.

On my visits to Soweto, whether on the bus, or on other,

more private occasions, I have been faced with the bewildering complexity of things as they are, and of things as they are perceived. I have encountered little hostility. This is perhaps worth recording, since the idea put about that it is some kind of jungle into which the White man strays only when heavily armed and full of fear is not only inaccurate but in many ways grimly amusing. As a matter of fact, I was accosted once, I recall, though it took me some time to realise what was happening. Three young boys came up to me, very thin teenagers with angry eyes who told me they had not eaten. They were in school, they said, it was their lunch hour but they had no money for food. Would I give them money? They stood around me in a semi-circle, blocking my path but they were so thin and so frail, so *young*, that the realisation that I was being threatened came very slowly and combined a feeling of incredulity that these skinny kids imagined they could mug anybody, with a touch of admiration at their brazen nerve. It is all of a piece, this braggadocio, with the ill-lettered and clumsy name changes painted on the walls of the smashed schools, burned-out beer-halls; large aspirations founded on threadbare foundations. Such desperate pretensions which mask a desire to be taken seriously, a wish still a long way from fulfillment, are closer to the nature of this place than the riots that hit the headlines. I gave them some money, truth be told, because I felt sorry for them. They asked me where I was from and when I said 'London' an extraordinary change occurred; they visibly relaxed in front of my eyes.

The small one patted my shoulder. 'Are people free in London – like they say?'

It is a difficult question to answer in a few words so I said, 'Yes, compared with this, I suppose you could say that people are free.'

The bigger boy asked; 'Is there apartheid?'

Again, impossible to answer, except in blunt terms. 'No, not in this way,' and, again, I waved my arms to include all of Soweto.

'I would like to go to London,' said the tall youth and his eyes glittered briefly, but I could see on his face that he did not bother to disguise the hopelessness of his ambition.

'All we have here is P.W. Botha,' said the smallest boy, 'and apartheid. That gets in the way of everything.'

The tall boy spotted my pen in my shirt pocket. He asked for it. He was going back to lessons soon and he had no pen. I hesitated about that. My first impulse was to refuse. I am a writer and I am lost without my pen. Besides, I wanted to make notes on this meeting. Then I realised that I did not need notes, this was the sort of thing I could not forget, even if I wished to do so. For those who do not believe in bullets and bombs memory is the truly subversive weapon; the recollection of what people would like to forget, of the way we were, and are. The authorities, of course, fear such resurrections. 'What's gone is gone, what's done is done. Can't you leave it alone? Must you always be dragging it up again?' These are questions one faces constantly. And not only from those responsible for this horrible comedy. But I cannot forget. It is like an illness. I expect that these boys, too, whether they grow up to be cabinet ministers or archbishops one day, will prefer not to recall our meeting here at a time when they were so poor and desperate. We all wish to forget, or avoid or ignore what a patched-up, hopelessly inept, ridiculous lot we are. What the hell! – I gave the boy my pen.

Back on the bus, passing the Tsabalala Cinema, which is over the road from the Tsabalala squatter camp, and quite possibly one of the worst slums you will see in South Africa, with desperately tiny paper and tin shacks, crowding what used to be a soccer field, beside a filthy, stinking stream. Along the road, beside the camp, are half a dozen chemical toilets which seem almost insulting in their white pristine shine. And here is Indaba Drive where the Protea police station is found. It is to this place you are brought when information is sought, according to one of my friends. 'When they take you in there, even what you don't know you do know by the time you get out,' he says. 'They got ways of making statues sing in there. That's where the interrogation branch gets to work. People sing like birds.' The police stations are ringed with fences and stiff with sentries. Soweto may have only one fire station and two fire trucks for its two and a half million people, but it is definitely rich in police stations. And here now is the last remaining functioning beer-hall in Soweto. It's called the *Jabulani* or 'Happiness' beer-hall, and I suspect it owes its survival to the close proximity of the police fortress nearby.

And so we leave, passing the 'Lie to Me Restaurant' and the 'Try Again Fish and Chip Shop', dazed by what we have seen, crawling back to Johannesburg along the main road crowded with the small vans the Sowetans use as taxis. Behind me a small green kite hovers high in the air above the town. A taxi carries a wry declaration of faith on its back bumper: 'Even God Loves Soweto'.

An old contention in this country is that the Nationalist Party, from which the White supremacist government is drawn, bears resemblances to the National Socialists in Germany in the 'thirties and 'forties. But any direct comparison is inaccurate, for National Socialism was in every sense a fatally serious venture; genocide was a programme at which the Nazis did not baulk. Apartheid, by contrast, is to a degree an opportunist, patchwork affair born as much of expediency as ideology. One can say about apartheid that the overt fraudulence of the scheme is always threatening to overwhelm the philosophy. To some degree you could say that South African Whites are, at least in this sense, too African for real resemblances to the Nazis to apply, and that is possibly their saving grace. However, there is one thing in which we do bear a living likeness, and this becomes clear when you visit a place like Soweto, or, for that matter, if you go to any Black township, dumping ground, transit camp, rubbish heap for people. For it was not upon Jews as Jews that Germans first turned, but upon Germans. In other words, they turned on their own. And that is what we have done. Apartheid is not to be seen as something that we have done to others; rather it is a wound which we have deliberately inflicted upon ourselves. And a further consideration flows from this: apartheid is often considered in the terms of its victims – less widely realised is what fools it has made of those who have administered the system.

An invitation to read something of my work to a group in Soweto; it is to be an informal, private gathering of writers and readers. There is also to be some dancing, though its theme and nature are not revealed. Like the rest of the arrangements for the evening, they are left strategically vague.

I travel into the township at nightfall and find the arts centre where the reading is to take place already busily preparing for the evening. The place works hard for a living, every corner is used to offer space to dancers, actors, musicians, writers, playwrights; leotards hanging behind the door; someone practising a sax next door, the notes a smooth growl deep in the brass throat.

The seats in the small amphitheatre are taken by about seven o'clock and my audience is varied: young children, middle-aged women, and a good number of brooding young men who exude a sense of scepticism, even hostility, which their courteous attention to my opening remarks cannot disguise.

We are all aware of the strangeness of the situation. I am, in the first place, a White South African and these days Whites are not much given to visiting Soweto and sitting around with people, in any capacity. As the young playwright who introduces me explains – it seems as if there is an invisible barrier between Soweto and the City of Johannesburg which Whites will not cross. Then, too, I am a South African writer who lives a long way away and while this is, I suppose, somewhat reassuring, since it presupposes certain disagreements on my part with the way things are done in South Africa, it also means that I am going to be out of touch with the important details of everyday life, the crucial nuances which only those directly involved in the tremendous struggle now taking place can comprehend. The fact that I live abroad is double-edged; in the first place it means I am removed from direct involvement in the machinery of oppression that has put troops and armoured cars on the streets of Soweto; yet I am a White South African so my complicity is also quite apparent. But then strangeness is not something that is going to bother very many of us because it is second nature to us, in a sense we expect to be strange to each other, at odds, out of tune, out of touch, familiar gulfs and hard-won misunderstandings loom between us, and it would be very strange, after nearly half a century of policies aimed at preventing fraternisation between the races, if they did not.

The audience sit in two blocks of seats on either side of me and I sit in the corner of the room upon a low stage or dais. I begin by reading a poem, a kind of soliloquy called 'In the Middle of Nowhere', in which a speaker whom I suppose would be best described as a refined and more articulate version of the man I met in the Balfour bar, Philip of the beautiful Greek ears, who believed himself and his right-wing friends to be the future... The poem mimics the sense of injured benevolence and blind good sense found among many Whites who resent the rejection of their best efforts to help Blacks, to lend a hand, to supply medicines, to teach better methods of farming, and encounter the growing resentment of Black people to these charitable enterprises and their unshakeable desire to repudiate Whites and all their works and even to dream of driving them into the sea. The poem concludes with a line which might be either threat or promise: 'Dying will be the last thing we do for them'.

I never get as far as the last line. Just ten lines into the poem and I am interrupted by a suspicious questioner in the front row, a man with woolly bangs and angry eyes. He wants to know who is speaking in the poem. I sketch as best I can in outline the creature of refined paternalism, backed by the kind of murderous self-certainty that allows some people to kill, if they believe this is the only thing that will do the victim any good. But why, the questioner persists, write a poem about such a creature? So there it goes – out of the window – my poem along with what I had hoped were carefully controlled ironies, nuances; the detached, musing tone of the speaker, and gone too was any notion that I could disclaim responsibility for the attitudes of the speaker in the poem. I had written it, had I not? There were murmurs of approval to this challenge. After all writing was a way of showing where one stood and from where the audience stood, the speaker in my poem did not deserve a line, he was the enemy, and that was the end of it.

I put the poem aside unfinished. I get the point. This is the front line and it will not do to read to front-line troops subtle analyses of the psychological perversions of the enemy.

I contemplate the rest of the reading with foreboding, this is not the usual literary evening. I move swiftly on to my novel, *The Hottentot Room*. I choose a section which describes the flight of the informer, Caleb Looper, to Berlin with the ashes of his elderly friend, Frau Katie, in a cardboard tub concealed in a shopping bag. Before I begin reading I explain very carefully where Berlin is and the way in which the city is divided by a wall into an eastern and western sector; how the eastern sector is controlled by the Russians and the western sector by the forces of Britain, France and the USA. A nurse in the back row says she has been to Berlin and remarks on the ugliness of the Wall which, she points out, is really two walls with minefields and other devices sown in the trench between them. Interest quickens slightly. I describe the position of West Berlin stuck way in the middle of East Germany like a Bantustan. I tell the story of Looper who, in an attempt to fulfil his promise to Frau Katie to return her ashes to her home in Berlin, follows Friedrichstrasse along its western length until he finds he cannot go any further because his way is blocked by the Wall which cuts the street in two at Checkpoint Charlie. An intense boy in the back row wearing a camouflage jacket says: 'We got a wall here.' I say yes, I believe it's called the Berlin Wall. (I had in fact seen their wall on my way in; several kilometres of concrete fencing.) A couple of people chuckle. Fifteen minutes into the reading and the first signs of relaxation.

A photographer begins taking pictures using a dazzling flash. The room is already brightly lit; I am about to ask if the lights can be turned down when I realise that my reading is being videotaped. I begin to feel like a man taking a lie-detector test. I read the section where Looper, aboard a tourist bus, crosses the Wall at Checkpoint Charlie and enters East Berlin, still with the ashes of his friend in the shopping bag on his lap. I describe the search of the bus, standard practice in East Berlin, the self-important demeanour of the guards, the mirror on the end of a pole, like a giant dentist's mirror with which the underside of the bus is examined. I remark on Looper's observation, as they drive into East Berlin with the official guide pointing out the architectural achievements of the socialist state, that he feels the place to be

very like South Africa, quite uncannily like home. Immediately I am challenged again. What do I mean – like home?
After all this is South Africa, and Looper is in the German
Democratic Republic – surely there is no comparison? I
explain that these are personal reactions and that my feeling
when I visited East Germany was that the bureaucracy and
tone of the party line which I encountered reminded me so
much of South Africa that I felt positively homesick. A very
pretty girl who does not look more than fifteen, with a severe
and aggressive manner, demands to know whether perhaps
the Wall is not a good thing in that it protects the integrity of
East Germany. I respond by saying that I dislike intensely
people who support walls, build them, or encourage their use.
I say that there is no difference in the intensity of my dislike,
whether measured against the monstrosity in Berlin or its
little brother down the road in their own backyard, and I jerk
a thumb over my shoulder. Again a ripple of laughter and I get
the chance to press on with the story. I tell how Looper arrives
amid a snow storm at the memorial to the Russian dead, one of
the stops on the trip, and how he is confronted by someone
who had been pursuing him throughout the book and whom
he was sure he had escaped, a large, enigmatic Zulu who has
been ordered by his masters in the South African Government to get Looper home at all costs, and in any condition.

There is consternation at the mention of the Zulu, mixed
with close interest. Why is he a Zulu? What is he wearing?
Why is he working for the South African Government? The
mention of the Zulu in this company raised a real issue, one
that I did not envisage in such sharpness. I used the Zulu
because Zulus are an ambiguous force today in South Africa;
at once the largest of all the Black groups, they outnumber all
others and uncertainty about their precise political status in
the struggle for freedom, symbolised in the ambiguous
position of their leader Chief Mangosuthu Buthelezi, is of
enormous concern and interest to Black radicals, and to many

256

others. In this company the huge, urbane, anonymous, beautifully groomed Zulu who hunts the renegade White agent Looper takes on an importance never intended in the novel, but then, as I discovered earlier with my poem, a work is capable of two very different readings – one which is merely literary and the other which is felt in the flesh. More than that, what is happening here is that my novel is being written by the audience, a task in which I am invited to join by way of speculating on the reasons behind the Zulu's treachery, on what action might be taken against him and how Looper might outsmart his pursuer. My novel becomes more novel by the minute. A more conventional audience would not put these questions. A more pedantic author might reply loftily; 'What I have written, I have written!' But this is no place for pedantry.

Again I take the chance offered to continue the story and read the sections in which Looper does find a last, desperate way to escape the indefatigable Zulu, and how he dies in the snow, but not before scattering the ashes of his old friend, Frau Katie, upon German soil. In doing so he carries out a solemn promise, finally but imperfectly. The German Jewess has come back to Berlin.

Again a challenge: home is home and a promise is a promise. If Looper has not found the very spot where Frau Katie once lived before the German madness set in, then he has failed in his promise. I reply that he has done his best; Looper feels that Frau Katie will have understood why he was unable to fulfil his vow to the letter. But how could he *know* she would understand since Frau Katie is dead? Because the old lady had been through something very similar herself, as a Jew hunted by the Gestapo, and had predicted that Looper would one day be confronted by his pursuers and would have to find a way of escaping them. But Looper was dead, wasn't he? Yes, Looper was dead, but he was also free; he had outwitted and outsmarted his pursuers by taking the only road he knew they could not follow him down. And he had come as close as possible to returning his friend to her home.

So then Looper was not in the end a traitor? demands the brooding young man who had challenged me earlier. No, perhaps not. Now the photographer puts down his camera and becomes one of the audience. Had I perhaps recognised the African connotations of my book, particularly in the relationship between Looper and Frau Katie, because his understanding of her, even after her death, suggested a kind of ancestral loyalty? No, I confess that this has not occurred to me but I am grateful for the comparison; although my book is set a long way away, in England and Germany, it is, I hope, an African novel. But what would have happened if Looper had escaped? asks the nurse; what sort of end would I have imagined for him then? Was there any chance of reconciliation with the Zulu? After all, it was not enmity but solidarity which one prayed for. Certainly it was, but I was unable to imagine any end for Looper other than the one I had written.

Though I feel unable to do so, this does not stop members of the audience, now that they have a firm, even an obsessive, grip on the story, from suggesting a variety of other resolutions to the novel which has never occurred to me. I thank these other writers of a book other than mine for their suggestions, grateful that the mood of the evening has changed from hostility and impatience to a far more cordial encounter, the price for this being that my listeners have taken over, my novel is no longer my property.

What more could a writer ask? I do not think I have experienced as much pleasure, or trepidation, since I managed to amuse and intrigue my friends thirty years before, in my hostel days, when getting people who believed that reading was bad for the eyes, or grew hair on their hands, to pick their way through twenty lines of closely worked rhyming couplets, not because they cared a hoot for something called poetry, or even because they enjoyed seeing justice done to themselves and vengeance wreaked upon enemies and considered themselves the only appropriate judges of such pleasures and rewards, but because they appreciated an accurate depiction of themselves and their world.

Having endured my ordeal, and been acquitted, or at least having been given a suspended sentence, the evening moves on to the dance and I am allowed to join the audience to watch a troupe of perhaps twenty young people, all of them in their early teens, go through a very rigorous routine, a set of dances, beautifully choreographed, carried out with considerable energy but admirable discipline on the small floor. The material is eclectic, and influences range from *West Side Story* to *Fame*, and the music pumped through the speakers, to which the dancers sometimes mime, comes from an inoffensive roundup of singers ranging from Michael Jackson to Lionel Richie, with a great deal of emphasis on love and understanding. This might have been where we left it, a good bunch of kids who show style and precision and who turn in a performance of considerable class, all the more admirable for having been created from very limited means, a message of love and affection in the heart of the ghetto. But this is not all. Into this rather bland, pleasant spectacle a new note is introduced with a tableau framed by electronic music, which depicts the arrival of a group of explorers, or conquerors, among a community of gentle people who welcome the visitors and put them at their ease. Now the audience sit forward in their seats when it becomes clear that we are close to home. The gentle people are rewarded with kicks and fists, are rounded up like cattle and cry out in their pain and astonishment as the invaders turn their guns on them. The sound track explodes into a hail of machine-gun fire, ugly, rasping, lengthy and so loud it hammers on the ear drums. One burst follows another, and another ... the volume increasing to a pitch that makes me cover my ears and we watch the dancers falling beneath the bullets. So loud I think it must carry to the soldiers outside, patrolling the streets of Soweto, beneath the high, skinny floodlights, with their armoured cars, and rifles and real bullets. Will they come bursting into the hall fearing that, in some mysterious revolutionary ploy, the children of Soweto have opened fire on themselves?

When I leave at the end of the evening one of my inquisitors offers me his hand. Without thinking, I shake it. A look of astonishment, almost of pain, spreads across his face. I have remembered too late the special 'Soweto shake' – a clasp of the hands, a circling of thumbs, and a final hand clasp. His surprise gives way to pity.

'Ah, Chris –' a rueful shake of the head – 'you've been away too long!'

I left South Africa in 1974, quite calmly, deliberately and voluntarily, I had specific reasons for leaving yet at the same time felt that I had no option but to do so. I think my decision to leave grew out of the realisation that, as I had always suspected, spirited claims to the contrary notwithstanding, there were really no South Africans. A sense of superfluity haunted me. It translated, among people I knew, into a kind of levity, a buoyancy that allowed us to float above things – an incorrigible lightness. We had the kind of problem my nanny George would have recognised immediately – we had no teeth. More precisely, I felt the growing irrelevance of my position as that increasingly threatened species, a White English-speaking South African caught between the entrenched nationalism of the White Afrikaner and the rising nationalism of the dispossessed majority of Blacks. We were out of sympathy with the Government, yet out of touch with Black aspirations, caught somewhere in the middle, not waving but drowning, outvoted, outnumbered, outgunned and, worst of all, outmoded. It seemed to me that the English-speaking liberal had made a considerable contribution to his own irrelevance. You might say that people of my persuasion were damned by the very qualities and ideals which they most admired and strove to uphold; a sense of fairness and tolerance were precisely the qualities which prevented us from attacking the everyday idiocies of our Government with proper ferocity. This also undermined our resistance to the co-option of English Whites into the ruling tribe, something which has proceeded inexorably over the past four decades and speeded up considerably in the last five years.

I believed that the only possible response to the system under which we lived in South Africa was not understanding, or fairness, impartiality, patience, or tolerance, or any of these things; but to find a way of attacking it from some new vantage point. When I left the country in 1974 it was with no sense of finality; it was, I suppose, more of a tactical withdrawal, an escape. I felt then, and still do, like an escapee, and perhaps this is partly to be explained by the institutional nature of South African society where no corner of life, private or public, is not touched by the shadow of racial obsession, the religion of pigmentation, and the result is to create a country more bizarre than anything a writer could dream up. South Africa is a deeply inventive asylum where the inmates long ago took over the running of the institution, dressed up in white coats, and have been giving orders ever since. For so long indeed that they have begun to take themselves seriously; worse than that, so have the rest of the population.

I left because I suppose I had a theory to test. On the one hand South Africa outwrote its most inspired novelists and poets. It was its own best book. It seemed to me that the only thing to do that would successfully convey something of the horrifying comedy of the place would be to attempt to set down one's experience with as little elaboration as possible.

It occurred to me that if only I could hold up a mirror, we

might glimpse in it a vision of ourselves – unexpected, ridiculous, sad, and quite laceratingly amusing. By this method one might also hope to expose the nursing staff who patrolled the wards of our asylum pretending to be angels of sweetness and light for the hard-faced harridans they really were. I think I also hoped that by putting down my recollections of the place I had left, I would begin at long last to persuade myself that it existed.

Accordingly I wrote, many miles from home, a novel about a teenager who did not know what colour he was. I set the story back in the mid-'fifties in an unnamed provincial town in the Transvaal, and I called the book *A Separate Development*, which is a euphemism for apartheid (itself a euphemism for something called *baasskap* – quite literally 'bosshood').

The result was both a disaster and a discovery. Although I had taken the precaution of setting my story back a quarter century, and despite the anonymity of the town, what I had considered to be a gentle little tale, with one or two comic gleams, aroused considerable feeling. Perhaps even more importantly, it was just beginning to find readers when a notice appeared in the Government *Gazette* banning *A Separate Development* and it disappeared from the shelves overnight.

The reasons given for the banning were large and excessively weighty for what was, after all, a little comedy. It was stated that my novel amounted to an incitement to racial hostility (this in a country dedicated to racial hostility as a way of life) and that it displayed hostility towards certain groups: 'policemen' was one of the groups and I think the other was 'Afrikaners', hardly the sorts of people who start at shadows. But then it has always been a principle in South Africa that you should not kick a man when he is up. I felt sorry about the disappearance of my novel, of course, but perversely grateful that if all else failed I had found in the censors careful readers and when starting out a writer is grateful for readers wherever he finds them. But above all I had made a discovery; it was not the condemnation of others which bothered the people in charge in South Africa – what really disturbed them were glimpses of themselves.

The day before the election, May 5th, and half a million Black workers have stayed away from work; a series of explosions has taken place and the tension is palpable. But as always we must take comfort where we can; this morning's newspaper announced that the World Avocado Congress is being held in South Africa at the moment. Also in the paper an advertisement by the Soweto Civic Association; it is a direct appeal to White voters to abstain: 'By what right do you vote for a government which passes oppressive laws against us? Which sets its army against us? Which jails our leaders and our children? Which bans our meetings and organisations?

MAY 6 IS NO SOLUTION
ABANDON APARTHEID!
ABANDON NAT RULE!

More evidence of the Jericho principle.

But there are many Sowetos, besides the Soweto that might be said to put on a show, a place of public clamour, rioting, and political insurrection, an occupied camp. It would be a shame if its political energies disguised the fact that the majority of its citizens lead private lives of quiet tumult, much like people anywhere.

Consider Marina, daughter of a Black mother and a White father. She works as a public relations officer for a building contractor who is doing considerable trade in the new estates of middle-class housing which are being developed in Soweto for teachers, government employees and the growing number of highly paid young Black professionals increasingly eager for a standard of living closer to that of their White counterparts in Johannesburg. Marina's dealings with the contractors who supply kitchens for these new estates are sharp, efficient and mercilessly direct. The carousel of files holding different kitchen designs spins past her manicured nails; the salesmen approach her with respect. Marina is one mean lady: about thirty-five, tall, slim, bold, attractive and she has a blistering line in scatological invective which leaves her Black clients awestruck and has the sweat popping out on the foreheads of her White suppliers. This is Marina the business woman.

She is also a Sowetan and a number of things take priority over business. There are, for example, the frequent stay-aways, which she emphatically supports.

'Not good for business perhaps, but they're my people, my brothers and sisters – how can I not support them? Their struggle is my struggle. We all strike together. Only certain categories are allowed to go to work during a stay-away ...' A shadow of a smile slides across her makeup which is generously applied and has an almost metal gleam to it which increases her daunting reputation as a hard woman.

'Which categories, Marina?'

The smile deepens. 'Nurses. Let me tell you that there is a big demand for nurses' uniforms, during the stay-aways ...'

Beyond business and politics, there is another story more extraordinary than either of those deeply mundane universes can provide. For no particular reason, Marina decides to tell me the story about her lost brother. The search begins in a deep mist of hatred felt for the White man, who fathered her in some small town in the bush and walked out on her mother. 'May his soul rot,' Marina declares with grim piety. Yet it was not hatred that sent Marina off on her search for her brother but love.

'I knew there was a brother, a little boy, back where I came from and so I went to find him. I promised. He was a little baby when my mother left him. I had never seen him. I took a train, it was a long way, and when the train stopped I caught the bus and when the bus stopped I walked until I came to this place where I thought he was and I asked the people who lived there: Where is my brother? This is what I said to the people I found there, in this place. It was to these people that my mother had given the boy, and some money to look after him, when she went away to find work. She could not look after him herself. So now I said to them – Where is he? – And they said to me: He is in there, in the hut. And so I went in and there was this boy, very thin, and I just looked at him and knew, yes, this is my brother. And so I went outside to these people who were supposed to look after him, and I could see that they had not been good to him, and I said to them – OK I am taking my brother away from here. He is coming with me – I went to my brother and said to him – Go and get your things. I, Marina, am taking you away from this place. I have a house in Soweto and I earn enough money and I am taking you home with me. And my brother he just started crying, he could not believe this, he could not believe anything! He was wearing a shirt, nothing else, and he was as thin as this!' Marina holds up one slim, manicured finger. 'The boy went to the hut and he came out with a bag, one small plastic bag, still wearing no pants, just the shirt, and I said – What is this? "These are my things," he says, "all my things are in the bag." Marina opens an imaginary bag and peers inside, sniffs and wrinkles her nose in disgust. She will not deign to tell me what her little half-naked brother numbered among his worldly possessions. Her flame-red nail points at the ground. 'I said to him – bury it! We need none of this rubbish in Soweto where we are going, your sister will buy you everything. And so we walked all the way to the bus and the bus took us to the train and the train took us back to Soweto, which is where we are today, my brother and his sister...'

Marina pauses and stares at the ground. Her face is firmly set, her expression one of towering pride mixed with unbearable sadness. Her rescue of her brother is undoubtedly a triumph, she has saved the boy and taken him home as she promised, but home is now the big city, Soweto, and he is a shy, country boy exposed now for the first time to the lures of the metropolis. Her brother, it seems, has had a difficult time adjusting. He sits home a lot. And he has succumbed to a familiar temptation.

'He went to a party and got drunk. I told him – you must be mad!' But then her face softens, he is after all many years younger than she, a kid. 'He wants to play professional football. But he smokes!' She shakes her head with rueful affection. 'I worry about that boy!'

A friend gives me copies of the anonymous leaflets distributed by the thousand in Soweto, scrappy, poor little pamphlets encouraging the stay-away on May 5th and 6th; the leaflet instructs that there is to be no shopping, no schooling, shebeens are to close, no one is to work except health workers and journalists. Health workers are reminded to wear uniforms, journalists must show identity cards. No buses or taxis are to be taken to town, 'town' being Johannesburg (the workplace of most of the people of Soweto); the tone is bold and uncompromising but one can't help detecting a certain note of desperation beneath it. White voters going to the polls are warned that there is no future in a racist Parliament or the Botha regime. It demands one person one vote in a united South Africa; it is all, no doubt, heady stuff but it is not the conflagration predicted, the explosion of violence so frequently prophesied and, in a curious way, depended upon by the radicals in the townships, and, for that matter, by the White government which has been using the fear of Black violence to compellingly good purpose in these last weeks.

The newspaper advertisement war between the parties has gone full page in the Sunday papers. The Progressive Federal Party have run perhaps their most effective campaign yet, listing, year by year, the catastrophic progress of White nationalism from the first forcible removal of 'Surplus Natives' in 1951 to emergency camps; the Sharpeville shootings of 1960; the eruption of Soweto in 1976 and the longed-for, and much touted, break-away of Afrikaner academics, sportsmen and journalists from the Nationalist Party in 1987. This advertisement is run in response to a particularly effective campaign of advertisements put out by the Nationalist Party, which goes in boots and all:

OVER MY DEAD BODY
WOULD I VOTE FOR THE ANC
SO WHY VOTE PFP?

Though tremendously dismayed not only by the savagery of this attack but by the growing suspicion that a good many people may well believe it, impossible though that is to comprehend, the PFP and its opposition allies continue to talk up their spirits. Their leader speaks of the dawn of a 'New Era'; in the last few hours before polling the English newspapers predict losses for the government and gains for the opposition, both left and right.

The long-awaited change of name has taken place at Barclays Bank. It is now to be called the 'First National Bank'.

I wonder if the sign painters are out in force at the Balfour branch? The fact that the bank's former British owners have severed links seems to have done nothing to endear Barclays to the Government which announced recently, and with

evident satisfaction, that a judicial investigation has con-
cluded that the chief executive of the bank, a man named Ball,
made a loan to a client who used it to pay for advertisements
supporting the illegal Black organisation, the African
National Congress. It looks as if a decision has been taken to
damage the man's reputation beyond repair. Nothing strange
about that. What is new is the decision of the bank's directors
to defend their man. In former years, such was the supine
nature of the relationship between banks and government, the
chances are that the board of this particular institution would
have immediately assumed that well-known and highly
characteristically grovelling position often demanded, and
willingly given, by captains of commerce and industry. But
this time, they have decided to stand their ground. Perhaps, at
last, the realisation is dawning that a readiness to lie down
when told to do so has never saved the victim from a heavy-
booted ramble upon his recumbent form. Why, at this late
stage, English-speaking businessmen should be making a stand
I have no idea. Unless perhaps somebody pointed out to them
Benjamin Franklin's warning that, when *in extremis*, those who
do not hang together are likely to hang separately. At any rate
I see that somebody approves of the banks' refusal to perform
a collective act of penance, for a rather interesting graffito
has appeared around town. It reads: 'FIRST NATIONAL BANK –
WITH BALLS!'

May 6th, D-Day, I awake to the sound of birds and burglar
alarms. Today is the fiftieth anniversary of the destruction of
the airship *Hindenburg*. Half a million Black people stay away
from work, and the centre of town is silent. There have been
land-mine explosions in the Northern and Eastern Transvaal.
Two limpet mines exploded in the centre of the city. The
polling stations are virtually armed camps; most of them are

at local schools which are closed for the day of course and large tents have been pitched in the grounds, gaily coloured affairs they are, rather like tea tents. But they are not serving tea in those tents, that is where the squads of police are billeted. At some polling stations there appéar to be more uniformed men than voters.

In my travels around the place I meet an Afrikaner Mormon just back from a conference in Salt Lake City. This man kicks off by giving a very believable impression of a dyed-in-the-wool right-winger. All Black people in South Africa, he informs me, belong to separate nations, and therefore were confined to separate territories and this plan was full of justice, light and truth. For reasons best known to himself he then varies this line without any encouragement from me. I am becoming quite used to people thinking out loud in my presence.

'On the other hand maybe we should face up to the truth. Maybe we should admit to ourselves that the time has come to have a general election with a vote for everybody. Yes, I mean *everybody*! Let them release Mandela. Let us take our chances now and see what result we get, rather than prolong the agony and end up with the same position anyway. Because that's what's going to happen, you mark my words.'

The pace of his enlightenment is too quick for me, but I manage to say it sounds like a sensible idea. He is ahead of me once again.

'In actual fact, you know, I sometimes believe that the White man has no business in Africa. Maybe Africa is for the Africans and our mistake was arriving here in the first place. Maybe all the White people in South Africa should leave for somewhere else; after all, everybody is entitled to their own country.'

I am getting ever further out of my depth. 'Where do you think we should all go?'

'To America. What do you think of that?' He gives me a sidelong glance. 'Mind you, we'd have to do something about the Red Indians, of course . . .'

Night falls and televisions flicker behind closed curtains. The television people are putting on quite a show, energetically going through the motions. Tonight they are playing charades. Tonight they are pretending this is a real election. They have pundits and pointers; shifts are being analysed, graphs plotted in pretty colours on the computers and incoming results flashing up on the screen. This is a fine exercise in democracy.

By midnight it is clear that something is going very wrong. Or is it going very right? Across the country the National Party, suspected these past weeks of being about to suffer a great loss of academics, a haemorrhage of clerics, a flight of intellectuals, is picking up votes. Worse still, where they are not gaining the parties of the White Right are doing so. The Conservative Party, the movement led by Dr No, is doing astonishingly well. Even the commentators are looking rather pale in the early morning strain of it all. A pundit declares, with a look of quiet terror, that if things go on like this the Conservative Party may even put the Progressive Party out of its long agony as official opposition. A few hours later this funereal prediction seems closer than ever to fulfilment. The Conservative Party and the Progressive Federal Party are now running neck and neck. A single Independent has won a seat.

In the cold light of the following morning the slaughter is complete and the unthinkable has happened. The Nationalists have increased their total of seats from 116 to 123. The

Progressive Federal Party, until yesterday confident of winning perhaps 40 or 50 seats, together with its allies the New Republic Party now holds just 19, a loss of 6. And safe seats have gone with it, some of the safest in the country, and even Helen Suzman's majority has been slashed by the suddenly formidable Mr Pagan. That warm embrace of Winnie Mandela did indeed cost a few thousand votes. The New Republican Party has been reduced to a single seat. The real winner has been the Conservative Party which has increased its number of seats from 18 to 22, supplanting the Progressives as the official opposition. When the Progressive leader declared that a new era was at hand I do not think this is what he had in mind. Taking the figures together, over eighty per cent of the electorate has voted for either the established governing party or parties of the far right. That is to say they have chosen to be governed by the dying or the dead. Large numbers of English-speaking voters have crossed to the Nationalists, or gone to the far right; the Conservative Party has polled half as many votes as the ruling Nationalist Party, and the extent of their support in the country and their rate of growth show them to be the most dynamic party in the country – and, it should be added, the youngest, having been founded just five years ago.

So there we have it. The election that was supposed to jolt the Government more cruelly than any election since 1948 has given them more support than they ever had before. And should they think of proceeding with real reforms, well then, the Visigoths of the far right have just come riding into town ready to shoot first and talk later, and to see to it that the Government watches its back.

The President appears on television and is to be seen graciously accepting the 'mandate' the electorate has given him. Gratitude, modesty and a certain satisfaction are in order – this is perfectly natural. The National Party has won its biggest victory in twenty years. Consider the proportions of those who voted for the parties: the NP received 52.45 per cent; the PFP 14.11 per cent; CP 26.37 per cent; NRP 1.92 per cent; HNP 3.14 per cent; and the three independent candidates between them 1.32 per cent. Maybe these figures ought to be branded on the brow of every opposition newspaper editor in town. For those who believe in parliamentary democracy, or peaceful change, this is a disaster. Perhaps the most restrained reaction comes from the Zulu leader, Chief Buthelezi. It is all the more commendable in its bleak, bare honesty. He is quoted as saying: 'the Whites would rather destroy South Africa than institute a policy of real change'.

Looking at these words, bold and despairing, they seem to state something we have always known but which for years, for decades, none but the craziest wanted to believe, not then, or ever. Well, we better start believing it.

The star of White, moderate, liberal opposition must have exploded many light-years ago and yet the news is only now filtering through. The sun is shining but it does not fool anyone. This is funeral weather. People who set out to talk calmly about the results suddenly get tears in their eyes. There has never been anything like this, a defeat so complete. They are too dazed to take it in. Yet so many were sure that this time it would be different. Graveside hours, a feeling of numbness and disbelief; but the pain of our bereavement will be difficult to ease, as it always is among grieving friends when there is nothing to lay to rest.

I set out on a walk very early in the morning; I am quite alone; the sunshine is lavish, brilliant in the whitewash of the high suburban walls. I mutter to myself my election mantra:

Malan, Strydom, Verwoerd, Vorster, Botha... Today the charm does not seem to be working, but I persist. I find if I say it slightly more quickly, I build up a rhythm, like a train pulling uphill. I begin to run in time to the rhythm, not because there is anybody after me, or anybody about to see me, but because somehow it is appropriate to keep moving. At the sound of my footsteps, behind the beautiful walls, all the dogs in the neighbourhood begin to bark.

THE PANAMA HAT TRAIL

TOM MILLER

Panama hats don't come from Panama; they are made two countries away in Ecuador, in South America. Tom Miller travelled there to find the origins of the hats. Learning how a Panama hat is made and marketed – from the harvesting of raw straw in the middle of a jungle to the purchase of a finished hat in a store in San Diego – is more than a travel adventure and a cultural study; it is also an off-beat lesson in the workings of world trade. How is a hat, sold for seventy cents by the peasant who had painstakingly woven it by hand, eventually bought for thirty-five dollars? Why do the impoverished peasants have little knowledge of this – and less interest? Tom Miller perceptively and personally leads us around the old Inca Empire, across the equator, through American foreign policy, and along one of the least travelled and most remarkable trails in the world –

'A lovely little gem of a book. THE PANAMA HAT TRAIL is part reportage, part travelogue, and all pleasure; it is rewarding and entertaining on many counts. It is filled with lively anecdotes, pungent asides, vivid scenes and – best of all in a travel book – delightful characters . . . a pleasure on every page of the journey' WASHINGTON POST

0 349 10018 7   NON-FICTION   £3.99

Under A Sickle Moon

A Journey Through Afghanistan

PEREGRINE HODSON

In the spring of 1984, Peregrine Hodson left London to travel through Afghanistan. It was not an easy time. He covered a distance of some thousand miles, mostly on foot; he nearly drowned; and later made a narrow escape from Russian commandos, after being caught up in a major offensive.

This is an extraordinary and illuminating book, charting the author's growing awareness of that country, its people, and of the complexities surrounding the Soviet occupation. But he also captures that dilemma peculiar to the solitary traveller: an almost total dependence on local inhabitants for basic requirements and companionship, on the one hand; on the other, the often irrational yearning for solitude and space to think in mother tongue.

'*A highly readable book which casts light not only on the suffering in Afghanistan, but also on the Islamic revival throughout the world*'
HARPERS & QUEEN

0 349 10006 3   NON-FICTION   £3.99

An Unfinished Journey

SHIVA NAIPAUL

AN UNFINISHED JOURNEY comprises the last writings of Shiva
Naipaul before his death in 1985 – six articles and the beginnings of his
projected book on Australia. All the pieces are rich and vital, fine
examples of Shiva Naipaul's determination to harass the issues which
troubled him and demanded his attention: his search for his own identity
within his family and within the world, his utter contempt for racism of
any kind and his fascination with India and the so-called 'Third World'
and, not least, his energetic yearning to understand mankind. AN
UNFINISHED JOURNEY is a memorial to a great writer and a
celebration of his art.

*This collection of pieces is magnificent . . . beautifully written, utterly honest,
and curiously uplifting. And I should not forget to say that it is also often very
funny' LITERARY REVIEW*

0 349 10009 8   NON-FICTION   £3.50

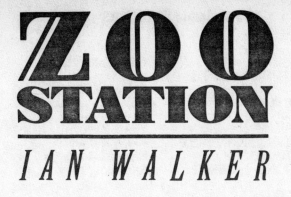

ZOO STATION

IAN WALKER

BERLIN   For most of us, the word whips up images of decadence, a dangerous *melange* of artistry, politics, and design extravagances; red-gashed mouths in smoky nightclubs, gaudy and melancholy. But qualified by 'East' and 'West' those images merge and disappear.

IAN WALKER lifts and separates the two zones, revealing Berlin as it is today: a two faced city where every single thing is mirrored and echoed in an undeclared war of buildings, cars, clothes, flags, food, music and street-signs. Drinking and dancing, talking to friends, exiles, ex-prisoners, and runaways, he shuttles in between communism and capitalism, a regular commuter on the smugglers' express . . . in awe of the faceless power of the Wall, yet crashing through it with addicted frequency.

'Will raise a pang of nostalgia in all who have fallen under the city's spell'
Daily Mail

0 349 10045 4   NON FICTION   £3.99

Also available in ABACUS paperback: